Catholic Theological Formation

General Editor: Christopher J. Thompson

MW00783072

The Catholic Theological Formation Series is sponsored by The Center for Theological Formation at The Saint Paul Seminary School of Divinity, the graduate school of theological formation for both Roman Catholic seminarians and laity enrolled at the University of St. Thomas in Saint Paul, MN. As a premier institution of theological formation for the region and beyond, The Saint Paul Seminary School of Divinity seeks to form both men and women for the task of fulfilling the specific call God has for them grounded in their common baptismal vocation to serve one another in Christ.

As an institution of the Archdiocese of Saint Paul and Minneapolis, the school is intentional in its commitment to priestly formation for the archdiocese and the broader region. As an institution of graduate theological education, the school prepares the laity for the equally compelling task of making Christ known and loved in the world. Though distinct in their various ministries, the common goal of intense theological formation is shared across the curriculum.

It is precisely this challenge of theological formation, faithfully informing one's understanding, that serves as the focus of this series, with special attention given to the task of preparing priests, teachers, and leaders within the Roman Catholic tradition. While academic in its tenor, the aim is intellectual — that is, we seek to promote a form of discourse that is not only professional in its conduct but spiritual in its outcomes. Theological formation is more than an exercise in academic technique. Rather, it is about the perfecting of a spiritual capacity: the capacity on the part of the human person to discern what is true and good. This series, then, aims to develop the habits of mind required of a sound intellect, that spiritual aptitude for the truth of God's living Word and His Church. Most often the series will draw from the more traditional specializations of historical, systematic, moral, and biblical scholarship. Homiletics and pastoral ministry are anticipated venues as well. There will be occasions, however, when a theme is examined across disciplines and periods, for the purposes of bringing to our common consideration a thesis yet undeveloped.

Despite the variety of methodologies and topics explored, the aim of the series remains constant: to provide a sustained reflection upon the mission and ministry of Catholic theological formation of both priests and laity alike.

The General Editor of the Catholic Theological Formation Series, Christopher J. Thompson, serves as the Academic Dean of The Saint Paul Seminary School of Divinity and Director of The Center for Theological Formation.

Verbum Domini and the Complementarity of Exegesis and Theology

Edited by

Fr. Scott Carl

WILLIAM B. EERDMANS PUBLISHING COMPANY
GRAND RAPIDS, MICHIGAN / CAMBRIDGE, U.K.

Published 2015 by

Wm. B. Eerdmans Publishing Co.

2140 Oak Industrial Drive N.E., Grand Rapids, Michigan 49505 /

P.O. Box 163, Cambridge CB3 9PU U.K.

Printed in the United States of America

21 20 19 18 17 16 15   7 6 5 4 3 2 1

Library of Congress Cataloging-in-Publication Data

Verbum Domini and the complementarity of exegesis and theology / edited by Fr. Scott Carl.
     pages   cm.   — (The Catholic theological formation series)
    Includes bibliographical references and index.
    ISBN 978-0-8028-7148-0 (pbk.: alk. paper)
    1. Bible — Criticism, interpretation, etc.   2. Bible — Hermeneutics.   3. Bible — Use.
    4. Catholic Church — Doctrines.   5. Catholic Church — Clergy — Training of.
    6. Catholic theological seminaries.   I. Carl, Scott.

BS511.3.V47   2015
220.088′282 — dc23
                                   2014026851

www.eerdmans.com

For the greater glory of God to the benefactors of the
Monsignor Jerome D. Quinn Institute of Biblical Studies

Contents

Part II: The Word of God in the Formation of Seminarians

Acknowledgments

This volume marks a significant juncture in the history of the Monsignor Jerome D. Quinn Institute of Biblical Studies, since it is the first published work under its auspices and stands as the first volume of the Catholic Theological Formation Series of The Saint Paul Seminary School of Divinity of the University of St. Thomas. The volume is dedicated to the benefactors of the Quinn Institute. First among them are Mr. Ray Quinn and Mrs. Sheila Ham, brother and sister to Msgr. Quinn who passed away in 1988, whose energies, resources, and promotion make our work possible. Secondly, I would like to thank Fr. James Swetnam, S.J., a personal friend of Msgr. Quinn, emeritus professor of the Pontifical Biblical Institute in Rome, and keynote presenter at our inaugural conference in 2009; his interest in the work of the Institute has given great impetus to our success. Then thanks are in order to all those who participated in the first two Quinn Conferences held in 2009 and 2011, including the contributors to this volume and all the other participants. Next, thanks goes to Msgr. Aloysius Callaghan, Rector of The Saint Paul Seminary School of Divinity and Vice President at the University of St. Thomas, for his support and encouragement of the Institute and for appointing me its first director. Thanks to Rev. Peter Laird, STD, priest of the Archdiocese of St. Paul and Minneapolis, who as Vice Rector of The Saint Paul Seminary School of Divinity gave me important guidance as to what direction the Institute should take at its outset. Thanks to Mr. Thomas Ryan, Vice President of Institutional Advancement of The Saint Paul Seminary School of Divinity for his work with Fr. Laird and the Quinn Family in making the Institute a reality in 2008. Moreover, I would like to thank Dr.

Christopher Thompson, Academic Dean of The Saint Paul Seminary School of Divinity, whose interest, enthusiasm, and wise guidance is a real benefit for this effort in the life of the Church. Lastly, I offer thanks to Dr. Christian Washburn and his wife Gretchen for their work in helping to prepare the manuscript. It is true that many hands go to the development and production of such an effort. For those whom I have not mentioned specifically, a sincere thanks to you as well. Most of all we thank God for our gift of faith in Jesus Christ.

FR. SCOTT CARL
Director of the Monsignor Jerome D. Quinn Institute of Biblical Studies
September 2014

Introduction

Scott Carl

The Monsignor Jerome D. Quinn Institute of Biblical Studies at The St. Paul Seminary School of Divinity of the University of St. Thomas in St. Paul, Minnesota seeks to improve the teaching of Sacred Scripture for our students and to make a contribution to the broader life of the Church by hosting scholarly conferences. The family and friends of Msgr. Quinn established this endowed institute as a way of continuing his legacy of scholarly study of Sacred Scripture in service of the Church. Msgr. Quinn, who passed away in 1988, was a world-renowned biblical scholar, serving on the Pontifical Biblical Commission (1978-84), being president of the Catholic Biblical Association (1970-71), publishing in the Anchor Bible Commentary series, and being twice an invited professor at the Pontifical Biblical Institute in Rome. He was the author of more than twenty books and articles, including the commentary on Titus in the Anchor Bible Commentary. All the while he maintained a deep concern for the formation of Catholic priests, remaining a faculty member throughout his entire scholarly life (1961-88) at The St. Paul Seminary. The present volume is a manifestation of these two dominant aspects of Msgr. Quinn's life: a scholarly biblical contribution whose primary aim is the formation of Catholic seminarians in preparation for the priesthood.

The Quinn Institute began in 2008, just prior to the XIIth Ordinary General Assembly of the Synod of Bishops, which gathered to discuss "The Word of God in the Life and Mission of the Church" in Rome in October of that year. This synod would eventually lead to Pope Benedict XVI's 2010 Apostolic Exhortation, *Verbum Domini.* These two events became the subject matter for the first two Quinn Conferences hosted in June 2009 and 2011. The overarching goal of these conferences has been to think about the implications of these acts of the magisterium for our lives as biblical scholars teaching in Catholic seminaries. To this end, Pope Benedict XVI urges that

> the study of the word of God, both handed down and written, be constantly carried out in a profoundly ecclesial spirit, and that academic formation take due account of the pertinent interventions of the magisterium. . . . Care must thus be taken that the instruction imparted acknowledge that "sacred Tradition, sacred Scripture and the magisterium of the Church are so connected and associated that one of them cannot stand without the others" [*Dei verbum* 10]. It is my hope that, in fidelity to the teaching of the Second Vatican Council, the study of sacred Scripture, read within the communion of the universal Church, will truly be the soul of theological studies. (*Verbum Domini* 47)

Thus, this volume seeks to respond concretely to these exhortations and concerns.

Part one speaks of the complementary relationship of exegesis and theology, with special attention to their tendency to be seen as separate in the exegetical endeavor. Part two speaks more specifically about the role of the Word of God in the formation of seminarians.

The renewal that the Church seeks is in part a response to the modern-day risk of splitting the exegetical and theological meaning of the Sacred Scripture (cf. *Verbum Domini* 35); this is the topic of part one of this volume. It begins with the article, "Inspiration and Incarnation," by Denis Farkasfalvy. This subject is stressed in *Verbum Domini*:

> [T]he theme of inspiration is clearly decisive for an adequate approach to the Scriptures and their correct interpretation [*Propositiones* 5 and 12], which for its part is to be done in the same Spirit in whom the sacred texts were written [*Dei verbum* 12]. Whenever our awareness of its inspiration grows weak, we risk reading Scripture as an object of historical curiosity and not as the work of the Holy Spirit in which we can hear the Lord himself speak and recognize his presence in history. (*Verbum Domini* 19)

Farkasfalvy explores the patristic parallelism between inspiration and incarnation. He addresses how this concept came to influence Vatican II's *Dei verbum* through the work of theologians such as Henri de Lubac, Hugo Rahner, and Hans Urs von Balthasar. The author proposes that more attention be paid to the analogous meaning of "inspiration" as applied in a subjective sense to *inspired authors* and, in an objective sense, to *inspired texts.*

Francis Martin, in "Spiritual Understanding of Scripture," seeks to demonstrate how an ancient tradition of interpreting Scripture by means of prophetic graces is being recovered and integrated by solid historical work done in recent centuries. He seeks to accomplish this goal by explaining how recent advances in the methodology of history have modified the aspects of other approaches that obstructed the spiritual or mystical sense of Sacred Scripture. Moreover, he reflects on some remaining deficient aspects of recent theories of history and cognition, demonstrating how they have impeded many believers from appropriating the Sacred Text. In his conclusion, he proposes that understanding human history and cognition in light of the Incarnation of Christ will dispose us to encounter Christ in the Sacred Text, where he is uniquely present to those who seek him in faith.

The next article, "*Verbum Domini* and Historical-Critical Exegesis," by Brant Pitre, summarizes five key points that Pope Benedict makes about the historical-critical method, showing its indispensability, the false dichotomy between "scientific exegesis" and "spiritual interpretation," the need to implement the three components for interpretation from *Dei verbum* 12 (the unity of all of Scripture, the living tradition of the Church, and the analogy of faith), the dangers of a dualistic approach to Scripture, and the need for an explicitly theological exegesis. In the end, Pitre draws out implications of these points, including the challenge that the training of most Catholic exegetes has focused on scientific exegesis without regard to the broader interpretative aspects mentioned by Benedict XVI and necessitated by Catholic theology.

Pablo Gadenz, in "Overcoming the Hiatus between Exegesis and Theology: Guidance and Examples from Pope Benedict XVI," directly addresses a key concern about dualistic interpretation stressed in *Verbum Domini.* Gadenz demonstrates in the work of Cardinal Ratzinger/Pope Benedict XVI how dogma is essentially the explanation of Scripture and how the Church is the living subject of biblical interpretation. He thereby begins to fill in the lacuna identified (and experienced) by Pitre.

Lastly in part one comes Christian D. Washburn's article, "The Catholic Use of the Scriptures in Ecumenical Dialogue." Ecumenism, too, is stressed by Pope Benedict XVI in *Verbum Domini:* "Conscious that the Church has her foundation in Christ, the incarnate Word of God, the Synod wished to emphasize the centrality of biblical studies within ecumenical dialogue aimed at the full expression of the unity of all believers in Christ" (*Verbum Domini* 46). Washburn describes how the centrality of biblical studies in ecumenical dialogue has focused in particular on the historical-critical method. He then addresses the role of the ecclesiological, patristic, and theological interpretations of the Scriptures, which are stressed in *Verbum Domini* and in the articles already introduced above. Washburn argues that these means of interpretation must be seen as part of the organic structure by which divine revelation is handed on, or else the entire Christian message is threatened by a fundamental disarticulation.

Part two focuses on how *Verbum Domini* is concerned with the role of the Word of God in seminary formation. Thus, the particular role of professors of Sacred Scripture in Catholic seminaries comes to the fore in these words: "Candidates for the priesthood must learn to love the word of God. Scripture should thus be the soul of their theological formation, and emphasis must be given to the indispensable interplay of exegesis, theology, spirituality and mission" (*Verbum Domini* 82, quoting *Propositio* 32).

Peter S. Williamson, in his article "Preparing Seminarians for the Ministry of the Word in Light of *Verbum Domini*," provides a broad picture of refashioning the teaching of Sacred Scripture in seminaries. Drawing from the work of the synod and Pope Benedict XVI, Williamson stresses important orientations for the formation of seminarians in the Word, including the priority of the Word in the ministry of priests, its centrality in a seminarian's spirituality, the special place of *lectio divina,* and the importance of integrating prayerful reading of Scripture and exegetical study. The paper distinguishes between foundational scriptural formation, such as *lectio continua* or introductory courses, and professional Scripture formation, such as learning a practical method of pastoral exegesis that enables the student not only to carry out the various aspects of priestly ministry but also to form a habit of ongoing biblical study.

In his paper, "Searching for the Obvious: Toward a Catholic Hermeneutic of Scripture with Seminarians Especially in Mind," James Swetnam, S.J., gives an outline of Catholic hermeneutics based on the Catechism of the Catholic Church. He stresses the intrinsically vertical orientation of hermeneutics since the Holy Spirit is the crucial element both in the ascertaining of the original text in terms of Catholic faith and in the application of this original meaning to the contemporary life of the faithful believer. Moreover, he gives tips to seminarians as to how they can best benefit from his Scripture courses. Throughout the text, Swetnam stresses the need for both seminary professor and student to take explicit consideration of their faith tradition. In so doing, Swetnam in a practical manner addresses the following concern of Pope Benedict XVI: "The lack of a hermeneutic of faith with regard to

Scripture entails more than a simple absence; in its place there inevitably enters another hermeneutic, a positivistic and secularized hermeneutic ultimately based on the conviction that the Divine does not intervene in human history" (*Verbum Domini* 35).

Mary Healy's article, "*Verbum Domini* and the Renewal of Biblical Preaching," boldly challenges the reality that Catholic preaching is often biblically impoverished. She manifests how Pope Benedict XVI in his Apostolic Exhortation points toward a means of renewing Catholic preaching by emphasizing two crucial factors. First, he calls for a renewed appreciation of the unique authority of Sacred Scripture as the inspired word in which Christ is truly present and which calls for a response of obedient faith. Second, he invites a rediscovery of the traditional understanding of the fourfold sense, in which all Scripture is recognized as a single word bearing witness to a unified plan of salvation in Christ. Healy concludes her article by reflecting on the implications of these two points and illustrating how they might be applied to homiletic preparation, using an example from Numbers 13–14.

The next article, "The Word of God and the Textual Pluriformity of the Old Testament," by Stephen Ryan, O.P., is the most technical of the volume, helping to demonstrate the interplay between exegesis and theology regarding inspiration. He discusses the issue of inspiration from the perspective of textual pluriformity in Old Testament texts. He shows how the patristic tradition (Origen, Augustine, Jerome), magisterial teaching (e.g., *Dei verbum, Liturgiam authenticam*), and the liturgical practice of the Catholic Church demonstrate that the Word of God revealed to the prophets and apostles is received by the Church in several authentic forms (e.g., Greek, Hebrew, Latin). The conclusion takes the form of brief theses about inspiration and textual pluriformity and offers reflections on how best to introduce this topic to students in introductory courses of Old Testament exegesis.

Kelly Anderson integrates well the role of exegesis and spirituality in teaching the psalms in her paper, "How the Liturgy of the Hours Provides an Effective Means for Teaching the Book of Psalms." She proposes integrating both ancient and new methods of interpretation when teaching in a seminary. The professor should first present the most recent findings of modern criticism, including form and canonical criticism of the Psalter. But given that the students are seminarians who pray the psalms daily, a further step is pedagogically advantageous and spiritually formative. By presenting the psalms in the context of the Liturgy of the Hours, professors can teach the seminarians about the role of the psalms in the life and tradition of the Church and how to hear the voice of Jesus Christ resounding in these ancient prayers. Thus, by studying the psalms using modern critical methods, but within the structure of the Liturgy of the Hours, the students will learn to integrate modern research with the traditional understanding of the psalms in the Church.

Lastly, Michael Magee proposes a helpful integration of exegetical methods to aid seminarians' reception of the development of the Pentateuch and its content in his article, "Combining Synchronic and Diachronic Methodology in Teaching the Pentateuch." This article is certainly helpful for anyone teaching a seminary course on the first five books of the Bible. Magee's experience in the classroom has shown that narrative criticism and other synchronic methods prove especially helpful because they hold the students' interest and prove more useful than historical-critical methods in drawing from the readings a message that can be preached to a congregation. Nonetheless, some familiarity with diachronic methodologies is essential so that the student will be able to utilize the contributions of many scholars over the past century. The article proposes a way of combining the various methodologies to achieve optimal results for the candidates in priestly formation.

One of the fruits of these conferences is that the work of the Monsignor Jerome D. Quinn Institute of Biblical Studies has been internationally recognized. The 2011 Quinn Conference was noted by His Eminence Marc Cardinal Ouellet, P.S.S., Prefect of the Congregation for Bishops, at the Synod on the New Evangelization on October 9, 2012, in his intervention on the reception of Pope Benedict XVI's Apostolic Exhortation *Verbum Domini*. Twice he singled out as noteworthy the paper presented by Mary Healy.

In conclusion, quoting his own intervention at the synod, Pope Benedict XVI said, "[W]here exegesis is not theology, Scripture cannot be the soul of theology, and conversely, where theology is not essentially the interpretation of the Church's Scripture, such a theology no longer has a foundation" (*Verbum Domini* 35). Such a union of exegesis and theology is crucial if we are to teach seminarians that "[t]he study of Scripture ought to lead to an increased awareness of the mystery of divine revelation and foster an attitude of prayerful response to the Lord who speaks," words that Pope Benedict XVI wrote explicitly to address the needs of candidates for Holy Orders (*Verbum Domini* 82). This volume seeks to address such fundamental challenges directly and practically, helping to form priests who will not only know Sacred Scripture and how to work with it in an exegetical classroom but also find in it a source of renewal for their vocations and offer well-grounded spiritual insight for the good of that portion of Christ's flock entrusted to their care.

PART I

The Complementarity of Exegesis and Theology

CHAPTER 1

Inspiration and Incarnation

Denis Farkasfalvy, O.Cist.

At a relatively early point in time Christian theological reflection on the Scripture perceived the analogy between incarnation and inspiration. But while the concept of incarnation, closely following the terminology of John 1:14, early on received the technical name of σάρκωσις, for the concept of biblical inspiration it has taken several centuries to appropriate a technical or "quasi-technical" vocabulary. However, the topic leads us back in any case to patristic times with a number of Church Fathers increasingly perceiving the parallelisms between the flesh in which God's Word dwelt among us and the letter which, in a similar way, veiled and revealed, transmitted and also expressed in appropriately human ways what God meant to express in human beings' oral or written instruments of communication. In this essay I will attempt, in the form of a brief survey, to present the main aspects of the analogy of inspiration and incarnation in the hope of providing a vantage point from which the theology of inspiration may be reexamined.

The History of This Analogy before Vatican II

Analogies between incarnation and inspiration have been found in Christian antiquity; Luis Alonso Schökel quotes some examples in his book *The Inspired Word*.[1] Before him, Henri de Lubac pointed out the importance of

1. In *The Inspired Word* (New York: Herder, 1965), p. 49, Schökel quotes St. Hippolytus, who wrote that the same Word was made "visible" and "audible" (Contra Noetum 12: PG 10,

this analogy in the works of Origen. His book on Origen, *Histoire et Esprit*, contains a long chapter under the title "Les incorporations du Logos" in the Scriptures.[2] A man sensitive to ensure the precision of nuances, de Lubac cautiously chose his terminology. In this context he avoided the word "incarnation," because in Catholic theology "incarnation" cannot be used in the plural. More importantly, Scripture has a twofold relationship to the incarnation of the Son: it is both derived from and analogous to the incarnation. So de Lubac uses another term that he finds in Origen: what is "incorporated" into the Scriptures is God's word as a divine message about Christ, not his divine nature subsisting in the person of the Son. But de Lubac dares to imitate Origen and his manner of speaking about a certain corporeal dimension that God's word obtains as he becomes accessible through the scriptural word.

Hugo Rahner, an older brother of Karl Rahner and a Jesuit, but a fellow patristic scholar to de Lubac, began to study Origen's theology of Scripture at about the same time as de Lubac did. In 1947, he published an article in which he coined the term "Schriftwerdung" in imitation of the German word for incarnation: *Menschwerdung*.[3] Shortly thereafter, in 1958, Karl Rahner published his very influential book with the title *Inspiration in the Bible*, which also includes several remarks about this analogy between "incarnation in the flesh" and "becoming human word."[4] However, Karl Rahner did not use the term "Schriftwerdung." But he employed the concept of an analogy between inspiration and incarnation throughout his book when referring to the "genesis" or the "coming about" *(Entstehung)* of Scripture, and its similarity to *Menschwerdung* (God becoming man). Another genius, the Swiss Jesuit Hans Urs von Balthasar, while in his young years still a Jesuit and personally acquainted with both de Lubac and the Rahner brothers (as well as a student of Origen), also took over Origen's analogy of incarnation and inspiration on some meditative pages, where comparing the Word made Flesh with the word becoming Scripture.[5]

---

820). He also quotes St. John Chrysostom's famous passage about divine "condescension" (Hom. in Gen 3:8 no 17, 1; PG 53, 134). The rest of the references about the analogy between Incarnation and inspiration come from medieval authors.

2. Henri de Lubac, *Histoire et Esprit. L'intelligence de l'Écriture d'après Origène* (Paris: Aubier, 1950). An English translation appeared only fifty-eight years later: *History and Spirit: The Understanding of Scripture according to Origen*, trans. A. E. Nash (San Francisco: Ignatius, 2008).

3. Hugo Rahner, "Das Menschenbild des Origenes," *Eranos-Jahrbuch* 15 (1947): 197-248.

4. Karl Rahner, *Über die Schriftinspiration* (Freiburg: Herder, 1958), p. 22, n. 5.

5. Hans Urs von Balthasar, *Verbum Caro, Skizzen zur Theologie* (Einsiedeln: Johannes Verlag, 1960), pp. 12-27.

4

A few years later, when, by the Preparatory Commission of the Council, the first outline of a document about Scripture and Tradition was presented to the Second Vatican Council ("De fontibus revelationis"), this new outlook was missing from the proposed text. As we know, the narrow, neo-Thomistic "schema" failed to obtain enough support, and after some stormy exchanges, thanks to a personal intervention by Pope John XXIII, was taken off the council's agenda. Two years later, however, at the last session, following the appointment of a new commission, this outlook made a comeback under a new title and within a new perspective. The new text eventually became the Dogmatic Constitution *Dei verbum,* the first conciliar document ever in which the patristic analogy between incarnation and inspiration appears.

Incarnation and Inspiration in *Dei verbum*

Dei verbum consists of six chapters. As its title reveals, it treats Divine Revelation and its transmission. Therefore, biblical inspiration and interpretation are included only as a secondary topic and in a somewhat sketchy way. The first two chapters deal with revelation as the process of God's self-disclosure offered to chosen persons to accept it in faith and then hand it over to their fellowmen. It is in such a context that Scripture is first mentioned in the second chapter (no. 10). Then, in the third chapter the document lays down in broad outline the theology of inspiration, with explicit references to previous statements of the magisterium on the matter.[6] In paragraph no. 13, the analogy between incarnation and inspiration is explicitly stated. Of course, we find in this passage no reference to previous magisterial documents, leaving the impression that the analogy of incarnation and inspiration has never been previously mentioned in any magisterial statement. The text reads:

> [For] the words of God, expressed in human language, have been made like human discourse, just as the Word of the Eternal Father, when he took to himself the weakness of the human flesh, was in every way made like men.[7]

6. 10-12 are heavily footnoted, with references to the Council of Trent, *Providentissimus Deus* by Leo XIII, *Divino afflante Spiritu* by Pius XII, and *Spiritus Paraclitus* by Benedict XV.

7. Although no footnote says so, this passage is nothing but a rectified version of *Divino afflante Spiritu* by Pius XII, in which the analogy between Scripture and God's Incarnate

This was a short reference to the Incarnation, yet afterward the idea of an analogy with the Incarnation did not completely disappear. When both subsequent chapters (the fourth chapter about the Old Testament and the fifth about the New Testament) begin with the term "the Word of God," the document harks back to "the Word of the Eternal Father" (cf. no. 11), proceeding from the Father, an expression that certainly evokes the Incarnation.

More significant is the parallelism that the opening lines of the sixth and last chapter of *Dei verbum* make between the Eucharistic and the Scriptural Word. They speak about transmitting God's life-giving nourishment to the faithful from *the double "table" of word and sacrament,* with an obvious parallelism between verbal and sacramental signs as the means by which God's self-disclosure and self-giving are continually offered to mankind. Through this reference to the Eucharist, the parallelism with the Incarnation is brought to mind again.

Implications for a New Theology of Inspiration

In the way I see it, after Vatican II and due to various causes, the theology of inspiration collapsed, causing both neglect and ignorance with regard to this topic. *Dei verbum* broke with the neo-Scholastic framework, an approach that lost its credibility well before the Council, while the Roman textbooks like those of Bea, Tromp, Höpfl-Gut-Metzinger-Leloir,[8] etc. were still in Roman use. But they became largely "unteachable," so that theology programs began to look for replacements.[9] The issues about the

---

Word appears in the following way: "Sicut enim substantiale Dei verbum hominibus simile factum est quoad omnia 'absque peccato' (Hebr 5:12), ita etiam Dei verba humanis expressa quoad omnia humano sermoni assimilia facta sunt excepto errore. . . ." It seems to me that the commission, which originally wanted to leave out the concept of inerrancy, suppressed any reference to this sentence of *Divino afflante Spiritu,* which contains the phrase *excepto errore.* As we know, *Dei verbum* has eventually, in spite of the Committee's reluctance but due to a papal intervention calling on the Theological Commission of the Council, finally included the words "sine errore." One must also notice that in this same paragraph, *Divino afflante Spiritu* quotes the term "condescension" in both Latin and Greek with a reference to John Chrysostom (cf. above note 1), which *Dei verbum* welcomed into its text, yet made no reference to the document of Pius XII.

8. This was the last edition of the *Introductio Generalis in Sacram Scripturam,* updated decade after decade by Benedictine professors succeeding each other, which reigned for over half a century in the Pontifical School of theology at Sant'Anselmo in Rome.

9. The story is a bit more complicated. By the early 1960s in almost every program,

"hagiographers" and the double authorship of Scripture, one divine and one human, lost their Thomistic speculative context, because Thomistic epistemology was losing ground. Already at the Council it became clear that, due to the lack of monographic studies about the patristic and medieval teaching of inspiration, there was little knowledge about what tradition really said about these matters. At the same time the hardening militancy of critical exegesis, which bracketed or excluded theological issues, resulted in biblical scholarship expressing little or no esteem for much of what ancient and medieval tradition offered, and biblical and patristic studies became further alienated.

Most biblical scholars realized that Karl Rahner in his book on inspiration, a tiny volume of eighty-three pages, made substantial challenges to the traditional scholastic treatise about this topic. He called for a complete rethinking of the doctrine of inspiration; yet beyond the response by Luis Alonso Schökel in his *The Inspired Word* and a few critical pages of assorted book reviews, nothing of significance happened in response.

The Outline of a Theology of Inspiration in an Incarnational Perspective

Before a question in Catholic theology is reshaped and renewed, one must assess and recover what tradition has achieved and preserved. This task is not as huge today as it was forty years ago, because the history of exegesis has been successfully studied and, as a collateral benefit, we have begun to understand a little better what our tradition has taught about inspiration.

The most beneficial contribution comes from *Dei verbum,* which inserts the question of inspiration into the general topic of the transmission of revelation in the context of salvation history. It thereby saves inspiration from the narrow confines of an interaction between God and man as joint authors of literary products, books that contain God's word without error. In other words, Sacred Scripture must be regarded as the product of one single sacred history that brought about the coming of Christ at its peak, with the people of Israel in its first phase and the Church in its second phase as the recipients of revelation. Revelation is not a set of propositional statements,

---

inspiration and inerrancy became part of "Fundamental theology," absorbing what was previously taught in "General Introduction to Sacred Scripture" so that the topic of inspiration often fell through the cracks between newly organized subjects.

but happens in "words and deeds."[10] While walking down this path, we come to the realization that the Word becoming flesh results also in the Word becoming Tradition and brings about the Word becoming Scripture — all these belong to one single process by which God has come into the world for the sake of our salvation.

We are now at the point where we can make some helpful distinctions in order to create adequate conceptual tools for outlining a theology of inspiration, or even, we might say, a theology of the Bible. A first distinction is very important although rarely made. Biblical inspiration can be studied from two sides: an objective side treating the inspired books, and a subjective side treating the biblical authors or "hagiographers." The distinction of these two aspects makes it possible to examine separately each set of questions concerning "inspired authors" (inspiration as charism) and the "inspired books" ("inspiredness" or inspiration as a property of the biblical text).

The inspired authors are recipients of charisms that they receive as mediators of God's word. Their role is analogous to that of the patriarchs, Moses, and his successors, the other prophetic figures, including those whose names mark various books of the Old Testament. In the New Testament, the mediators of God's new word of revelation are the apostles as well as their collaborators, whom the early church calls "viri apostolici," apostolic men. In both Testaments the "mediators" of the word must be seen as a subordinated mediatory function to the earthly Christ as they extend the mediation of him who is now in glory. Thus these mediators of the word are truly instruments of transmission, but Christ remains God's only full and fully authentic self-disclosure. As the prophetic leaders anticipate, the apostolic leaders extend the supreme office and role of Christ, the only mediator between God and man. This whole structure of transmitters of the divine word must be seen as emanating from *and* providing participation in the one Word of the Father. That some of these figures transmitted the prophetic or the apostolic message orally and some did it in writing is an important distinction, but remains of secondary importance. The word of God addresses man *viva voce,* forms a community, and functions in a role of establishing and maintaining remembrance. In both its written and oral form, God's word, when transmitted in human words, provides lasting instruments by which the word constituting the community of God's people may enable that people to hear the word in its original force and authenticity.

10. See the phrases "verbis gestisque inter se connectis" (no. 2) and "facta et verba" (no. 17).

The outline laid out here posits an intimate connection between Scripture and tradition. Usually oral tradition precedes Scripture, but tradition also keeps the Scriptures secure, well defined, and stabilized. Tradition also serves as the living and actual interpretive framework of God's word, while the written texts offer more objective standards of authenticity, precision, solid verbal expression, and accurately focused memory.

What I have described so far is only one dimension of the genesis of Scripture, a dimension that we can call historical or temporal. In this process, God reveals, while man listens, believes, accepts, responds, remembers, and, for the sake of future generations, transmits both memory and text. The one and same God, who initiates revelation by offering himself to mankind, keeps this very process in motion. He accompanies his word so that it might be retained, remembered, and passed on. Biblical inspiration is the grace that accompanies God's word, all the way up to its written consolidation in the finalized and canonized form of Scripture.

There is, however, a second dimension. The written word that comes about in the course of this process is the sacred text; it can be called an "inspired text." The sacred text enshrines and solidifies what God has told the human creature in the process of salvation history, and can be accessed as such by new generations. Scripture contains a blueprint of God's dealings with man so that it becomes a map for man's journey to God. The objective aspect of inspiration is a specific quality of the text. The inspired text resembles all human literary productions, insofar as it also represents in some objective and solidified terms human states of consciousness in written form. But the sacred text is not merely a human product. At its greatest depth, it makes God's word accessible in audible-legible form; it provides for the ongoing availability of God's self-disclosure for any human being who can read and/or understand the particular human idiom. It brings God, in search of man, to potentially every human being who seeks God in faith.

Further Clarifications

The relationship between incarnation and inspiration is manifold.

First, there is a cause-effect relationship. The economy of salvation not only aims at, but also derives from the Incarnation of the Son. Scripture is part of the "scaffolding" on which the Incarnation, the Son's hypostatic union with human nature, is set in both its pre-resurrectional and resurrected state. The Incarnate and glorified Word is the fulfillment of all other words. This creates a specific reference system of all parts of Scripture to Jesus born, crucified, and glorified.

Second, there is an analogy between the Incarnate Word and the word of God presented in the Holy Scriptures. Their structures resemble each other insofar as in both, the human element is linked to the divine by its instrumental role and by its function of bringing to the realm of sense perception what is beyond the senses. Consequently both can be approached by the senses, specifically the eyes and ears. Just as in the sacraments, human tools are needed for communicating both what is human and what is divine. Both must be explored by "fides quaerens intellectum." On the surface, the Word Incarnate may create disappointment or scandal; at its depth He offers a revelatory encounter with God on all levels of human existence: physical, intellectual, emotional, moral, and ontological. The various senses of Scripture in ancient and medieval exegesis examine these various yet connected levels.

Third, inspiration involves divine condescension. This term does not only signify God stooping to man so that man's slow intellect or unyielding selfishness may be overcome. When offering his word in permanently deposited, written form, God allows man to approach him according to the needs of his nature. In the Incarnation, God's condescension makes possible what was first impossible even to Moses: fellowship with God. Now man begins to "converse with God as a man converses with a fellow human being" (Exod. 33:11). Regardless of the kind of vision that Moses was given, only in Jesus' earthly life can mortal flesh possibly carry a fully divine personal presence. But, of course, the mortal body of human beings handicaps the fullness of revelation. Far from simply revealing the Deity, it both veils and hides the Deity. When Jesus is raised, he appears to his apostles and transmits both the gift of the Holy Spirit and the gift of the Scriptures, explaining the meaning of both to the apostles. Three gifts constitute the Church:

1. the presence of Jesus' risen humanity in the Eucharist,[11]
2. the gift of the Holy Spirit, and
3. the meaning of the Scriptures, which the apostolic church takes into its possession while depositing its understanding of Christ in the writings of the New Testament.

---

11. Of course, I subsume to this point the whole sacramental order and the liturgical life of the Church.

Rather than attempt to write a concluding paragraph for an essay that was meant to remain sketchy and incomplete, I provide here as a reminder a rather lengthy passage from the Gospel of Luke by which, in the framework of the divine word, he authentically condenses all that can be said summarily about inspiration and incarnation and the further relationships they invoke.

While they were talking about this, Jesus himself stood among them and said to them, "Peace be with you." They were startled and terrified, and thought that they were seeing a ghost. He said to them, "Why are you frightened, and why do doubts arise in your hearts? Look at **my hands and my feet**; see that it is I myself. Touch me and see; for a ghost does not have flesh and bones as you see that I have." And when he had said this, **he showed them his hands and his feet**. While in their joy they were disbelieving and still wondering, he said to them, "Have you anything here to eat?" They gave him a piece of broiled fish, and he took it and ate in their presence. Then he said to them, "**These are my words that I spoke to you** while I was still with you — that everything **written** about me in the law of Moses, the prophets, and the psalms must be fulfilled." Then he opened their minds to understand the scriptures, and he said to them, "Thus it is written, that the Messiah is to suffer and to rise from the dead on the third day, and that repentance and forgiveness of sins is to be proclaimed in his name to all nations, beginning from Jerusalem. You are witnesses of these things. And see, **I am sending upon you what my Father promised**; so stay here in the city until you have been clothed with power from on high." (Luke 24:36-49)

My last comment spells out a tall task. The incarnational context of inspiration offers to the theology of inspiration a new chance for what Karl Rahner asked for in 1958: a complete overhaul of the concept, in order to rethink, redevelop, and repossess it for the sake of renewing biblical theology.[12]

---

12. He proposed that *the concept of inspiration be thought through anew* ("den Begriff der Inspiration neu zu durchdenken"). K. Rahner, *Über die Schriftinspiration* (Freiburg: Herder, 1958), p. 16.

CHAPTER 2

Spiritual Understanding of Scripture

Francis Martin

Introduction: The Fire of Sinai

There is a rabbinic tradition that those who earnestly seek to enter into the mystery of the Sacred Text will be brought to the source of all revelation and experience the fire of Sinai. This method of pondering the Sacred Text is called "stringing pearls" and it consists in elucidating texts by "piercing" and "stringing" them together. One moves from the Torah to the Nebiim, to the Ketubim, back to the Torah, to the Nebiim, and the Ketubim until the very source of revelation is accorded to the seekers. A tale from the Jerusalem Talmud recounted by Rabbi Elisha b. Abuyah illustrates this tradition:

> Abuyah my father was one of the leading men of Jerusalem. It happened on a Sabbath day, when I was to be circumcised, that he invited all the leading men of Jerusalem and he seated them in one room; but R. Eliezer and R. Joshua he put in another room. When they (all the guests) had finished eating and drinking, they began to clap and dance.
>
> R. Eliezer said to R. Joshua: As they are busy about their affairs let us be busy about ours. And they sat down and busied themselves with the words of the Torah, from the Torah to the Prophets and from the Prophets to the Writings. And a fire came down and enveloped them. Abuyah said to them: Masters have you come to burn my house down on me?

I would like to thank Crystal Grothoff, whose invaluable editing has improved this contribution.

They said to him: Far be it from us! But we were sitting and stringing together the words of the Torah, from the Torah to the Prophets and from the Prophets to the Writings. And the words were full of joy as when they were delivered from Sinai. The fire was lapping at them, coming from Sinai. Originally, when they were given from Sinai, they were only given in fire: "And the mountain was burning with fire right up to the heart of heaven" (Dt 4:11).[1]

This connection between the revelatory power of the Sacred Text and the fire of Sinai lies behind the Lucan passage that recounts Jesus' meeting with the two disciples leaving Jerusalem. Jesus takes the disciples through "Moses and all the prophets," and then through the Torah, the Nebiim, and the Ketubim (here abbreviated as "the psalms"):

Then beginning with Moses and all the prophets, he interpreted to them what referred to him in all the scriptures. . . . "Were not our hearts burning (within us) while he spoke to us on the way and opened the scriptures to us?" . . . He said to them, "These are my words that I spoke to you while I was still with you, that everything written about me in the Law of Moses and in the prophets and psalms must be fulfilled." Then he opened their minds to understand the scriptures. (Luke 24:13-45)

In this passage, St. Luke makes two theological statements. First, Jesus is the fire of Sinai, the revelatory light and unifying reality of all Scripture. Second, the experience of being instructed by him is one of the proofs of his resurrection. This second point is elaborated upon by St. Thomas, who describes the spiritual understanding that pertains to the grace of prophecy:

After the level of those who receive revelation directly from God, another level of grace is necessary. Because men receive revelation from God not only for their own time but also for the instruction of all who come after them, it was necessary that the things revealed to them be passed on not only in speech to their contemporaries but also as written down for the instruction of those to come after them. And thus it was also necessary that there be those who could interpret what was written down. This also

---

1. y. Ḥagigah 2:1. For a slightly more ample account of this theme, one could consult Francis Martin, *Narrative Parallels to the New Testament,* SBL Resources for Biblical Study 22 (Atlanta: Scholars Press, 1988), p. 35. For a modern appreciation of the importance of this theme, see Rickie D. Moore, "Deuteronomy and the Fire of God," *Journal of Pentecostal Theology* 7 (1995): 11-33.

must be done by divine grace. And so we read in Genesis 40:8, "Does not interpretation come from God?"[2]

In this brief contribution, I wish to reflect on the ancient tradition that the Sacred Text is interpreted by means of prophetic graces and point to the manner in which this tradition is being recovered and integrated with what is sound in the historical work that has been done in recent centuries. First, I will discuss how recent advances, both practical and theoretical, in the understanding of history have modified those aspects of historical study of the Sacred Text that have prevented it from bringing us to the "fire of Sinai." Second, I will institute a comparable reflection on the deficiencies that remain in recent theories of history and cognition, indicating how they have prevented many believers from appropriating the Sacred Text. I see this effort as following the course laid out for us in Pope John Paul II's encyclical letter, *Fides et Ratio:*

> [T]he relationship between philosophy and theology is marked by a kind of circular progress. The beginning and primal source of theology is the Word of God revealed in history, while its ultimate purpose is necessarily the understanding of that Word which grows gradually with the progress of time. But since the Word of God is Truth (cf. *Jn* 17:17) the human search for truth — the philosophical mind observing its own laws — can only help God's Word to be better explained. . . . It is very evident that, moving between these two poles — that is between the Word of God and its deeper comprehension — reason is offered guidance and is warned against paths which would lead it to stray from revealed truth and to stray in the end from truth pure and simple: rather, reason is in this way spurred on to exploring new paths which, left to itself, it could hardly imagine that it could find. *From this circular movement philosophy* [read here: historical and literary study and its presuppositions] *emerges the richer from its contact with the Word of God in its attainment of new and unexpected ends.*[3]

---

2. Thomas Aquinas, *Summa Contra Gentiles* Bk. 3, c. 154.

3. Pope John Paul II, *Fides et ratio,* 14 September 1998. Translation taken from *Restoring Faith in Reason,* ed. Laurence Paul Hemming and Susan Frank Parsons, trans. Anthony Meredith and Laurence Paul Hemming (London: SCM Press, 2002), pp. 285-314. Italics added.

An Understanding of History[4]

The basic principle of a spiritual understanding of the Sacred Text is well articulated by Alister McGrath: "Scripture is read in order to encounter Christ."[5] My approach, therefore, is to allow the faith experience of the past and present to confront the often sterile results of modern exegesis and thus "spur" reason to correct what is faulty in the underlying presuppositions of some fundamental approaches.

History and Immanence

Perhaps the single most misleading presupposition in the historical study of the Bible is that there is no transcendent cause operative in history. This position was clearly articulated by Baruch Spinoza, who maintained that the Bible must be approached like any other imaginative literature.[6] One of the founders of the sociological method, Emile Durkheim, maintained that religious expressions in a culture were due to social and immanent causes.[7] He saluted the atheistic position of Auguste Comte and was, in turn, a powerful influence upon Hermann Gunkel, who exercised a decisive influence in the formation of form criticism. These thinkers held that the Gospels were the result of a progressive sociological process of transmission. Since the information concerning Jesus' words and actions passed through a grid of communal interpretation, there is no certitude as to the actual agent of what is recounted.

Although some Christian commentators maintained that one could prescind from the sociological laws developed by the Durkheim school, little genuine theology emerged from this historical approach. Pierre Benoit was

---

4. Some of the material that follows will be published in a forthcoming book of my essays.

5. Alister McGrath, "Reclaiming Our Roots and Vision: Scripture and the Stability of the Christian Church," in *Reclaiming the Bible for the Church,* ed. Carl E. Braaten and Robert W. Jensen (Grand Rapids: Eerdmans, 1995), pp. 63-68, at 67.

6. See David Laird Dungan, "Baruch Spinoza and the Political Agenda of Modern Historical-Critical Interpretation," in *A History of the Synoptic Problem: The Canon, the Text, the Composition, and the Interpretation of the Gospels,* The Anchor Bible Reference Library (New York: Doubleday, 1999), pp. 198-260.

7. See Emile Durkheim, *The Elementary Forms of the Religious Life* (New York: George Allen & Unwin Ltd., 1915; reprint, New York: Free Press, 1965).

an early and astute critic of this interpretive procedure and the presuppositions upon which it was based. In 1946, he wrote:

> By the "Community" is meant the mass of earliest Christians taken all together as a social group, and an anonymous one. An unknown quantity, and a very convenient one, which is made to endorse everything.
>
> For eyewitnesses are an embarrassment. They have lived through the events. We hesitate before attributing reports that are too untruthful to them. If others ascribe to Jesus deeds and words of which he is not the author, it is open to us to say that they do so without realizing that they are deceived by popular rumour. But for eyewitnesses it is different. The only thing that remains is to eliminate them. And that is what these critics do.[8]

More recently, several authors have challenged the position of form criticism and its sequelae by considering the contribution of both eyewitnesses and the oral tradition in the composition of the Gospels. Among these authors are James D. G. Dunn, Richard Bauckham, Paul Rhodes Eddy, and Gregory Boyd.[9] Another line of critique is taken by Christopher Seitz, who accents the "canonical shaping" of the Old Testament text and challenges the atomizing tendency of much historical criticism.[10]

In addition to the criticisms of the biases present in historical studies of the Bible, there are also several studies that reflect on the philosophical positions that influence historical studies. Among the earlier critics was Joseph Ratzinger:

---

8. Pierre Benoit, "Reflections on 'Formgeschichtliche Methode,'" in *Jesus and the Gospel* (New York: Seabury Press, 1973), p. 35.

9. James D. G. Dunn challenges the concentration on written material in approaching the Synoptic material in "Altering the Default Setting: Re-Envisaging the Early Transmission of the Jesus Tradition," *New Testament Studies* 49, no. 2 (2003): 139-75; and accents the role of the oral tradition in *A New Perspective on Jesus: What the Quest for the Historical Jesus Missed,* ed. Craig A. Evans and Lee Martin McDonald, Acadia Studies in Bible and Theology (Grand Rapids: Baker Academic, 2005). For a solid portrayal of eyewitnesses and the oral tradition, one should consult Richard Bauckham, *Jesus and the Eyewitnesses: The Gospels as Eyewitness Testimony* (Grand Rapids: Eerdmans, 2006); and Kenneth E. Bailey, "Informal Controlled Oral Tradition and the Synoptic Gospels," *Themelios* 20, no. 2 (1995): 4-11. Bailey has extensive experience in the cultural milieux of various Semitic languages where the same means of narrative transmission have been in force for many centuries. See also Paul Rhodes Eddy and Gregory A. Boyd, *The Jesus Legend: A Case for the Reliability of the Synoptic Jesus Tradition* (Grand Rapids: Baker Academic, 2007).

10. Christopher R. Seitz, *Word without End: The Old Testament as Abiding Theological Witness* (Waco, TX: Baylor University Press, 2004).

The real philosophical presupposition behind the whole enterprise seems to me to lie in the Kantian turn. According to Kant, man cannot perceive the voice of being in itself; he can hear it only indirectly, in the postulates of practical reason, which remain so to say as the last narrow slit through which contact with the really real, with his eternal destiny, can still reach him. For the rest, for what the activity of his reason can substantively grasp, man can go only so far as the categorical allows. He is therefore limited to the positive, to the empirical, to "exact" science in which by definition something or someone Wholly Other, a new beginning from another plane, has no room to occur. Translated into the language of theology, this means that revelation must retreat into the pure formality of the "eschatological" attitude, which corresponds to the tiny chink left open by Kant. Everything else must be "explained": what otherwise may have appeared to be a direct disclosure of the divine can only be a myth governed by ascertainable laws of development. . . . The debate about modern exegesis is not at its core a debate among historians, but among philosophers.[11]

In the Kantian system, there is no "direct disclosure of the divine," and approaching the "fire of Sinai" is not deemed feasible.

Relying on recent philosophical discussions concerning the nature of history and history writing,[12] I wish to integrate a more extended critique of the weaknesses lying behind the modern understanding of history. The proposal here is to integrate what linear history can teach us about the meaning of the Sacred Text with an understanding of how the events recounted also participate in the mystery of the Word become flesh. A full development of this theme would require a treatment of Christ himself as "auctor doctrinae" both as God, the First Truth, and as man, the unique and privileged manifestation of that truth.[13]

11. Joseph Ratzinger, "Biblical Interpretations in Conflict: On the Foundations and the Itinerary of Exegesis Today," in *Opening Up the Scriptures,* ed. Jose Granados, Carlos Granados, and Luis Sánchez-Navarro (Grand Rapids: Eerdmans, 2008), pp. 1-29, at 18-19.

12. These studies include Matthew Lamb, *Eternity, Time, and the Life of Wisdom* (Naples, FL: Sapientia Press at Ave Maria University, 2007); Francis Martin, "Historical Criticism and New Testament Teaching on the Imitation of Christ," *Anthropotes* 6 (1990): 261-87; "The Spiritual Sense (Sensus Spiritualis) of Sacred Scripture," in *Sacred Scripture: The Disclosure of the Word* (Naples, FL: Sapientia Press, 2006), pp. 249-75. These arguments are referred to and developed in the ample study by Matthew Levering, *Participatory Biblical Exegesis: A Theology of Biblical Interpretation,* ed. Gary A. Anderson, Matthew Levering, and Robert Louis Wilken (Notre Dame: University of Notre Dame Press, 2008).

13. See Yves Congar, "Tradition et 'Sacra Doctrina' Chez Saint Thomas D'Aquin," in

History, as we presently use the term, refers to human activity past and present. The Christian position is that this activity, individual and collective, is not ultimately intelligible unless it is seen in its "interior dimension." Human beings are not merely agents but also subjects: their activity has an interior dimension which relates to God and which affects every other human being. This understanding of history derives its ultimate direction and meaning from the economy of the Incarnation. Jesus Christ is the center of the history of humankind. In the Letter to the Colossians, Paul writes, "He himself is before all things, and in him all things hold together" (1:17). The phrase "all things" refers not merely to cosmic events but also includes all human activity from the beginning of creation until its completion. The passage continues: "He is the head of the body, the church; he is the beginning, the firstborn from the dead, so that he might come to have first place in everything" (1:18). Within this economy of the Incarnation, the Church participates in the uniqueness of the presence of God in Christ. This is the Church that began with Abraham and will continue until the end of our present mode of history.

Following Aquinas, we must distinguish between the anticipated presence of the grace of Christ in the history and the worship of Israel, and the *status* (stable form) of that grace in the New Covenant. According to Augustine, Aquinas, and the general tradition of the Church, devout Israelites belonged not only to the economy of the Incarnation but actually to the Body of Christ. To illustrate this position, allow me to cite three passages, all of which are from Aquinas but which have their counterparts elsewhere in the tradition.

First, the unique presence of God in Christ is the basis of the economy of the Incarnation:

> God is said to be in a thing in two ways; in one way after the manner of an efficient cause; and thus He is in all things created by Him; in another way He is in things as the object of operation is in the operator. . . . In this second way God is especially in the rational creature which knows and loves Him actually or habitually. . . . There is, however, another special mode of God's existence in man by union.[14]

This economy of the Incarnation reaches back into the history of the Jewish people:

Église et Tradition, ed. Johannes Betz and Heinrich Fries (Le Pye/Lyon: Xavier Mappus, 1963), pp. 173-74.
14. *Summa Theologiae* I, q. 8, a. 3, cor. and ad 4; cf. III, q. 2.

The Jewish people were chosen by God in order that Christ be born of them. Therefore it was necessary that the whole state *(status)* of that people be prophetic and figural as Augustine says in *Contra Faustum* (22,24).[15] And for this reason even the judicial precepts handed on to that people are more figural than the judicial precepts handed on to other peoples. And thus even the wars and actions of that people are expounded mystically [i.e., have a spiritual sense] but not the wars and actions of the Assyrians or Romans even though they were by far better known among men.[16]

Elsewhere, Aquinas explicitly teaches that the Jews belong to the Body of Christ. In answering the objection that the New Testament uses the word "shadow" to speak of the Old Testament liturgical observances, Aquinas writes:

It should be said that the holy Fathers did not stop at the sacraments of the Law as mere things, but as images and shadows of future realities. For the movement toward an image, in so far as it is an image, is the same as the movement toward the reality as the Philosopher says in his work *On Memory and Recall.* And therefore, the ancient Fathers, by observing the sacraments of the Law, were brought toward Christ through the same faith and love by which we are still brought toward him. For this reason the ancient Fathers belonged to the same Body of the Church to which we belong.[17]

15. Augustine writes, "not only the speech of these men, but their life also, was prophetic; and the whole kingdom of the Hebrews was like a great prophet, corresponding to the greatness of the Person prophesied" (*St. Augustin: The Writings Against the Manicheans and Against the Donatists,* ed. Philip Schaff [reprint, Peabody, MA: Hendrickson, 1992], p. 282). So powerful was this understanding of the early church that Didymus the Blind (d. 398), commenting on 1 Peter 1:10-13, was able to say: "Those who lived before the coming of Christ were less well informed, not because of their wickedness but because of God's dispensation of time. Therefore it is said that the prophets examined how and at what time the salvation of their souls would be fulfilled by the sufferings of Christ and his subsequent glory. They preached these things, knowing that they were not going to be revealed directly to them but would appear at some future time. Therefore it is wrong to say that their sanctification was somehow inferior to ours." See *James, 1-2 Peter, 1-3 John, Jude,* Ancient Christian Commentary on Scripture, New Testament, 11, ed. Gerald Bray (Downers Grove, IL: InterVarsity Press, 2000), pp. 73-74.

16. *ST* I-II, q. 104, a. 2, ad 2. Note that Aquinas is speaking here about *realities* (wars and actions) and not only about the words by which these realities are mediated.

17. *ST* III, q. 8, a. 3, ad 3. I am indebted here to the study by Colman O'Neill, "St. Thomas On the Membership of the Church," *The Thomist* 27 (1963): 88-140. The latter part of Aquinas's response is his translation. For a more ample discussion of this point, I refer the reader to my article, "The Spiritual Sense (Sensus Spiritualis) of Sacred Scripture."

This rather surprising understanding of the manner in which the just among the people of Israel related to Christ/the Word is only one aspect of a concerted conviction of the early theologians and mystics.[18] I will cite two of the many texts that witness to the early conviction that Christ was, in some way, present to Israel. One of the clearest examples is found in 1 Corinthians 10 in a series of warnings against imitating the infidelity of Israel. Paul writes: "All ate the same spiritual food, and all drank the same spiritual drink, for they drank from the spiritual rock that followed them, and the rock was Christ" (10:3-4).[19] Alluding to the incident of the bronze serpent (Num. 21:4-7), Paul continues: "Let us not test Christ as some of them did, and suffered death by serpents" (1 Cor. 10:9), substituting "Christ" for "God" in Psalm 78:18 which reads "and they tested God in their hearts, demanding the food they craved."[20]

It is as well a patristic commonplace to consider that in some mysterious way the Word was present to his people before the Incarnation. An example would be:

The Son of God has been sown everywhere throughout the Scriptures [of Moses]. Sometimes He speaks with Abraham, sometimes with Noah, giving him the measurements of the ark; He looks for Adam, brings judgment on the Sodomites. . . . Thus the Word of God always showed to men, so to speak, the outlines of the things He was to accomplish in the future, the contours of the Father's saving plan, thereby teaching us the things of God.[21]

To conclude this section, I wish to suggest that the modern study of history can be integrated with a biblical understanding only if the transcen-

18. For a good discussion of this point, see Angela Russell Christman, *"What Did Ezekiel See?": Christian Exegesis of Ezekiel's Vision of the Chariot from Irenaeus to Gregory the Great* (Leiden: Brill, 2005).

19. This summary of the manner in which God cared for Israel in the desert is close to that of the themes in the liturgy of Sukkot as well as those in Nehemiah 9:20: "You gave them your good spirit to instruct them, you did not withhold your manna from their mouths, you gave them water for their thirst."

20. A certain number of texts read "the Lord" rather than "Christ" but this kind of substitution (i.e., not understanding how Christ could have been present) is more understandable than its opposite. For a discussion of this point, see Gordon D. Fee, *The First Epistle to the Corinthians,* The New International Commentary on the New Testament (Grand Rapids: Eerdmans, 1987), p. 456.

21. Irenaeus, "Against the Heresies," IV, 10, 1; 20, 8-11; Hans Urs von Balthasar, ed., *The Scandal of the Incarnation: Irenaeus Against the Heresies* (San Francisco: Ignatius Press, 1990), p. 90, #90.

dent dimension of time is restored. For modern history, time is succession, a dubious and uneven march toward an indeterminate future. The study of history, now capable of genuine reconstruction and insight, records this march. As we have seen, it resolutely eschews any consideration of transcendence, any search for a causality that exceeds the forces and resources of what is fundamentally a closed system.[22] Just as physics reduces the material universe to the "superior" language of mathematics, so critical history reduces the mystery of human temporal existence to the "superior" viewpoint of a certain understanding of causality and the attainability of knowledge of the past: both are prisoners of the loss of transcendence.[23]

Cognition

As an understanding of creation requires an appreciation of participation, so does an adequate grasp of knowledge itself require what Robert Barron recently has called "epistemic participation."[24] In a similar vein, Aquinas writes:

> Though there be many participated truths, there is but one absolute Truth which by its own essence is Truth, namely the Divine Being itself, by which Truth all words are words. In the same way there is one absolute Wisdom, raised above all, namely the Divine Wisdom by participation in whom all wise men are wise. And in the same way the absolute Word by participation in whom all who have a word are said to be speaking. This is the Divine Word, which in himself is the Word raised above all.[25]

22. The relation between this view and the pre-Christian pagan view of reality can be seen in the study by Robert Sokolowski, *The God of Faith and Reason: Foundations of Christian Theology* (Notre Dame: University of Notre Dame Press, 1982).

23. For an admirable analysis of this reductive viewpoint, see Louis Dupré, *Passage to Modernity: An Essay in the Hermeneutics of Nature and Culture* (New Haven and London: Yale University Press, 1993). Much of the material in the following paragraphs is taken from my article, "*Sacra Doctrina* and the Authority of Its *Sacra Scriptura* According to St. Thomas Aquinas," *Pro Ecclesia* 10, no. 1 (2001): 84-102.

24. Robert Barron, *The Priority of Christ* (Grand Rapids: Brazos Press, 2007). The phrase and its application occur in chapter 10: "The Nature of the Christ Mind."

25. Thomas Aquinas, *Commentary on the Gospel of John*, ch. 1, lect. 1. A consequence of this view was already enunciated by Aquinas's predecessor, Hugh of St. Victor: "The Word of God comes to man every day, present in the human voice." *The Word of God*, I, 2-3 (*Sources Chrétiennes* 155, 60). The translation is mine.

We have seen that a lack of appreciation for God as creator of the universe and as author and Lord of history to whom all things are present leads to the reduction of history to a mere succession of events. It now remains to be seen that a failure to understand human rationality in view of the Divine Word who is the fire of Sinai, "the light enlightening all men," leads to a reduction of knowledge to a solely human activity. The act by which God confers light on the mind is unique to him and, in this sense, only God can teach. Aquinas says that the interior light of reason is itself a "certain participation in divine light"; it is, in fact "nothing else but the imprint of the divine light in us."[26] God also can instruct in the manner of a human teacher, ministering to the light he first supplies. In commenting on the words of Romans 1:19, "God made it [what can be known about him] manifest to them," Aquinas speaks of God's activity in creating as that of a teacher "proposing exterior signs of his wisdom" (Sir. 1:10) and also "conferring an interior light by which a person actually knows."[27]

In speaking of *sacra doctrina,* St. Thomas uses much of the same terminology that he applies to the exercise of the natural light of reason in learning from God through creation. He says of *sacra doctrina,* a term he often equates with *sacra scriptura,* that it is "a certain imprint of the divine knowledge."[28] This generation of knowledge is active from the side of God but passive from the side of the one who receives it.[29] Thus, in conferring knowledge through revelation, God acts as a teacher. Revelation is given imperfectly in prophecy and perfectly in the beatific vision.[30]

Along with apostleship, prophecy can be a general category by which to designate those who received normative revelation at its origin:

> [P]rophecy is a knowledge imprinted by divine revelation *(impressa ex revelatione divina)* on the mind of a prophet, in the form of teaching. Now the truth of knowledge is the same in the disciple as in the master. The disciple's knowledge is, in effect, a reproduction *(similitudo)* of that in the master, just as in things of nature the form of what is generated is a certain likeness of the form of that which generates.[31]

---

26. *ST* I, q. 12, a. 11, ad 3; I-II, q. 91, a. 2.

27. *Ad Romanos* §116, in *Super Epistulas S. Pauli Lectura* (Rome: Marietti, 1953).

28. Francis Martin, "*Sacra Doctrina* and the Authority of Its *Sacra Scriptura* According to St. Thomas Aquinas"; *ST* I, q. 1, a. 3, ad 2.

29. *On III Physicorum*, c. 3, l. 5 (Leonine ed. II, 113).

30. *ST* II-II, q. 171, a. 4, ad 2.

31. *ST* II-II, q. 171, a. 6. Translation by Roland Potter (London: Blackfriars/Eyre & Spottiswoode, 1972), vol. 45, p. 25.

The use of the notion of *doctrina* or teaching in connection with prophecy enables Pierre Benoit to give the following as a generic description of prophecy:

> By "prophecy" St. Thomas understands essentially knowledge, supernaturally given to man, of truths exceeding the present reach of his mind, which God teaches him for the benefit of the community.[32]

With similar words to Benoit, Aquinas holds that "all supernatural influence can be reduced to prophecy," if prophecy is taken in a broad sense.[33]

The principle that it requires a certain prophetic grace in order to understand the Scriptures is a commonplace in the Christian tradition. For Origen and most of the Fathers, the relationship between the content of the Old Testament text and the mystery of Christ is perceived through an experiential knowledge of the reality that is conferred by the Holy Spirit and is mediated in and through the Old Testament now understood in the light of Christ. This Spirit-conferred knowledge is described by Henri Crouzel in the striking phrase of "prophecy in reverse":

> Spiritual exegesis is in a kind of way the reverse process of prophecy: the latter looks to the future, but the former looks back from the future to the past. Prophecy follows the course of time forwards and in a historical or contemporary event sees darkly the messianic or eschatological fact that is prefigured. Spiritual exegesis follows the course of time backwards and, starting from the Messiah already given to the People of God, recognizes in the old Scriptures the preparations and seeds of what is now accomplished.[34]

The knowledge of Christ as the "fire of Sinai," the inner mystery of the Sacred Text, is conferred by the Spirit.

Origen's irreplaceable role in Christian thought is found in his prophetic insight into what we call today the economy of salvation. He brought to greater consciousness and clarity the plan of God in regard to Israel and its

---

32. Paul Synave and Pierre Benoit, *Prophecy and Inspiration: A Commentary on the Summa Theologica II-II, Questions 171-78,* trans. Avery Dulles and Thomas Sheridan (New York: Desclée, 1961), p. 61.

33. Thomas Aquinas, *De veritate,* q. 12, a. 13c. The following several paragraphs have been published as part of the study, Francis Martin, "The Spiritual Sense (Sensus Spiritualis) of Sacred Scripture."

34. Henri Crouzel, *Origen,* trans. A. S. Worrall (Edinburgh: T. & T. Clark, 1989), p. 71.

Scriptures as that economy is now seen in Christ. He articulated the New Testament presupposition that the events and persons mediated to us in the Old Testament are somehow anticipated and partial realizations of the mystery of Christ, now fully present in history and yet awaiting its own completion at the end of history. Origen and the other great theologians of antiquity mediate to us their experiential knowledge of the mystery, its "name," its "Logos," its "image," and its "knowledge." They show us in this way the reality to be contacted in and through the text for the building up of the Church, the Body of Christ.

Conclusion: The Glory of Sinai

The last line of the Book of Exodus (Exod. 40:34) recounts that, when the Tabernacle was completed, "The cloud of YHWH *was* upon the Dwelling by day, and fire was in it by night, in the sight of all the house of Israel, through-out all their journeys." M. Weinfeld's observation that "In P and Ezekiel the *kābōd* of Yahweh is conceived as a blazing fire surrounded by a cloud" calls attention to the fact that the presence of the kabod at the Meeting Tent, and later in the Temple, is understood as a continuation of Sinai.[35] In order to return to this fire, one must pass through the glorious cloud. The fire of the divinity of Christ is veiled by his humanity and shines forth in anticipation at the Transfiguration and definitively at the Resurrection. Understanding human history and cognition in light of the Resurrection of Christ disposes us to encounter him in the Sacred Text, where he is uniquely present to those who seek him in faith. Those who seek this fire in the cloud of the Scriptures must persevere in an attentive and purifying search. The spiritual or mystical sense of Scripture, its inner life, is not a "meaning" as much as it is a "fire," a touch of divine realities. As Henri de Lubac once described it, it is the mystical life itself:

> [S]ince Christian mysticism develops through the action of the mystery received in faith, and the mystery is the Incarnation of the Word of God revealed in Scripture, Christian mysticism is essentially an understanding of the holy Books. The mystery is their meaning; mysticism is getting to

35. See Exod. 19:9; 24:16-18; 29:43; 40:34-38; Lev. 9:6, 23-24; Ezek. 1:4; 10:4; 1 Kgs. 8:10-12. See also Deut. 4:11; 5:24. M. Weinfeld, "Kabod," in *Theological Dictionary of the Old Testament,* vol. 7, ed. Helmer Ringgren and Heinz-Josef Fabry (Grand Rapids: Eerdmans, 1995), p. 53.

know that meaning. Thus, one understands the profound and original identity of the two meanings of the word *mystique* that, in current French usage, seem so different because we have to separate so much in order to analyze them: the mystical or spiritual understanding of Scripture and the mystical or spiritual life are, in the end, one and the same.[36]

36. Henri de Lubac, "Mysticism and Mystery," in *Theological Fragments* (San Francisco: Ignatius, 1989), p. 58.

CHAPTER 3

Verbum Domini and Historical-Critical Exegesis

Brant Pitre

As anyone familiar with contemporary Catholic biblical studies knows, the historical-critical method is currently the subject of widespread and often heated debate. On the one hand, the method has some staunch defenders. For example, in 2008, after a lifetime of historical-critical work, the prominent Catholic exegete Joseph A. Fitzmyer, S.J., published a collection of essays bearing the subtitle: *In Defense of the Historical-Critical Method.*[1] On the other hand, various aspects of historical criticism, if not the entire method, have been seriously called into question by other equally prominent Catholic scholars. For example, in 2002, in the opening essay of the *The Future of Catholic Biblical Scholarship,* Luke Timothy Johnson describes the method as "bankrupt."[2]

In this context of intense debate over the value of historical criticism, in 2010, Pope Benedict XVI released what is arguably one of the most detailed and explicit magisterial teachings on "historical-critical exegesis" ever promulgated.[3] In light of this historic publication, the goal of this paper is to

1. Joseph A. Fitzmyer, S.J., *The Interpretation of Scripture: In Defense of the Historical-Critical Method* (Mahwah: Paulist, 2008).

2. Luke Timothy Johnson, "What's Catholic about Catholic Biblical Scholarship?," in *The Future of Catholic Biblical Scholarship: A Constructive Conversation,* ed. Luke Timothy Johnson and William S. Kurz, S.J. (Grand Rapids: Eerdmans, 2002), p. 14.

3. Benedict XVI, *Verbum Domini* ["The Word of the Lord"], Post-Synodal Apostolic Exhortation on the Word of God in the Life and Mission of the Church (September 30, 2010) (Boston: Pauline, 2010), pp. 31-36. To be sure, in the modern papal encyclicals on Scripture, various aspects of the historical-critical method — textual criticism, attention

provide a concise overview of the section in the Apostolic Exhortation that deals most directly with historical-critical exegesis: *Verbum Domini,* nos. 31-36. During the course of this overview, I will highlight what I consider to be the five most significant points made by the exhortation, given the landscape of current scholarly debate over historical criticism. Finally, I will conclude with some brief reflections about the implications of *Verbum Domini* for Catholic biblical scholars, especially those of us teaching in twenty-first-century Catholic seminaries. The overall thesis of the paper is that *Verbum Domini* presents us with clear guidelines for the future of Catholic exegesis in general, and the role of historical criticism in particular. Significantly, the document may well provide us with some much-needed keys to overcoming the current, widespread, and lamentable divide between biblical exegesis and theology.

Historical-Critical Exegesis Is "Indispensable" Because History Is Indispensable

The first mention of historical-critical exegesis in *Verbum Domini* takes place in Part 1 of the document, "Verbum Dei," in the subsection titled "The Interpretation of Sacred Scripture in the Church."[4] After affirming the Church as the primary setting for biblical hermeneutics and repeating Vatican II's teaching that "the study of the sacred page should be, as it were, the very soul of theology,"[5] *Verbum Domini* raises the question of the relationship between "historical research" and "a hermeneutic of faith."[6] In this context,

---

to literary forms, etc. — are of course discussed, often in some detail. But it is interesting to note that even Pius XII's encyclical *Divino afflante Spiritu* (1943), the Dogmatic Constitution on Divine Revelation *Dei verbum* (1965), and the section on Sacred Scripture in the *Catechism of the Catholic Church* (1992) never once explicitly speak of "historical criticism" or "the historical-critical method." Cf. Fitzmyer, *The Interpretation of Scripture,* p. 5, who points out that Pius XII "never named the method" in his famous encyclical. Of course, the Pontifical Biblical Commission's 1993 *Interpretation of the Bible in the Church* has a lengthy definition and discussion of the historical-critical method. However, in its current form, the PBC is "not an organ of the magisterium" but rather a commission of scholars that enjoy the confidence of the magisterium. See Joseph Cardinal Ratzinger, "Preface to the Document of the Biblical Commission," 1993, in *The Church and the Bible,* ed. Dennis J. Murphy (New Delhi: St. Paul's/Alba House, 2007), p. 690.

    4. Benedict XVI, *Verbum Domini* 29-49 (here 31).

    5. Vatican II, *Dei verbum* 24.

    6. Benedict XVI, *Verbum Domini* 29, 31.

the exhortation begins by acknowledging with "heartfelt gratitude" the work of many exegetes and theologians in recent decades, especially the members of the Pontifical Biblical Commission. It then proceeds to examine "the state of biblical studies and their standing within the field of theology," with specific reference to the question of the "relationship between exegesis and theology."[7] It is in this broader context of the question of how Sacred Scripture relates to theology that *Verbum Domini* begins its specific discussion of historical-critical exegesis, in which it has this to say:

> Before all else, we need to acknowledge the benefits that historical-critical exegesis and other recently developed methods of textual analysis have brought to the life of the Church. For the Catholic understanding of Sacred Scripture, attention to such methods is indispensable, linked as it is to the realism of the Incarnation: "This necessity is a consequence of the Christian principle formulated in the Gospel of John 1:14: *Verbum caro factum est.* The historical fact is a constitutive dimension of the Christian faith. The history of salvation is not mythology, but a true history, and it should thus be studied with the methods of serious historical research." The study of the Bible requires a knowledge of these methods of enquiry and their suitable application.[8]

Several aspects of this section are worth highlighting. First, Pope Benedict clearly wishes to begin with a *positive* acknowledgment of the benefits of modern historical-critical exegesis and analysis. Given the fact that he has already acknowledged the benefits of modern exegesis in the previous paragraphs, he is clearly at pains here to offset an overly negative estimation of modern historical-critical work.

Second, *Verbum Domini*'s affirmation of the value of historical-critical exegesis is remarkably strong: for Catholic exegesis, attention to historical method is not merely "useful," or "advisable"; it is *"indispensable."* These are strong words, which may come as something of a disappointment to those who consider the historical-critical project as a whole to be "bankrupt," and, as a result, quite dispensable.

Third and finally — and this is important — for *Verbum Domini,* the *reason* historical-critical exegesis is indispensable is not because this is the consensus of modern exegetes (it certainly isn't); nor is it because the results of source-critical, form-critical, and redaction-critical hypotheses are

---

7. Benedict XVI, *Verbum Domini* 31.
8. Benedict XVI, *Verbum Domini* 32.

"assured" (they certainly aren't). Rather, it is because "*the historical fact* is a *constitutive dimension* of the Christian faith."[9] Quoting his own Intervention in the 2008 Synod of Bishops, Pope Benedict states: "*The history of salvation is not mythology, but a true history,* and it should thus be studied with the methods of serious historical research."[10] After several centuries of biblical scholarship claiming that much of the history of salvation recorded in Scripture *is* in fact mythology and not true history, these are remarkably bold statements. For *Verbum Domini,* Christianity is an intrinsically historical religion; it cannot dispense with history without undermining the fundamental *factum* of the Incarnation itself. For this reason, authentic Catholic exegesis not only suggests but in fact "*requires* a knowledge of historical methods" and "their suitable application."[11]

In light of these statements, it seems clear that any wholesale rejection of historical-critical exegesis and sound historical method is clearly at odds with the teaching of the Church as proposed by *Verbum Domini.* As we will see in a moment, this does not mean that historical-critical exegesis is untouched by error or free from dangers, but it does mean that it is not in fact entirely "bankrupt" and has an essential role to play in the interpretation of Sacred Scripture.

The False Dichotomy between "Scientific Exegesis" and "Spiritual Interpretation"

The second aspect of *Verbum Domini*'s treatment of historical criticism that merits attention occurs in its overview of the history of magisterial interventions regarding "the introduction of new methods of historical analysis."[12] In this section, Pope Benedict highlights in particular the encyclicals of Pope Leo XIII, *Providentissimus Deus* (1893), and Pope Pius XII, *Divino afflante Spiritu* (1943). In doing so, he applies the insights from these encyclicals on Scripture to the current question of the relationship between exegesis and theology:

9. Benedict XVI, *Verbum Domini* 32.

10. Benedict XVI, *Verbum Domini* 32 (emphasis added), quoting Benedict XVI, Intervention in the Fourteenth General Congregation of the Synod (October 14, 2008): *Insegnamenti* 4, no. 2 (2008); 492; cf. *Propositio* 25.

11. Benedict XVI, *Verbum Domini* 32 (emphasis added).

12. Benedict XVI, *Verbum Domini* 33.

Pope Leo XIII's intervention had the merit of protecting the Catholic interpretation of the Bible from the inroads of rationalism, without, however, seeking refuge in a spiritual meaning detached from history. Far from shunning scientific criticism, the Church was wary only of "preconceived opinions that claim to be based on science, but which in reality surreptitiously cause science to depart from its domain." Pope Pius XII, on the other hand, was faced with attacks on the part of those who proposed a so-called mystical exegesis which rejected any form of scientific approach. The encyclical *Divino afflante Spiritu* was careful to avoid any hint of a dichotomy between "scientific exegesis" for use in apologetics and "spiritual interpretation meant for internal use"; rather it affirmed both the "theological significance of the literal sense, methodically defined" and the fact that "determining the spiritual sense . . . belongs itself to the realm of exegetical science." In this way, both documents rejected "a split between the human and the divine, between scientific research and respect for the faith, between the literal sense and the spiritual sense."[13]

Two aspects of this analysis of the papal encyclicals on Scripture are worth highlighting. First, in contrast to the narrative sometimes constructed, in which *Divino afflante Spiritu* is depicted as "liberating" Catholic biblical scholars from the constraints of *Providentissimus Deus, Verbum Domini* presents both encyclicals as *complementary* responses to the dangers of *rationalistic* exegesis on the one hand (Leo XIII) and *spiritualistic* exegesis on the other (Pius XII).[14] Second, in the light of this complementary reading of the encyclicals, *Verbum Domini* makes absolutely clear that authentic Catholic interpretation must refuse to give way to the all-too-common "dichotomy" between "scientific exegesis" and "spiritual interpretation." Although a detailed discussion of the relationship between the literal and spiritual senses of Scripture is beyond the bounds of this brief paper,[15] *Verbum Domini* stresses that the *theological* significance of the *literal* sense of Scripture is an essential aspect of "exegetical science."

As the footnotes to this section make clear, in all this, Pope Benedict is drawing directly on Pope John Paul II's 1993 discourse on the centenary and fiftieth anniversaries of the two papal encyclicals on Scripture. In this discourse, John Paul not only rejected any such split between historical exegesis and spiritual interpretation, but also rooted the unity of the two approaches

---

13. Benedict XVI, *Verbum Domini* 33.

14. Cf. Fitzmyer, *The Interpretation of Scripture,* p. 5.

15. Cf. Benedict XVI, *Verbum Domini* 37.

directly in "the Church's faith in the mystery of the Incarnation."[16] In the debate over the value of historical criticism, it is all too easy to simply choose sides: either to defend historical-critical exegesis as opposed to spiritual and theological interpretation (often decried as "eisegesis"), or to reject historical criticism as dangerous to faith and retreat to a spiritual interpretation not solidly grounded in the literal sense of the text. *Verbum Domini* reiterates that neither of these responses is a viable option for authentic Catholic exegesis, which must avoid both the Scylla of rationalism and the Charybdis of ahistorical fideism as equally dangerous. In other words, however strong the tension may be between historical analysis and theological exegesis, the two must be held together, as surely as the mystery of the human and the divine in the Incarnation.

The Need to Implement the "Three Criteria" of *Dei verbum* 12

The third aspect of *Verbum Domini*'s treatment of historical criticism that I wish to highlight here may, to my mind, be its most significant positive contribution. It is all well and good to recommend that Catholic exegetes avoid the dichotomy between exegesis and theology, between scientific analysis and spiritual interpretation — Vatican II recommended as much over forty years ago — but how does one actually go about doing so? What practical and exegetical guidelines should be followed?

In the next section, Pope Benedict teaches with magisterial authority something he has said as a private theologian for decades: the way beyond the impasse between exegesis and theology is to actually *implement* the exegetical directives of the Second Vatican Council's Dogmatic Constitution on Divine Revelation, *Dei verbum* 12, regarding how to ascertain the intention of the divine author of Scripture.[17] By my count, over the course of its discussion of the interpretation of Scripture in the Church, *Verbum Domini*

---

16. John Paul II, "Discourse on the Occasion of the Centenary of the Encyclical *Providentissimus Deus* and the Fiftieth Anniversary of the Encyclical *Divino afflante Spiritu* (23 April 1993)," in Murphy, *The Church and the Bible,* pp. 680-82.

17. See, e.g., Cardinal Joseph Ratzinger, "Biblical Interpretation in Conflict: The Question of the Basic Principles and the Path of Exegesis Today," in Joseph Cardinal Ratzinger, *God's Word: Scripture, Tradition, Office* (1989; reprint San Francisco: Ignatius, 2008), pp. 91-126 (here 96); Joseph Cardinal Ratzinger, *Jesus of Nazareth, Part Two: Holy Week: From the Entrance into Jerusalem to the Resurrection,* trans. Philip J. Whitmore (San Francisco: Ignatius, 2010), pp. xiv-xv.

explicitly refers to "the criteria set forth in number 12 of the Dogmatic Constitution *Dei verbum*" at least *five* times.[18] This is a considerably heavy emphasis. It seems clear that Pope Benedict is going to great lengths to stress the following point:

> On the one hand, the Council emphasizes the study of literary genres and historical context as basic elements for understanding the meaning intended by the sacred author. On the other hand, since Scripture must be interpreted in the same Spirit in which it was written, the Dogmatic Constitution indicates *three fundamental criteria* for an appreciation of the divine dimension of the Bible: (1) the text must be interpreted with attention to *the unity of the whole of Scripture;* nowadays this is called canonical exegesis; (2) account is be taken of *the living Tradition of the whole Church;* and, finally, (3) respect must be shown for *the analogy of faith.* "Only where both methodological levels, the historical-critical and the theological, are respected, can one speak of a theological exegesis, an exegesis worthy of this book."[19]

In other words, an authentically Catholic interpretation of Scripture must not only engage in historical-critical analysis, examining the language, literature, history, and culture of the biblical texts with the aim of discovering the intention of the human authors.[20] It must also take into account the three pillars of Catholic theology: Scripture, Tradition, and the teachings of the magisterium. Only when it does this, can one speak of a properly *theological* exegesis that is worthy of inspired Scripture. As *Verbum Domini* goes on to say: "While today's academic exegesis, including that of Catholic scholars, is highly competent in the field of historical-critical methodology and its latest developments, it must be said that comparable attention needs to be paid to the theological dimension of the biblical texts, so that they can be more deeply understood in accordance with the three elements indicated by the Dogmatic Constitution *Dei verbum.*"[21]

In other words, while Catholic exegetes have expended an enormous amount of energy and attention on the *first* half of *Dei verbum* 12, regarding the intention of the human author(s), we have not adequately integrated and given enough attention to the *second* half of the paragraph, regarding the

18. Benedict XVI, *Verbum Domini* 34 (twice), 38, 39, 47.
19. Benedict XVI, *Verbum Domini* 34 (some emphasis added).
20. Vatican II, *Dei verbum* 12.
21. Benedict XVI, *Verbum Domini* 34.

intention of the *divine author,* and the necessity of interpreting any given text in the broader context of the whole canon of Scripture, the living Tradition of the Church, and "the analogy of faith" — that is, "Catholic doctrine, as authoritatively proposed by the Church."[22] One does not have to be very familiar with the major journals in biblical studies published in the last four decades to know that these three criteria from Vatican II are hardly operative in most of the exegetical work being done by historical critics today.[23] I for one cannot recall the last time I found any references to the analogy of faith in any major work of exegesis, and references to the living Tradition of the Church are often slim or nonexistent.

In fact, in the foreword to volume 2 of *Jesus of Nazareth,* Pope Benedict XVI makes the same point even more pointedly. Strikingly, he describes his exegetical project as "fundamentally" being "a matter of finally putting into practice the methodological principles formulated for exegesis by the Second Vatican Council (in *Dei verbum* 12), *a task that unfortunately has scarcely been attempted thus far.*"[24] This is an arresting claim: from Pope Benedict's perspective, over forty years after the Second Vatican Council ended, its vision of exegesis has "scarcely been attempted," even by Catholic exegetes. Surely this is a situation that must change, and change soon, if we ever hope to bridge the lamentable gulf between exegesis and theology and reap the fruits of the biblical renewal that led to the Second Vatican Council.

The Three Dangers of a Dualistic Approach to Scripture

Significantly, in addition to describing historical-critical exegesis as indispensable and worthy of praise, *Verbum Domini* also levels a remarkably detailed magisterial *critique* of the errors that often accompany modern exegesis. In a lengthy section, Pope Benedict enumerates the dangers that attend the "dualistic approach to Sacred Scripture" common "nowadays" and the "barrier between exegesis and theology" that such an approach often leads

22. Leo XIII, *Providentissimus Deus* 14, in *The Scripture Documents: An Anthology of Official Catholic Teachings,* ed. Dean P. Bechard (Collegeville, MN: Liturgical Press, 2002), p. 48. See also Pius XII, *Divino afflante Spiritu* 24 and *Catechism of the Catholic Church* 114.

23. For example, in his programmatic essay on "The Second Vatican Council and the Role of the Bible," Joseph Fitzmyer makes no mention of the three criteria taught in *Dei verbum* 12; he skips over them as if they were not part of the conciliar teaching on Catholic exegesis. See Fitzmyer, *The Interpretation of Scripture,* pp. 8-9.

24. Ratzinger, *Jesus of Nazareth, Part Two,* p. xv.

to, something that occurs "even at the highest academic levels."[25] He then lists three of the "most troubling consequences" of the tendency to separate or oppose the historical and theological levels of the biblical text.

First, this dualistic approach leads to a *historical reductionism,* in which "the work of exegesis is restricted to the first level alone."[26] As a result, "Scripture ends up being *a text belonging only to the past:* One can draw moral consequences from it, one can learn history, but the Book as such speaks only of the past, and exegesis is no longer truly theological, but becomes pure historiography, history of literature."[27] One sees abundant evidence for this result in the universities in the shift from "Theology" departments to "Religious studies" programs, as well as in the abundance of "Bible as literature" courses, in which one of the operative principles is that the biblical text is treated *only* as a piece of human literature, and not as divinely inspired Scripture.

Second, the dualistic approach that often accompanies modern exegesis frequently if not inevitably leads to the replacement of a hermeneutic of faith with a *hermeneutic of secularism:*

> The lack of a hermeneutic of faith with regard to Scripture entails more than a simple absence; in its place there inevitably enters another hermeneutic, a positivistic and *secularized hermeneutic* ultimately based on the conviction that the Divine does not intervene in human history. According to this hermeneutic, whenever a divine element seems present, it has to be explained in some other way, reducing everything to the human element. This leads to interpretations that deny the historicity of the divine elements.[28]

This is a very significant paragraph. For one thing, it makes clear that for Pope Benedict, at least one philosophical error against which Leo XIII wrote at the end of the nineteenth century — the error of rationalism — is alive and well at the beginning of the twenty-first century, under the guise of modern (and now postmodern) secularism. This important observation needs to be taken seriously by scholars who may still be under the impression, to quote the words of Athanasius Miller in his influential 1955 review of the *Enchiridion Biblicum,* that "the position of Catholic scholars at the turn of the

25. Benedict XVI, *Verbum Domini* 35.
26. Benedict XVI, *Verbum Domini* 35.
27. Benedict XVI, *Verbum Domini* 35.
28. Benedict XVI, *Verbum Domini* 35.

century, or the dangers that threatened Catholic teaching on Scripture and its inspiration on the part of liberal and rationalistic criticism" are no longer a significant problem. As he puts it: "[A]t present, the battle is considerably less fierce. . . ."[29] This diagnosis may well have been true in the 1950s, but anyone who has scanned the shelves of the religion section in a bookstore lately or read the recent works of Bart Ehrman knows that rationalistic and secularist attacks on Scripture are very much alive and well.[30] Moreover, *Verbum Domini's* critique of this dualistic approach to Scripture also shows that the reductionism that often attends modern exegesis is not merely historicist in character, it is also *philosophical* and *metaphysical.* According to a secularized hermeneutic, exegesis must not only restrict itself to the arena of the *historical* past, it must also restrict itself to the arena of the *human* and *earthly,* a human and earthly arena untouched by anything supernatural. This too is simply a kind of eighteenth-century exegetical deism dressed up in twentieth-century (and now twenty-first-century) garb.

Third and finally, the historicism and secularism of this dualistic approach ultimately results in a *hermeneutic of skepticism* toward the truth of Scripture, especially the historical truth of its supernatural elements. In a lengthy reflection on this secularized hermeneutic, *Verbum Domini* states:

> Such a position can only prove harmful to the life of the Church, casting doubt over fundamental mysteries of Christianity and their historicity — as, for example, the institution of the Eucharist and the resurrection of Christ. A philosophical hermeneutic is thus imposed, one which denies the possibility that the Divine can enter and be present within history. The adoption of this hermeneutic within theological studies inevitably introduces a sharp dichotomy between an exegesis limited solely to the first level and a theology tending towards a spiritualization of the meaning of the Scriptures, one which would fail to respect the historical character of revelation.
>
> All this is also bound to have a negative impact on the spiritual life and on pastoral activity; "as a consequence of the absence of the second meth-

29. Athanasius Miller, O.S.B., "Review of *Enchiridion Biblicum* (1954)," *Catholic Biblical Quarterly* 18 (1956): 24; quoted in Murphy, *The Church and the Bible*, p. 301.

30. See Bart D. Ehrman, *Forged: Writing in the Name of God — Why the Bible's Authors Are Not Who We Think They Are* (San Francisco: HarperOne, 2011); Bart D. Ehrman, *Jesus Interrupted: Revealing the Hidden Contradictions in the Bible (And Why We Don't Know about Them)* (New York: HarperOne, 2010); Bart D. Ehrman, *Misquoting Jesus: The Story Behind Who Changed the Bible and Why* (New York: HarperOne, 2007).

odological level, a profound gulf is opened up between scientific exegesis and lectio divina. This can give rise to a lack of clarity in the preparation of homilies." It must also be said that this dichotomy can create confusion and a lack of stability in the intellectual formation of candidates for ecclesial ministries.[31]

This is a remarkably concise but accurate diagnosis of the contemporary situation. Once a dualistic approach to Scripture is adopted, the hermeneutic of *faith* is ultimately replaced, whether explicitly or implicitly, by a hermeneutic of *doubt.* Such doubt is rooted once again in the old *a priori* of deism and rationalism: the belief that God does not "enter" into or act "within history." Given the fact that Scripture is replete with accounts of such divine actions in history — above all in the form of miracles and prophecies — it is inevitable that such doubt would ultimately touch even the fundamental mysteries of the Christian faith, such as the institution of the Eucharist and the bodily resurrection of Christ, as well as miraculous events like the virgin birth and the healings of Jesus' public ministry, to say nothing of the miracles recounted in the Old Testament. In my own experience as a biblical scholar and professor, it is this aspect of modern exegesis — its hermeneutic of skepticism, even toward fundamental mysteries of faith — that leads many to reject modern biblical exegesis as dangerous, harmful to faith, and bankrupt of any value. And Pope Benedict is certainly correct to point out that such skepticism has had a deleterious effect on "the spiritual life" of many Christians, and in particular, "the intellectual formation" of candidates for ecclesial ministries.

The Need for Explicitly Theological Exegesis

The fifth and final aspect of *Verbum Domini*'s treatment of historical-critical exegesis that merits attention is in some ways the most remarkable of them all. At the end of his critique of a dualistic approach to biblical interpretation, Pope Benedict, once again quoting his own synodal intervention, sums up his point as follows:

> In a word, "*where exegesis is not theology,* Scripture cannot be the soul of theology, and conversely, *where theology is not essentially the interpretation of the Church's Scripture,* such a theology no longer has a foundation."[32]

31. Benedict XVI, *Verbum Domini* 35.
32. Benedict XVI, *Verbum Domini* 35, quoting Benedict XVI, Intervention at the Four-

This is a stunning challenge to both modern exegesis and modern theology. I must confess that I am hard pressed to think of many modern Catholic theologians whose theology could be legitimately described as *"essentially the interpretation of the Church's Scripture."* Joseph Ratzinger himself has certainly exemplified such an approach; but it seems to me that in this regard he stands in a relative minority. Likewise, I am equally hard pressed to think of many modern Catholic exegetes — I include myself in this critique — whose exegesis can be simply *equated* with "theology." That is not to say they do not exist; but, once again, they appear to be in the minority. Lest this seem to be putting it too strongly, notice that *Verbum Domini* describes the division that exists between exegesis and theology not merely as a "barrier" but as a "gulf."[33]

In sum, Pope Benedict ends his discussion of contemporary exegesis by calling for two radical renewals: first, a method of Catholic exegesis that is not incidentally but *essentially theological;* and second, a method of Catholic theology that is not incidentally but *essentially biblical and exegetical.*

Conclusion: Summary and Implications

In summary, a close reading of the section in *Verbum Domini* that deals with historical-critical exegesis reveals at least five significant observations that pertain to contemporary Catholic exegesis and theology.

First, *Verbum Domini* makes absolutely clear that, from a Catholic perspective, modern historical-critical exegesis, applied rightly, is indispensable. Whatever modifications, adaptations, and limitations it may be subject to, the historical analysis of Scripture cannot be dispensed with, simply because history itself — the history of salvation — cannot be dispensed with, unless we wish to undermine the very foundations of Christianity. Second, because of the inextricable bond between history and the mysteries of faith, authentic Catholic exegesis must reject the false (but widespread) dichotomy between historical-critical exegesis and the theological interpretation of Scripture. The mystery of the Incarnation itself demands that we hold history and theology, the natural and the supernatural, the human and the divine, faith and reason, together. Third, in order to accomplish this in the

---

teenth General Congregation of the Synod (October 14, 2008): *Insegnamenti* 4, no. 2 (2008): 493-94 (emphasis added).

33. Cf. Benedict XVI, *Verbum Domini* 35.

realm of exegesis, *Verbum Domini* repeatedly insists that Catholic exegetes actually follow and implement the methodological principles of Vatican II, *Dei verbum* 12: Sacred Scripture must be interpreted with both its human *and divine* authors in mind. In other words, the biblical text must be interpreted, not only in the light of the language, literature, history, and culture of the human authors, but in the light of the canon, the living tradition, and the doctrines of faith. All of these tools, the historical and the theological, are necessary for a proper interpretation of Scripture. Fourth, *Verbum Domini* exhorts Catholic interpreters to avoid three troubling consequences of the dualistic approach to Scripture that is often part and parcel of contemporary exegesis: historical reductionism, a secularized hermeneutic, and skepticism toward the historical truth of Scripture. In place of these, authentic Catholic exegesis must be characterized above all by a hermeneutic of faith in which "the harmony of faith and reason" are affirmed and maintained.[34] Fifth and finally, *Verbum Domini* calls for an unabashedly and essentially *theological* exegesis. Apart from such exegesis, theology itself will be robbed of its unifying and animating principle — its "soul" — which should be the interpretation of the Church's Scripture.

It should go without saying that the implications of these five points in *Verbum Domini* are manifold. Here, I will briefly draw out only a few that come to mind for those of us who teach in Catholic seminaries.

First, if historical-critical exegesis is in fact an "indispensable" method, and *Verbum Domini* shows that this is in fact the teaching of the Church, then Catholic seminary professors will need to follow Benedict's lead in stressing that the *reason* historical criticism is essential is not because its various theories are unassailable or rejected only by the ignorant. Rather, as Catholics, we simply cannot flee from history without betraying the very mystery of the Incarnation. The Catholic faith appeals to history; to history it must go. This kind of positive approach will take a great deal of effort, especially if seminarians have already formed negative opinions about historical criticism or have decided to reject the historical method as a whole. Moreover, any discussion of historical criticism's positive elements will have to be accompanied by a detailed and nuanced presentation of the false philosophical presuppositions and hermeneutical approaches outlined by *Verbum Domini* as characterizing much critical exegesis: a historicist reductionism, a hermeneutic of secularism, and a hermeneutic of skepticism toward the historical truth of Scripture, especially its supernatural elements. Catholic

---

34. Cf. Benedict XVI, *Verbum Domini* 36.

seminarians will need to be clearly taught that they can reject these errors without rejecting historical-critical exegesis as a whole. This too will be a difficult task, given the fact that so many critical works do call into question the historical truth of Scripture, including the fundamental mysteries of faith. Indeed, it seems to me that unless we provide students with concrete *examples* of historical-critical exegesis that is not characterized by historicist, secularist, and skeptical hermeneutics, we should expect them to continue to exhibit negative estimations of the historical-critical method.

Second, in the wake of *Verbum Domini,* along these lines, biblical professors in seminaries will need to stress to students that authentic Catholic interpretation rejects any kind of split or dichotomy between historical exegesis and spiritual interpretation. This too will be a difficult task, given the fact that precisely this split pervades much of the modern writing that has been done and continues to be done on Scripture. Moreover, in my limited years of teaching seminary, I have been struck by how many seminarians are quite content to retreat into spiritualizing or overly subjective interpretations of biblical texts, even after I have labored long and hard to show them how history and theology mutually illuminate one another. I have had to stress emphatically that by accepting the split between history and theology, between scientific exegesis and spiritual interpretation, they risk lapsing into a kind of exegetical docetism, in which the words of Scripture only appear to be fully human, but are in fact only divine. Despite my pleas, students, even very good ones, are often much more attracted to the spiritual exegesis of the Church Fathers than they are to what I consider some of the best works of modern exegesis.

Third and finally — and this is where I think *Verbum Domini* has issued its most consequential directive — Catholic professors in seminaries will have to make a deliberate and sustained attempt to actually implement the methodological principles of *Dei verbum* 12, employing the three criteria of the canon, the living tradition, and the analogy of faith in the interpretation of any given text of Scripture. This will be very difficult for some of us. My own graduate training in biblical studies — though highly excellent in many ways — was in other ways very narrow, highly focused on languages and extrabiblical literature, and remarkably limited to very few books in the actual canon of Scripture. Even more problematic, I had virtually *no* exposure to the living Tradition of the Church; any familiarity with the writings of the Church Fathers or their interpretation of Scripture that I have today is completely remedial in character. I have had to do all that work in my "spare time," and, even so, it plays virtually no role in the kinds of research

I have to do in order to publish articles in academic journals or full-length exegetical monographs. As far as the analogy of faith goes, again, speaking for myself, not only was I not trained to have recourse to Church doctrine as a guide for exegesis; I was trained to view with *suspicion* any interpretation that coheres with dogma as probably "apologetics" or eisegesis in disguise and not true exegesis. Hence, in my own attempt to interpret Scripture according to the directives of Vatican II, I have had to be very deliberate in the seminary classroom about balancing my assignments of modern exegetical articles and monographs with writings from the Church Fathers and the relevant teachings of the magisterium. To be frank, I have not yet figured out how to implement the vision of Vatican II at the level of my own academic, historical-critical work on Jesus.[35] For me, that is still very much a work in progress.

In short, in the Apostolic Exhortation *Verbum Domini,* Pope Benedict XVI has issued a rather tall order to Catholic exegetes, especially those of us teaching in Catholic seminaries. If the Church is calling for "exegesis" to truly *be* "theology," and if theology is to become "essentially the interpretation of the Church's Scripture,"[36] then a generation of Catholic biblical scholars and theologians have a great deal of work to do before the vision of both *Dei verbum* and *Verbum Domini* might come to its full flowering. May God grant us the grace, the ability, and the courage to answer this most noble call of the Church, so that the study of the Sacred Page might no longer be the source of division between exegesis and theology, but might truly be the very soul of sacred theology.

---

35. See Brant Pitre, *Jesus and the Last Supper* (Grand Rapids: Eerdmans, 2015); *Jesus, the Tribulation, and the End of the Exile: Restoration Eschatology and the Origin of the Atonement* (WUNT; Tübingen: Mohr-Siebeck; Grand Rapids: Baker Academic, 2005).

36. Benedict XVI, *Verbum Domini* 35.

CHAPTER 4

Overcoming the Hiatus between Exegesis and Theology: Guidance and Examples from Pope Benedict XVI

Pablo Gadenz

In the full, published version of his 1988 Erasmus lecture on biblical interpretation, the then Cardinal Ratzinger, commenting on the at times unqualified use of the historical-critical method in Catholic biblical scholarship since the Second Vatican Council, wrote that "in the realm of Catholicism, too, there is now a total hiatus between exegesis and dogma."[1] He was not the first or the last to make such a comment. Already back in 1961, Karl Rahner had written that there existed "a certain estrangement within Catholic theology" between exegetes and dogmatic theologians, due in large part to the practice of modern biblical criticism.[2] Two years after Cardinal Ratzinger's lecture, the International Theological Commission in its 1990 document "The Interpretation of Dogmas" also noted the "conflict between exegesis and dogma,"[3] and gave a similar explanation: "[f]ollowing on the 'age of

---

1. Joseph Ratzinger, "Biblical Interpretation in Conflict: The Question of the Basic Principles and Path of Exegesis Today," in Ratzinger, *God's Word: Scripture, Tradition, Office,* ed. Peter Hünermann and Thomas Söding, trans. Henry Taylor (San Francisco: Ignatius, 2008), pp. 91-126, at 98.

2. Karl Rahner, "Exegesis and Dogmatic Theology," in *Theological Investigations,* vol. 5: *Later Writings,* trans. Karl-H. Kruger (London: Darton, Longman & Todd, 1966), pp. 67-93, at 67.

3. International Theological Commission, "The Interpretation of Dogmas," in *International Theological Commission,* vol. 2: *Texts and Documents 1986-2007* (San Francisco: Ignatius, 2009), pp. 23-53, at 42. The following year, the document of the Pontifical Biblical Commission, *The Interpretation of the Bible in the Church* (Vatican City: Libreria Editrice Vaticana, 1993), sec. III.D.4, commented on this text, saying that "[t]here was not conflict in a generalized sense between Catholic exegesis and dogmatic theology, but only some

Enlightenment,' the tools of historical criticism were developed with the aim in mind also of favouring emancipation where dogmatic and ecclesiastical authority were concerned."[4] Non-Catholic authors likewise made similar observations. For example, in 1992, Brevard Childs, the pioneer of canonical criticism, explained how he had become "painfully aware that an iron curtain separated Bible from theology"; he thus indicated that "the pressing need for the next generation is to build strong links between the disciplines of Bible and theology."[5]

As a result of such assessments, various scholars in the last twenty years have indeed labored to advance theological approaches to the interpretation of Scripture.[6] From Ratzinger's perspective, the key principles for moving toward such interpretation were already outlined at the Second Vatican Council,[7] which spoke of the study of Scripture as the "soul of Sacred Theology,"[8] and which indicated two methodological levels of biblical interpretation, the historical-literary and the spiritual-theological.[9] In particular,

---

instances of strong tension." For this text, see Dean P. Béchard, ed., *The Scripture Documents: An Anthology of Official Catholic Teachings* (Collegeville, MN: Liturgical Press, 2002), pp. 244-315, at 302.

4. International Theological Commission, "The Interpretation of Dogmas," p. 42. Indeed, scholars who developed the methods of biblical historical criticism consciously sought to liberate the Bible from "the shackles of dogma": see, for example, the discussion in Max Turner and Joel B. Green, "New Testament Commentary and Systematic Theology: Strangers or Friends?" in *Between Two Horizons: Spanning New Testament Studies and Systematic Theology,* ed. Joel B. Green and Max Turner (Grand Rapids: Eerdmans, 2000), pp. 1-22, at 7.

5. Brevard S. Childs, *Biblical Theology of the Old and New Testaments: Theological Reflection on the Christian Bible* (Minneapolis: Fortress Press, 1992), pp. xv-xvi.

6. Francis Watson, *Text, Church and World: Biblical Interpretation in Theological Perspective* (Edinburgh: T. & T. Clark, 1994); Stephen E. Fowl, *Engaging Scripture: A Model for Theological Interpretation,* Challenges in Contemporary Theology (Oxford: Blackwell, 1998); Kevin J. Vanhoozer, ed., *Dictionary for Theological Interpretation of the Bible* (Grand Rapids: Baker, 2005); Matthew Levering, *Participatory Biblical Exegesis: A Theology of Biblical Interpretation* (Notre Dame: University of Notre Dame Press, 2008); and Daniel J. Treier, *Introducing Theological Interpretation of Scripture: Recovering a Christian Practice* (Grand Rapids: Baker, 2008). Raising important questions regarding the direction of "theological interpretation" is Markus Bockmuehl, "Bible versus Theology: Is 'Theological Interpretation' the Answer?" *Nova et Vetera* 9 (2011): 27-47.

7. Ratzinger, "Biblical Interpretation in Conflict," p. 98: "a careful reading of the *whole* text of *Dei verbum* will detect the elements essential for a synthesis between historical methodology and theological 'hermeneutics.'"

8. Second Vatican Council, Dogmatic Constitution on Divine Revelation *Dei verbum* (November 18, 1965) 24 (*Scripture Documents,* ed. Béchard, p. 29).

9. *Dei verbum* 12 (*Scripture Documents,* ed. Béchard, pp. 24-25). However, this does not

regarding the second level, the Council gave three criteria often repeated by the Pope: the exegete should pay attention to the content and unity of all of Scripture (canonical exegesis), the living tradition of the Church, and the analogy of faith.[10] The 1993 document of the Pontifical Biblical Commission likewise explained the task of Catholic exegetes with regard to these two levels. After making use of the historical-critical method and other methods of interpretation (at the first level), the work of Catholic exegetes is not finished, since they must (at the second level) "never forget that what they are interpreting is the *Word of God. . . .* They arrive at the true goal of their work only when they have explained the meaning of the biblical text as God's Word for today. . . . Exegetes should also explain the christological, canonical, and ecclesial meanings of the biblical texts."[11] More recently, in the "Foreword" to *Jesus of Nazareth, Part Two,* the Pope again speaks of the need to connect exegesis to theology: "If scholarly *exegesis* is not to exhaust itself in constantly new hypotheses, becoming theologically irrelevant, it must take a methodological step forward and see itself once again as a *theological* discipline, without abandoning its historical character."[12] He also again notes the two levels, explaining that exegesis "must recognize that a properly developed faith-hermeneutic is appropriate to the text and can be combined with a historical hermeneutic, aware of its limits, so as to form a methodological whole."[13] In the Pope's opinion, however, there is still much to do to put the second level into practice.[14] As a result, twenty-two years after his 1988 Erasmus lecture, in his 2010 Apostolic Exhortation *Verbum Domini,* the

imply a dualistic approach; see Benedict XVI, Post-Synodal Apostolic Exhortation *Verbum Domini* (Vatican City: Libreria Editrice Vaticana, 2010), 35.

10. *Dei verbum* 12; see also the *Catechism of the Catholic Church,* 2nd ed. (Vatican City: Libreria Editrice Vaticana, 1997), 112-14. More recently, see Joseph Ratzinger/Benedict XVI, *Jesus of Nazareth: From the Baptism in the Jordan to the Transfiguration,* trans. Adrian J. Walker (New York: Doubleday, 2007), p. xviii; and Benedict XVI, *Verbum Domini* 34.

11. Pontifical Biblical Commission, *The Interpretation of the Bible in the Church,* sec. III.C.1 (*Scripture Documents,* ed. Béchard, p. 296) (emphasis in original).

12. Joseph Ratzinger/Benedict XVI, *Jesus of Nazareth, Part Two: Holy Week: From the Entrance into Jerusalem to the Resurrection,* trans. Philip J. Whitmore (San Francisco: Ignatius, 2011), p. xiv (emphasis added).

13. Ratzinger/Benedict XVI, *Jesus of Nazareth, Part Two,* p. xv. See also Joseph Ratzinger/Benedict XVI, *Jesus of Nazareth: The Infancy Narratives,* trans. Philip J. Whitmore (New York: Image, 2012), p. xi: "good exegesis involves two stages."

14. Ratzinger/Benedict XVI, *Jesus of Nazareth, Part Two,* p. xv: "this is a matter of finally putting into practice the methodological principles formulated for exegesis by the Second Vatican Council (in *Dei verbum* 12), a task that unfortunately has scarcely been attempted thus far."

Pope still writes that "[u]nfortunately, a sterile separation sometimes creates a barrier between exegesis and theology."[15]

The Pope's concern is not merely a matter of academic interest but involves the life of the Church. As he explains, the absence of a "hermeneutic of faith" inevitably entails the adoption instead of "a positivistic and *secularized hermeneutic*"; "[s]uch a position can only prove harmful to the life of the Church, casting doubt over fundamental mysteries of Christianity and their historicity — as, for example, the institution of the Eucharist and the resurrection of Christ."[16] It can be especially harmful for those preparing for priestly ministry: "The adoption of this hermeneutic within theological studies inevitably introduces a sharp dichotomy between an exegesis limited solely to the first level and a theology tending toward a spiritualization of the meaning of the Scriptures, one which would fail to respect the historical character of revelation."[17] The barrier between exegesis and dogma can thus hinder the seminarians' necessary work of integration: "It must also be said that this dichotomy can create confusion and a lack of stability in the intellectual formation of candidates for ecclesial ministries."[18]

In view of the Pope's call for an integrated biblical hermeneutic, I will therefore consider in this essay the relationship between exegesis and dogmatic theology, with the goal of building bridges between the two disciplines.[19] Specifically, two aspects of this relationship will be considered: dogma as the Church's interpretation of Scripture and the Church as the living subject of biblical interpretation. These two aspects will be considered from the perspective of an exegete. Of course, the reflections here could be complemented by those of a dogmatic theologian.[20] For each aspect, the

15. Benedict XVI, *Verbum Domini* 35.

16. Benedict XVI, *Verbum Domini* 35 (emphasis in the original).

17. Benedict XVI, *Verbum Domini* 35.

18. Benedict XVI, *Verbum Domini* 35.

19. Or more precisely, with R. R. Reno, "Rebuilding the Bridge Between Theology and Exegesis: Scripture, Doctrine, and Apostolic Legitimacy," *Letter & Spirit* 3 (2007): 153-68, at 168, the goal is to build a bridge "from where we are now . . . to the intellectually vibrant project of interpretation that restores a living relationship between doctrine and Scripture."

20. Ratzinger, "Biblical Interpretation in Conflict," p. 93, notes that an unfortunate counter-reaction to the rise of historical criticism of the Scriptures is that some "systematic theologians are looking for a theology that is as independent of exegesis as possible." For a discussion from the perspective of two systematic theologians, see Gerald O'Collins and Daniel Kendall, *The Bible for Theology: Ten Principles for the Theological Use of Scripture* (Mahwah, NJ: Paulist, 1997), p. 2, and compare with Turner and Green, "New Testament Commentary and Systematic Theology," p. 1.

guidance provided by Joseph Ratzinger/Pope Benedict (and others) will be presented and then illustrated with some examples, again drawing on his writings.

Dogma as Interpretation of Scripture

"Now dogma is, in fact, essentially nothing other than the explanation of Scripture."[21] So spoke Cardinal Ratzinger in a 1983 lecture given in Lyons and Paris. It is claimed, however, that with the development of historical criticism, a new interpretation arose that made the dogmatic interpretation appear as "an unscientific first step"; in such a view, "the certainty of dogma necessarily appears to be either an outmoded, archaic stage of thought or else the emanation of the will to power of self-perpetuating institutions."[22] In countering this view, Ratzinger has at various times explained that the proper locus for understanding the Scriptures is the setting[23] or environment[24] of the community of faith (the People of God/the Church), wherein

---

21. Joseph Ratzinger, "Handing on the Faith and the Sources of the Faith," in Joseph Ratzinger, Dermot J. Ryan, Godfried Danneels, and Franciszek Macharski, *Handing on the Faith in an Age of Disbelief: Lectures Given at the Church of Notre-Dame de Fourvière in Lyons, France and at Notre-Dame Cathedral in Paris*, trans. Michael J. Miller (San Francisco: Ignatius, 2006), pp. 13-40, at 17. If indeed dogma is the Church's official interpretation of Scripture, the study of the Church's dogmas should be carried out with Scripture as the primary reference: see the International Theological Commission, "The Interpretation of Dogmas," p. 42: "The witness of Sacred Scripture then should be the starting point and the basis for the understanding of dogma."

22. Ratzinger, "Handing on the Faith and the Sources of the Faith," p. 17.

23. Benedict XVI, *Verbum Domini* 29: "Here we can point to a fundamental criterion of biblical hermeneutics: *the primary setting for scriptural interpretation is the life of the Church*. This is not to uphold the ecclesial context as an extrinsic rule to which exegetes must submit, but rather is something demanded by the very nature of the Scriptures and the way they gradually came into being" (emphasis in original).

24. See the discussion of this point in Scott W. Hahn, *Covenant and Communion: The Biblical Theology of Pope Benedict XVI* (Grand Rapids: Brazos, 2009), p. 31: "The modus operandi of 'scientific' exegesis would seem to be wrongheaded for scientific reasons. It would be comparable to a natural scientist deciding to study a plant or animal without any reference to its habitat or its natural environment." See also Thomas G. Weinandy, "Pope Benedict XVI: A Biblical Portrayal of Jesus," *Nova et Vetera* 7 (2009): 19-34, at 23: "Benedict is also attempting . . . to rescue Scripture from a pseudo-academic environment where it has languished for decades and to return it to its proper environment, that is, the living household of faith, the Church."

they were also written and gathered together as Scripture.[25] For example, as he said in the 1988 Erasmus lecture:

> If exegesis wishes to be theology, it must go a step farther: it must recognize that the faith of the Church is the kind of sympathy without which the text remains a closed book. It must recognize this faith as a hermeneutic key, as a locus of understanding that does not do dogmatic violence to the Bible, but offers the only chance we have of allowing it to be itself.[26]

Some non-Catholic scholars have voiced similar opinions. For example, Brevard Childs, in the face of the modern consensus that wants to read Scripture in a manner that is free from dogma, appropriately asks: "Can one actually read a text meaningfully without some sort of conceptual framework?"[27] He concludes that "the issue of the use of dogmatic categories for Biblical Theology calls for a careful reformulation. The often used cliché of 'freedom from dogma' seems now largely rhetorical. Nor can the categories of historical versus dogmatic be seen as intractable rivals."[28] Indeed, Childs later discusses Irenaeus, whose conceptual or "theological framework for scriptural interpretation" was provided by the rule of faith *(regula fidei),* without, however, "playing Bible and tradition over against each other."[29]

25. Ratzinger, "Handing on the Faith and the Sources of the Faith," pp. 37-38: "Today we see that only within the context of the communal faith of the Church is it possible to take the Bible at its word. . . . This provides, then, a historical justification as well for the dogmatic interpretation of Scripture: The hermeneutic locus 'Church' is the only one that can adhere to the writings of the Bible as Scripture and accept what they themselves say as meaningful and true. . . . [I]t has by now become quite clear that traditional faith is not the enemy but rather the guarantor of historical fidelity with regard to the Bible." See also his essay "The Spiritual Basis and Ecclesial Identity of Theology," in Joseph Ratzinger, *The Nature and Mission of Theology: Approaches to Understanding Its Role in the Light of Present Controversy,* trans. Adrian Walker (San Francisco: Ignatius, 1995), pp. 45-72, at 65.

26. Ratzinger, "Biblical Interpretation in Conflict," p. 126. Pope Benedict repeated these ideas almost verbatim in his Address to Academics of the Pontifical Biblical Institute (October 26, 2009), in *L'Osservatore Romano,* Weekly Edition in English, November 4, 2009, p. 4.

27. Childs, *Biblical Theology of the Old and New Testaments,* p. 12.

28. Childs, *Biblical Theology of the Old and New Testaments,* p. 12.

29. Childs, *Biblical Theology of the Old and New Testaments,* p. 32. See also Robert W. Wall, "Reading the Bible from within Our Traditions: The 'Rule of Faith' in Theological Hermeneutics," in *Between Two Horizons,* ed. Green and Turner, pp. 88-107. For a discussion of the *regula fidei* in Irenaeus, see Robert Barron, "Biblical Interpretation and Theology: Irenaeus, Modernity, and Vatican II," *Letter & Spirit* 5 (2009): 173-91, at 174-80.

In a 1964 essay, Ratzinger gives us further guidance on how Bible and tradition need not be played over against each other. In other words, he helps us understand how the "dogmatic interpretation" came about and why it is consistent with a "historical interpretation."

> *There is an ecclesial theology of the New Testament,* which we call dogmatics. It relates to the New Testament theology of the New Testament in the same way as the New Testament theology of the Old Testament relates to the Old Testament theology of the Old Testament. The particular "extra" element that accordingly distinguishes dogmatics from biblical theology is what we call, in a precise sense, tradition. Here, too, we should note once again that the ecclesial theology of the New Testament, even though it is not simply identical with the inner, historically ascertainable New Testament theology of the New Testament . . . , is nonetheless not something merely exterior to it. For here, too, within the New Testament itself, begins the ecclesial process of interpreting what has been handed down; the ecclesial theology of the New Testament reaches back, as a process, right into the midst of the New Testament.[30]

Ratzinger then clarifies that "in a precise sense, only dogma itself [is] the ecclesial theology of the New Testament" (since dogmatic theology in general includes as well "the private theology of the individual theologian").[31] What we can take from this explanation is that dogma is not exterior to the Bible, not imposed on it from outside, but is an ecclesial interpretation arising from within the Bible itself.[32] Some examples can hopefully clarify this line of thought.

Our first example is to consider how the teaching of the Christological Councils can be linked with the Gospel portrait and titles of Jesus. For instance, in his discussion of the title "Son of God," the Pope in *Jesus of Nazareth* refers to the term *homoousios* from the Nicene Creed:

> This term did not Hellenize the faith or burden it with an alien philosophy. On the contrary, it captured in a stable formula exactly what had emerged as incomparably new and different in Jesus' way of speaking with the Fa-

---

30. Joseph Ratzinger, "The Question of the Concept of Tradition: A Provisional Response," in Ratzinger, *God's Word,* pp. 41-89, at 61-62.

31. Ratzinger, "The Question of the Concept of Tradition," p. 62.

32. For a similar conclusion, see Reno, "Rebuilding the Bridge Between Theology and Exegesis," p. 168.

ther. In the Nicene Creed, the Church joins Peter in confessing to Jesus ever anew: "You are the Christ, the Son of the living God" (Matt. 16:16).[33]

The Pope has given this explanation of the term *homoousios* in a number of his writings dating back at least forty years, using it as an example of the continuity between biblical and dogmatic Christology.[34] By such an explanation, the Pope is trying to show that the meaning of the biblical text (as intended by the evangelist) is clarified, not obscured, by later dogmatic formulation.[35]

The Pope is not alone in making this connection. The Lutheran theologian David Yeago makes virtually the same argument, without apparent familiarity with Ratzinger's writings. He notes that "[o]ne of the consequences of the Western Church's two centuries of fumbling with the implications of the historical-critical method is a loss of any sense of the connection between the classical doctrines of the Church and the text of scripture."[36] This is in contrast to "the unanimous conviction of the Christian tradition that they are *the teaching of scripture*."[37] Yeago relates the teaching of Nicea to Paul's hymn in Philippians: "Philippians 2:6ff and the Nicene *homoousion* meet all our ordinary criteria of 'sameness': despite the conventional wis-

33. Ratzinger/Benedict XVI, *Jesus of Nazareth,* p. 355. See also the similar explanation earlier in the chapter: "This philosophical term serves . . . to safeguard the reliability of the *biblical* term" (p. 320, emphasis in original).

34. See, for example, Joseph Ratzinger, *Behold the Pierced One: An Approach to a Spiritual Christology,* trans. Graham Harrison (San Francisco: Ignatius, 1986), p. 32: "dogmatic and biblical Christology cannot be divorced from one another or opposed to one another." And again, a little later: "the term [*homoousios*] is used solely as a translation of the [biblical] word 'Son' into philosophical language" (p. 36). See also Joseph Ratzinger, *Introduction to Christianity,* rev. ed., trans. J. R. Foster (San Francisco: Ignatius, 2004), p. 227: "These declarations were not developed out of mythological notions of origin but out of the Johannine testimony." Ratzinger also discusses this example in *The God of Jesus Christ: Meditations on God in the Trinity,* trans. Robert J. Cunningham (Chicago: Franciscan Herald, 1979), pp. 77-84; and *Truth and Tolerance: Christian Belief and World Religions,* trans. Henry Taylor (San Francisco: Ignatius, 2004), pp. 92-95.

35. In contrast, Ratzinger, in *Behold the Pierced One,* p. 33, notes the common but erroneous view that the process of "putting the biblical testimony into the forms of Greek philosophical thought brought about a complete refashioning of what was once the plain witness to Jesus."

36. David S. Yeago, "The New Testament and the Nicene Dogma: A Contribution to the Recovery of Theological Exegesis," in *The Theological Interpretation of Scripture: Classic and Contemporary Readings,* ed. Stephen E. Fowl (Oxford: Blackwell, 1997), pp. 87-100, at 87. See also Trevor Hart, "Tradition, Authority, and a Christian Approach to the Bible as Scripture," in *Between Two Horizons,* ed. Green and Turner, pp. 183-204, at 188-89.

37. Yeago, "The New Testament and the Nicene Dogma," p. 88 (emphasis in original).

dom of the critics, it is not at all odd or naïve to claim that they 'say the same thing' about Jesus and the Father."[38]

Of course, such references to later Church teaching should not be made in a simplistic or ahistorical way. In this regard, it is helpful to explore the example a bit further by observing the nuanced way in which the Pope treats the title "Son of God" in parts of *Jesus of Nazareth, Part Two.* He is well aware, for example, that this phrase can mean various things in Scripture. Thus, when he considers the meaning of the words "Son of God"/"Son of the Blessed" (Matt. 26:63; Mark 14:61) in Caiaphas's interrogation of Jesus, the Pope comments as follows: "The high priest questions Jesus about his Messiahship and refers to it in terms of Psalm 2:7 (cf. Ps. 110:3), using the expression 'Son of the Blessed' — Son of God. In the context of the question, this expression refers to the Messianic tradition, *while leaving open the form of sonship involved.*"[39] However, at the level of the Gospel's redaction and narrative dynamics, the Pope notes the irony in Matthew's formulation of the high priest's question, which echoes Peter's confession (Matt. 16:16) precisely at the moment when Peter is himself denying Jesus.[40] Following Jesus' response to the question, the high priest's reaction of tearing his robes and charging Jesus with blasphemy (Matt. 26:65) indicates that he too understood Jesus to be making, at some level, a claim of divinity, not unlike what the Nicene Creed using philosophical terminology will later say about Jesus: "[I]t meant that Jesus was claiming to be close to the 'Power,' *to participate in God's own nature,* and this would have been understood as blasphemy. . . . [T]o the members of the Sanhedrin, the application of the noble words of Scripture to Jesus evidently appeared as an intolerable attack on God's otherness, on his uniqueness."[41] Later, the "Son of God" title appears again as the Pope briefly treats the centurion's confession of Jesus as "God's Son" (Mark 15:39), describing it as "an act of faith."[42] He thus again sees continuity between the biblical title "Son" and the later dogmatic formulation, although such a connection is here not expressed explicitly. Other scholars, by considering the intention of the evangelist in these verses, reach conclusions very similar to those of the Pope.[43]

---

38. Yeago, "The New Testament and the Nicene Dogma," p. 95.

39. Ratzinger/Benedict XVI, *Jesus of Nazareth, Part Two,* p. 179 (emphasis added).

40. Ratzinger/Benedict XVI, *Jesus of Nazareth, Part Two,* pp. 179-80.

41. Ratzinger/Benedict XVI, *Jesus of Nazareth, Part Two,* p. 181 (emphasis added).

42. Ratzinger/Benedict XVI, *Jesus of Nazareth, Part Two,* p. 224.

43. For example, see the discussion in Raymond E. Brown, *Death of the Messiah,* 2 vols. (New York: Doubleday, 1994), vol. 2, pp. 1146-52. Brown concludes that "there is no con-

In *Jesus of Nazareth, Part Two,* the Pope also provides another christological example, considering Jesus' prayer in Gethsemane in light of the monothelite controversy and the response of Maximus the Confessor. The Pope thus explains that "[t]he drama of the Mount of Olives lies in the fact that Jesus draws man's natural will away from opposition and back toward synergy, and in so doing he restores man's true greatness."[44] In particular, "the prayer 'not my will, but yours' (Luke 22:42) is truly the Son's prayer to the Father, through which the natural human will is completely subsumed into the 'I' of the Son."[45] As the Pope has explained in more detail elsewhere, the Third Council of Constantinople vindicated Maximus, and in doing so was simply explaining the testimony of Scripture, not only Jesus' prayer in the garden from the Synoptic Gospels (Matt. 26:39; Mark 14:36; Luke 22:42), but also a text from John's Gospel explicitly cited by the council: "I have come down from heaven, not to do my own will, but the will of him who sent me" (John 6:38).[46]

Related to the continuity the Pope sees between biblical and dogmatic Christology is the continuity he sees between the historical Jesus and the Christ of faith. In other words, the Pope argues that "the Jesus of the Gospels" is not some construct behind which the scholar must go in order to determine the real, historical Jesus; rather, the Pope considers this Jesus to be "a historically plausible and convincing figure."[47] Observing the Christology

---

vincing objection to the thesis that the predicate in the confession of the Marcan centurion meant 'the Son of God' in the full sense of the term" (p. 1150).

44. Ratzinger/Benedict XVI, *Jesus of Nazareth, Part Two,* p. 161.

45. Ratzinger/Benedict XVI, *Jesus of Nazareth, Part Two,* p. 161. See also Ratzinger, *Behold the Pierced One,* p. 41: "Jesus' human will assimilates itself to the will of the Son."

46. Ratzinger, *Behold the Pierced One,* p. 37: "The so-called Neo-Chalcedonian theology which is summed up in the Third Council of Constantinople (680-681) makes an important contribution to a proper grasp of *the inner unity of biblical and dogmatic theology*" (emphasis added; cf. DH 556 [= *Enchiridion symbolorum definitionum et declarationum de rebus fidei et morum,* ed. Heinrich Denzinger and Peter Hünermann, bilingual 43rd edition (San Francisco: Ignatius, 2012)]).

47. Ratzinger/Benedict XVI, *Jesus of Nazareth,* p. xxii. See also Joseph Ratzinger, *Gospel, Catechesis, Catechism: Sidelights on the Catechism of the Catholic Church* (San Francisco: Ignatius Press, 1997), p. 64: "The *Catechism* trusts the biblical word. It holds the Christ of the Gospels to be the real Jesus." For some helpful reflections on the Pope's treatment of the "Jesus of history" issue, see Roch Kereszty, "The Challenge of *Jesus of Nazareth* for Theologians," *Communio* 34 (2007): 454-74, at 460: "faith in the Jesus of the Gospels appears eminently reasonable in Benedict's book." See also William M. Wright IV, "A 'New Synthesis': Joseph Ratzinger's *Jesus of Nazareth,*" *Nova et Vetera* 7 (2009): 35-66, at 46-47: "Lest this position be taken as pre-modern naïveté, Ratzinger . . . maintains that the real, historical Jesus can be heard and known through the mediation of communities and the

of the New Testament authors, readers are led to ask "Where did this Christology come from?"[48] The Pope answers: "Isn't it more logical, even historically speaking, to assume that the greatness came at the beginning, and that the figure of Jesus really did explode all existing categories and could only be understood in the light of the mystery of God?"[49] Thus, the Pope arrives at a hermeneutic of faith: "[W]e take this conviction of faith as our starting point for reading the texts with the help of historical methodology."[50]

Not only in Christology but also in Mariology does the Pope try to show that the Church's dogmatic teaching is an interpretation of Scripture. For example, in his book *Daughter Zion,* Ratzinger explains that the teaching of the Council of Ephesus that Mary is *Theotokos,* Mother of God, is not the distortion of Christianity, introducing into the Christian faith the Hellenistic pagan piety associated with the "Great-Mother" goddess Artemis-Diana.[51] Rather, the Council teaching interprets Mary as does the New Testament (e.g., Luke 1:43), referring "back to the mothers of the Old Testament, to the theology of [Israel as] the daughter Zion, and probably also to Eve."[52] This "line of development in the Old Testament . . . acquires its definitive meaning for the first time in the New Testament: in the woman who is herself described as . . . the authentic daughter Zion, and who is thereby the mother of the savior, yes, the mother of God."[53] Especially in Ratzinger's biblical Mariology does one see an application of all three of the criteria of *Dei verbum* 12: attentiveness to the content and unity of all of Scripture, to the living Tradition of the Church, and to the analogy of faith.[54]

---

evangelists' compositional activity. The Gospel narratives do not obscure Jesus, but rather they bring his enduring significance to light."

48. Ratzinger/Benedict XVI, *Jesus of Nazareth,* p. xxii.

49. Ratzinger/Benedict XVI, *Jesus of Nazareth,* pp. xxii-xxiii.

50. Ratzinger/Benedict XVI, *Jesus of Nazareth,* p. xxiii. In contrast to this faith-hermeneutic, the Pope discusses how the figure of Jesus in a work by Schnackenburg "suffers from a certain unresolved tension because of the constraints of the method he feels bound to use, despite its inadequacies" (p. xiii).

51. Joseph Ratzinger, *Daughter Zion: Meditations on the Church's Marian Belief,* trans. John M. McDermott (San Francisco: Ignatius, 1983), p. 14.

52. Ratzinger, *Daughter Zion,* p. 25.

53. Ratzinger, *Daughter Zion,* p. 24.

54. Regarding the analogy of faith, Ratzinger explains that we "cannot assign Mariology to Christology alone or to ecclesiology alone. . . . Mariology underscores the *nexus mysteriorum* — the intrinsic interwovenness of the mysteries." Joseph Ratzinger, "Thoughts on the Place of Marian Doctrine and Piety in Faith and Theology as a Whole," in Joseph Ratzinger and Hans Urs von Balthasar, *Mary: The Church at the Source,* trans. Adrian Walker (San Francisco: Ignatius, 2005), pp. 19-36, at 29. The dogma of Mary's motherhood is thus

PABLO GADENZ

The Church as the Living Subject of Biblical Interpretation

One issue raised by the preceding discussion is how to account for the development of doctrine. The objection could be raised, for example, that all the examples of dogmas thus far considered are rather straightforward: they are rather explicitly contained in the New Testament and were defined in the early Church Councils. Can one maintain, however, that dogma is "essentially nothing other than the explanation of Scripture" even for dogmas not explicitly taught in Scripture and defined much later in Church history? For example, regarding Mary's Immaculate Conception and Assumption, Raymond Brown cautions against trying to read later dogmatic teaching back into Scripture:

> I do not find a single text of the NT that in its *literal sense* refers to either of these two dogmas. . . . A thesis positing that, despite the silence of the NT on the Immaculate Conception and the Assumption, the Spirit has led the church to penetrate the salvific significance of Mary as first Christian is a far safer approach than attempting to find dogmas in NT passages where the authors show no consciousness of them. Of course, once having defined the Immaculate Conception and the Assumption, the church has cited certain biblical texts as illustrating the dogmas; but that is often simply free application. The issue . . . is the relation of dogmas to what the NT meant to the people who wrote it and first read it.[55]

Elsewhere, Brown similarly explains that in such cases which go "beyond the biblical material," one "seeks lines of development within the early Christian picture . . . that would make the doctrine intelligible as a reflection of the revelation attested to in the Bible."[56] Thus, for the Immaculate Conception

---

also related to the image of "the *mater ecclesia*" (p. 28), itself a biblical image (e.g., Gal. 4:26, which alludes to Ps. 86:5 LXX).

55. Raymond E. Brown, *Biblical Exegesis and Church Doctrine* (Mahwah, NJ: Paulist, 1985), pp. 43-45. See also his chapter on "What the Biblical Word Meant and What It Means" in Raymond E. Brown, *The Critical Meaning of the Bible* (Mahwah, NJ: Paulist, 1981), pp. 23-44.

56. Raymond E. Brown, "The Contribution of Historical Biblical Criticism to Ecumenical Church Discussion," in *Biblical Interpretation in Crisis: The Ratzinger Conference on the Bible and Church,* ed. Richard J. Neuhaus (Grand Rapids: Eerdmans, 1989), pp. 24-49, at 29; cf. p. 40. This essay is Brown's lecture at the same conference in January 1988 at which Ratzinger presented his Erasmus lecture on biblical interpretation. The two were among the participants in the scholarly conversation that took place at the conference; for an account of this conversation, see Paul T. Stallsworth, "The Story of an Encounter," in *Biblical Interpretation in Crisis,* ed. Neuhaus, pp. 102-90.

and Assumption, "the doctrines stem from a reflection on the role of Mary in salvific history. The reflection took place in prayer, liturgy, popular imagery, and theology; the underlying role had its roots in the NT."[57] In this way, because of the lines of development that provide a link, the later Church dogma should not be perceived as without basis or as an arbitrary imposition of authority.[58]

Without detracting from Brown's careful treatment of a rather complex issue, it is interesting to attempt to compare his approach with that of Ratzinger.[59] In particular, it is helpful to ascertain whether Ratzinger says anything different regarding those cases where no "single text of the NT" refers "in its *literal sense*" to a particular dogma.

Now, when Ratzinger in his 1988 Erasmus lecture said that there currently exists a "hiatus between exegesis and dogma," he immediately noted that, as a consequence of this gap, "Scripture has become a word from the past. . . . Dogma, from which the ground of Scripture has been pulled away, no longer stands. The Bible that has freed itself from dogma has become a document about the past and, thereby, itself belongs to the past."[60] Again in 2010, when Pope Benedict in *Verbum Domini* refers to the "barrier between exegesis and theology," he likewise notes that as a consequence, "if the work of exegesis is restricted to the first level alone, Scripture ends up being *a text belonging only to the past.*"[61] How then, we might ask, is Scripture brought into the present? The response, the Pope explains, involves our understanding of inspiration: "[W]e get a glimmer, even on the historical level, of what inspiration means: The author does not speak as a private,

---

57. Brown, *Biblical Exegesis and Church Doctrine*, p. 44.

58. Brown, "The Contribution of Historical Criticism," p. 40: "When I apply church authority as my warrant for preferring one critical interpretation over another, I never think of this authority as juridical and external. It gives voice to the Bible lived within church history. . . . The 'lines of development' approach in my paper shows that the so-called moderate positions are accepted because of the thesis that the Bible is the book of the church and that liturgy, church history, and the *sensus fidelium* are major hermeneutical tools."

59. Such a comparison is suggested by considering that Ratzinger and Brown themselves had the opportunity to compare their thinking on biblical interpretation at the conference in January 1988. At the press conference held on January 28, 1988, Ratzinger expressed his respect for Brown; see *Origins* 17, no. 35 (1988): 595: "I would be very happy if we had many exegetes like Father Brown." For his part, Brown included a section of "Addenda" in the published version of his paper ("The Contribution of Historical Criticism," pp. 37-49), in which he discussed his reactions to Ratzinger's lecture, both convergences and divergences.

60. Ratzinger, "Biblical Interpretation in Conflict," pp. 98-99.

61. Benedict XVI, *Verbum Domini* 35 (emphasis in original).

self-contained subject. He speaks in a living community. . . . The People of God — the Church — is the *living subject* of Scripture; it is in the Church that the words of the Bible are always in the present."[62] This oft-repeated explanation has far-reaching implications. Historical continuity between the time in the past when the Scriptures were written under the inspiration of the Spirit and the time in the present when they are being interpreted in that same Spirit is to be found in the living subject of the Church.[63] It is in the Church that the Scriptures remain a living word. This explanation of course does not mean ignoring the past, which would result in an ahistorical reading tending toward fundamentalism; in this regard, Ratzinger insists on the necessity of the first methodological level. Even after the writing of the New Testament, however, the effects of inspiration continue as the living subject of the Church, interpreting the Scriptures in the same Spirit in whom they were written, grows in understanding of the Scriptures, and thus, "constantly advances toward the fullness of divine truth."[64]

Now, getting back to the later Marian dogmas, Ratzinger would agree with Brown that these dogmas are not explicitly taught in the New Testament in its literal sense.[65] He would also agree with Brown's assessment that

62. Ratzinger/Benedict XVI, *Jesus of Nazareth,* pp. xx-xxi (emphasis added). This is another key principle that Ratzinger has repeated on a number of occasions. See, for example, "The Spiritual Basis and Ecclesial Identity of Theology," p. 61. See also his essay "What in Fact Is Theology?" in Joseph Ratzinger, *Pilgrim Fellowship of Faith: The Church as Communion,* ed. Stephan Otto Horn and Vinzenz Pfnür, trans. Henry Taylor (San Francisco: Ignatius, 2005), pp. 29-37, at 34: "Without this surviving and living agent, the Church, Scripture would not be contemporary with us." More recently, see Benedict XVI, *Verbum Domini* 86. For further discussion of this principle, see Francis Martin, "Joseph Ratzinger, Benedict XVI, on Biblical Interpretation: Two Leading Principles," *Nova et Vetera* 5 (2007): 285-314, at 285-94.

63. Cf. Ratzinger/Benedict XVI, *Jesus of Nazareth: The Infancy Narratives,* p. xi.

64. *Dei verbum* 8 (*Scripture Documents,* ed. Béchard, p. 22). See Ratzinger/Benedict XVI, *Jesus of Nazareth,* p. 234: "The Church's remembering is not merely a private affair. . . . It is a being-led by the Holy Spirit, who shows us the connectedness of Scripture, the connection between word and reality, and, in doing that, leads us 'into all the truth.'"

65. The dogma of the Assumption is a particularly interesting example because it requires us to consider carefully our understanding of Tradition; see Joseph Ratzinger, *Milestones: Memoirs 1927-1977,* trans. Erasmo Leiva-Merikakis (San Francisco: Ignatius Press, 1998), pp. 58-59: "Altaner . . . had proven in a scientifically persuasive manner that the doctrine of Mary's bodily Assumption into heaven was unknown before the fifth century; this doctrine, therefore, he argued, could not belong to the 'apostolic tradition.' . . . This argument is compelling if you understand 'tradition' strictly as the handing down of fixed formulas and texts. . . . But if you conceive of 'tradition' as the living process whereby the

"the Spirit has led the Church to penetrate the salvific significance of Mary." However, Ratzinger seems to differ from Brown in emphasizing that the Spirit's guidance of the Church toward these truths is *not a move beyond or away from Scripture, but rather a move into the "depth dimension" of Scripture.*[66] The later Marian dogmas would thus not fall completely outside the scope of the task of exegetes, since they involve more than "simply free application" of Scripture. In this regard, note how Ratzinger in *Daughter Zion* explains "the distinctive structure of the Marian dogmas":

> [T]hey *cannot* be deduced from individual texts of the New Testament; instead they express the broad perspective embracing the unity of both Testaments. They become visible only to a mode of perception that accepts this unity, i.e., within a perspective which comprehends and makes its own the "typological" interpretation.... Wherever the unity of Old and New Testaments disintegrates, the place of a healthy Mariology is lost.... This in no way means that the New Testament texts lose their importance. We are merely indicating the perspective within which they can develop their full significance.[67]

Ratzinger's comments suggest that the Marian dogmas are still related to Scripture, if Scripture is understood in its full significance.[68] Specifically,

---

Holy Spirit introduces us to the fullness of truth and teaches us how to understand what previously we could still not grasp (cf. John 16:12-13), then subsequent 'remembering' (cf. John 16:4, for instance) can come to recognize what it had not caught sight of previously and yet was already handed down in the original Word." See also Ratzinger, *Daughter Zion,* pp. 72-73.

66. On the depth dimension of Scripture, see Ignace de la Potterie, "Biblical Exegesis: A Science of Faith," trans. Michelle Borras, in *Opening Up the Scriptures: Joseph Ratzinger and the Foundations of Biblical Interpretation,* ed. José Granados, Carlos Granados, and Luis Sánchez-Navarro (Grand Rapids: Eerdmans, 2008), pp. 30-64, at 33.

67. Ratzinger, *Daughter Zion,* pp. 32-33. Similarly, Thomas Guarino, "Catholic Reflections on Discerning the Truth of Sacred Scripture," in *Your Word Is Truth: A Project of Evangelicals and Catholics Together,* ed. Charles Colson and Richard John Neuhaus (Grand Rapids: Eerdmans, 2002), pp. 79-101, at 101.

68. Cf. Avery Dulles, "Revelation, Scripture, and Tradition," in *Your Word Is Truth,* ed. Colson and Neuhaus, pp. 35-58, at 57, who indicates that "[m]ost Catholic theologians today would hold that every revealed truth is in some way attested by Scripture, but that some revealed truths are not explicitly mentioned by any texts in Scripture." Similarly, Guarino, "Catholic Reflections on Discerning the Truth of Sacred Scripture," pp. 94, 98. Brown would certainly not disagree, but nonetheless he does not emphasize that Scripture may teach a doctrine in an implicit way. Indeed, in *Biblical Exegesis and Church Doctrine,* pp. 31-48, it seems that Brown too readily places doctrines that are not taught in any text "in its *literal*

with the mention of "typological" interpretation,[69] Ratzinger points to the importance of considering not only the literal sense but also the spiritual sense of Scripture.[70] As Aquinas might say, this involves understanding not just the meaning of the words, but also the meaning of the *realities* signified by the words, even so as to *participate* in the power of those realities through faith, hope, and charity.[71] In this regard, Ratzinger's view seems to correspond to what Levering calls "participatory" biblical interpretation.[72] On the other hand, Levering describes Brown's view as rooted in a linear concept of history: the bridge between past and present is not so easy to construct in this system.[73] At times, therefore, it seems to unduly separate

---

sense" (p. 43) into the category of "Doctrines about which the Scriptures are virtually silent" (p. 40).

69. For the dogma of the Immaculate Conception, Ratzinger, *Daughter Zion,* pp. 67-68, comments that "[o]ne need not search very far for a typological identification grounding Mary's freedom from original sin," namely the *"Ecclesia immaculata"* (cf. Eph. 5:27). "Here the doctrine of the *Immaculata,* like the whole of later Mariology, is first anticipated as ecclesiology. . . . Mary is presented as the beginning and the personal concreteness of the Church." For the dogma of the Assumption, Ratzinger, *Daughter Zion,* pp. 79-80, similarly refers to the Church-Mary typology; referring to Colossians 3:3 and Ephesians 2:6, he notes that "there is something like an 'ascension' of the baptized" which already finds its bodily fulfillment in Mary. Ratzinger also refers to the transfer of the ark of the covenant to Jerusalem as a type of the Assumption (pp. 81-82).

70. On the spiritual senses and typology, see Benedict XVI, *Verbum Domini* 37-41; cf. *Catechism of the Catholic Church* 115-18, 128-30.

71. See Thomas Aquinas, *Summa Theologiae,* I, q.1, a.10. On this point, see Francis Martin, "Reading Scripture in the Catholic Tradition," in *Your Word Is Truth,* ed. Colson and Neuhaus, pp. 147-68, at 152-53: "[T]hese four senses [the literal and the threefold spiritual sense] . . . are not four meanings of the words, but four dimensions of the *event* which is being mediated by the words: the words are important because they are a privileged means of mediating the realities. . . . We are dealing here with the metaphysical notion of participation."

72. Levering, *Participatory Biblical Exegesis,* pp. 60-61: "The biblical interpreter continually encounters realities that both are historical and break the boundaries of linear history: the biblical 'present' is greater and more capacious than our understanding of it. . . . [I]n order to interpret such realities, the interpreter, and his methods, must enter and be open to these participatory depths. . . . [L]inear-historical research, at its best, enables the realities depicted in the biblical text to be seen in their linear-historical past. Yet theological reading of the biblical text is no mere add-on that indicates the evolution of postbiblical thinking. Rather, theological reading explores the historical in its participatory dimensions."

73. Levering, *Participatory Biblical Exegesis,* pp. 58-59, citing Raymond E. Brown, *The Gospel According to John (I–XII),* Anchor Bible vol. 29 (New York: Doubleday, 1966), p. vi. See also Brown, *Biblical Exegesis and Church Doctrine,* p. 30.

the exegete's task from that of the theologian,[74] what the Bible meant then and what it means now.[75]

Indeed, according to Brown, "Tension is not an improper relationship between what the Scripture meant to its authors and what it has come to mean in the Church."[76] Other examples that can serve to illustrate his position in contrast to that of Ratzinger are the dogmas of the institution of the Sacraments by Christ. In this regard, the Council of Trent dogmatically defined a few verses, such as John 3:5 as referring to water Baptism (DH 1615) and John 20:22-23 as referring to the institution of Penance (DH 1703).[77] In commenting on such texts, Avery Dulles notes Brown's distinction, but also remarks that "[t]he theological meaning is a true meaning of the text, and cannot be dismissed as 'eisegesis,' as if the Church were reading something into the text that was not really there."[78] For the specific example of John 20:22-23 and the institution of the Sacrament of Penance, however, there have been wide-ranging reactions from Catholic exegetes, from rejection to acceptance,[79] such that this passage merits further investigation and invites

74. Barron, "Biblical Interpretation," p. 185, comments on Brown's "exaggerated bifurcation between biblical exegesis and theology."

75. See n. 55 above. Critical of Brown's distinction is Denis Farkasfalvy, *Inspiration and Interpretation: A Theological Introduction to Sacred Scripture* (Washington, DC: Catholic University of America Press, 2010), p. 123, n. 5: "The issue is rooted in the question about human 'authorial intent' being elevated and instrumentally used by God's transcendental action for conveying what he wants the Bible to express."

76. Brown, *The Critical Meaning of the Bible*, p. 41. Brown clarifies, however, that "personally [he] would not accept the opposite extreme which allows the literal meaning and the church interpretation to be contradictory in the strict sense."

77. See Brown, *Biblical Exegesis and Church Doctrine*, p. 46: "[T]he doctrine of 'institution by Christ' remains valid but is understood historically in a more subtle way as the church's interpreting the mind of Jesus."

78. Avery Dulles, "Vatican II on the Interpretation of Scripture," *Letter & Spirit* 2 (2006): 17-26, at 24. Dulles thus allows that, because of the divine authorship of Scripture, a text's meaning may "go beyond what the sacred writer might have grasped" (p. 20, n. 11).

79. Sandra M. Schneiders, "The Lamb of God and the Forgiveness of Sin(s) in the Fourth Gospel," *Catholic Biblical Quarterly* 73 (2011): 1-29, at 27-28, finds the interpretation of John 20:23 in terms of the Sacrament of Penance to be "completely anachronistic." In contrast, Raymond E. Brown, *The Gospel According to John (XIII–XXI)*, Anchor Bible vol. 29a (New York: Doubleday, 1970), vol. 2, pp. 1041-45, explains the verse by noting the distinction between the evangelist's meaning and the later Church meaning. More supportive of the idea that the Church meaning reflects an original meaning referring to the disciples' ministry of forgiving postbaptismal sins are James Swetnam, "Bestowal of the Spirit in the Fourth Gospel," *Biblica* 74 (1993): 556-76, at 572-74; and Scott W. Hahn, "Temple, Sign, and Sacrament: Towards a New Perspective on the Gospel of John," *Letter & Spirit* 4 (2008): 107-43, at 137-41.

further reflection regarding the ecclesial role and responsibility of Catholic exegetes. For his part, Ratzinger strongly affirms that the passage involves the disciples' ministry of forgiving sins, as he interprets John 20:23 in conjunction with Matthew 16:19 and 18:15-18: "If we bear in mind the parallel to the word of the risen Jesus transmitted in John 20:23, it becomes apparent that in its core the power to bind and to loose means the authority to forgive sins."[80] Ratzinger thus once again illustrates that Church teaching comes from moving into the depth dimension of Scripture ("in its core"), a move that occurs in this example through the application of the criterion of the content and unity of all of Scripture (*Dei verbum* 12).

One final example involving the Sacraments can serve to further illustrate that at times the "tension" is not between what the Bible meant and what it now means in the Church, but involves disagreement about what the Bible actually meant. In other words, the determination of the literal sense of a text is not as clear-cut and objective a process as some historical critics once assumed; the results may be conditioned by the presuppositions with which the historical-critical method is practiced. This becomes rather apparent when considering the example of the priesthood of Christ and the Christian priesthood in the New Testament. At the Council of Trent, the Church defined Luke 22:19 and 1 Corinthians 11:24 ("Do this in remembrance of me") as referring to the institution of the priesthood (DH 1752). On this topic, Brown comments that "[t]here is no evidence in the language of Jesus that he thought about a priesthood replacing the Jewish priesthood in the Temple. He had disciples . . . but he designated none of his followers as priests."[81] He nonetheless supports the dogma of Trent by explaining it in a nuanced way: "that establishment by Christ involves looking at what Jesus did historically on the night before he died in the light of the Christology, liturgy, and ecclesiology of the next 100 years which interpreted the original action and words."[82] Once again it seems that, according to Brown, the Church's dogma *moves away from Scripture,* even though Brown believes that such a move can be defended if appropriate lines of development can be drawn.

In considering Brown's position on the institution of the priesthood, it

80. Joseph Ratzinger, "The Primacy of Peter and the Unity of the Church," in *Called to Communion: Understanding the Church Today,* trans. Adrian Walker (San Francisco: Ignatius, 1996), pp. 47-74, at 64.

81. Brown, *Biblical Exegesis and Church Doctrine,* p. 47. See also Raymond E. Brown, *Priest and Bishop: Biblical Reflections* (New York: Paulist, 1970).

82. Brown, *Biblical Exegesis and Church Doctrine,* p. 48.

is helpful to recall one of the presuppositions of historical criticism that was critiqued by Ratzinger in his 1988 Erasmus lecture, namely, "the alleged antagonism of the prophetic against the 'legal' and, thus, in turn against what is cultic."[83] In this regard, Ratzinger traces the crisis in the Catholic priesthood following the Second Vatican Council to modern biblical criticism:

> In the new intellectual openness that had arisen as a result of the Council, the old Reformation-era arguments, combined with the findings of modern exegesis, which had itself been nourished to a large extent by Reformation presuppositions, suddenly acquired an obviousness that Catholic theology [on the priesthood] did not have sufficiently well-founded answers to refute.[84]

Brown is undoubtedly aware of the bias associated with this anti-cultic presupposition and thus explains, in response to it, how the Catholic Church has preserved the ordained priesthood.[85] However, his perspective on this issue may still be affected by the anti-cultic scholarly consensus of his time. For example, elsewhere he writes that "[f]or the emergence of the idea of a special Christian priesthood in place of the Jewish priesthood several major changes of direction had to intervene," the first of which is that "Christians had to come to think of themselves as constituting a new religion distinct from Judaism."[86] However, in light of recent studies on the Temple, priestly Messianic expectation, and the Jewish priesthood, such a statement ("a new religion") would seem exaggerated to many scholars. It now seems clearer, for example, that if Jesus at the Last Supper spoke about establishing a (new) covenant, this would also involve in some way a change in the priesthood as well as a change in sacrifice, the Temple, and the law (cf. Heb. 7:12), since

83. Ratzinger, "Biblical Interpretation in Conflict," p. 108. Ratzinger explains that at root is "Luther's view of the relationship between the two Testaments; in place of the previous model of analogy, he set a dialectical structure. Perhaps this turning point is the real rift dividing the old and the new exegesis."

84. Joseph Ratzinger, "On the Essence of the Priesthood," in *Called to Communion,* pp. 105-31, at 105.

85. Brown, *The Critical Meaning of the Bible,* p. 103: "We Catholics should think of the ordained priesthood as part of our God-given heritage from Israel, which brought into Christian life the wealth and mystery of the whole area of OT cult. We have managed to preserve, alongside the uniqueness of the sacrifice and priesthood of Christ, the Levitical consciousness of the sacred character of a special priestly service that brings contact with the cultic symbols of God's presence."

86. Brown, *Priest and Bishop,* p. 17.

these are all correlative terms. Thus, with the gradual overcoming of the bias against the study of cultic matters in Second Temple Judaism, we are beginning to see today, even *at the level of the literal sense,* a firmer critical foundation for the notions of Christ's awareness of his priesthood and of his instituting a new priesthood than Brown thought possible only a generation ago.[87] This example, therefore, invites Catholic exegetes to take up Ratzinger's suggestions to develop a theological approach to the text and to do so with humility,[88] recognizing that what seem today like definitive answers from a critical perspective might change in a few years' time, as new lines of inquiry are pursued and new evidence is uncovered.

To be fair, despite any contrast in perspective, Brown, far from objecting to Ratzinger's proposals in his 1988 Erasmus lecture, made the following comments: "Beyond historical-biblical criticism I see the fuller meaning of the text. This can be developed only by adding the theological. This is still exegesis. It still draws meaning from the text."[89] Hence, the difference may

---

87. See N. T. Wright, "Whence and Whither Historical Jesus Studies in the Life of the Church?" in *Jesus, Paul and the People of God: A Theological Dialogue with N. T. Wright,* ed. Nicholas Perrin and Richard B. Hays (Downers Grove, IL: InterVarsity Press, 2011), pp. 115-58, at 150, who comments about the future direction of Historical Jesus studies by noting that "[t]he study of the Gospels in the light of all we now know about first-century Judaism positively cries out for exploration of big, new subjects," including "Jesus and priesthood." See also Crispin H. T. Fletcher Louis, "Jesus as the High Priestly Messiah: Part 1," *Journal for the Study of the Historical Jesus* 4 (2006): 155-75, at 155, who, in contrast to the "scholarly consensus," considers "some important evidence that Jesus thought of himself as Israel's eschatological high priest." Of interest also are the works of Deborah Rooke, "Kingship as Priesthood: The Relationship between the High Priesthood and the Monarchy," in *King and Messiah in Israel and the Ancient Near East,* ed. John Day, Journal for the Study of the Old Testament Supplement Series 270 (Sheffield: Sheffield Academic Press, 1998), pp. 187-208; and "Jesus as Royal Priest: Reflections on the Interpretation of the Melchizedek Tradition in Heb. 7," *Biblica* 81 (2000): 81-94. See also Brant Pitre, "Jesus, the New Temple, and the New Priesthood," *Letter & Spirit* 4 (2008): 47-83.

88. See also Ratzinger's answers to various questions posed by Richard Neuhaus during the conference following his 1988 Erasmus lecture: Stallsworth, "The Story of an Encounter," pp. 133-37.

89. See Stallsworth, "The Story of an Encounter," p. 145. Brown further commented that "we need to preserve what is extremely valuable from the historical-critical method, and we need to preserve what is extremely valuable from the great church exegesis of the Fathers" (p. 147). Moreover, in his written response to Ratzinger's lecture, Brown, "The Contribution of Historical Biblical Criticism," pp. 27 and 37, briefly mentions "a broader sense of Scripture" and refers to the spiritual sense (pp. 27, 37), the *sensus plenior* (p. 37), or "more-than-literal exegesis" (p. 49). Brown's emphasis, however, remains on the literal sense. In this regard, David M. Williams, *Receiving the Bible in Faith: Historical and Theo-*

be more one of emphasis, with Ratzinger insisting more on that aspect of Tradition which considers it not so much as moving beyond or away from Scripture but as elucidating Scripture in its depth dimension.[90] The view of Ratzinger thus also seems more in keeping with the integrated approach of *Dei verbum,* which sees Scripture and Tradition more as coming "together into a single current,"[91] as opposed to the view of "two sources of divine revelation" (Scripture and Tradition) that was common before the Second Vatican Council.[92]

In summary, Ratzinger's insights regarding the Church as the living subject of Scripture enrich our understanding, not only of biblical inspiration, but also of biblical interpretation. The hiatus between exegesis and theology can be overcome by moving more fully into the depth dimension of Scripture.

Conclusion: Relationships between Exegesis, Theology, and Prayer

In this essay, with the help of Pope Benedict's writings, we have considered two aspects associated with the task of relating exegesis to theology: understanding dogma as interpretation of Scripture and viewing the Church

---

logical Exegesis (Washington, DC: Catholic University of America Press, 2004), p. 77, notes Brown's "gradual abandonment of specific interest" in meanings that go beyond the literal.

90. See Benedict XVI, *Verbum Domini* 17: "The living Tradition is essential for enabling the Church to grow through time in the understanding of the truth revealed in the Scriptures. . . . Ultimately, it is the living Tradition of the Church which makes us adequately understand Sacred Scripture as the word of God." Explaining Tradition in a way similar to Ratzinger is Dulles, "Revelation, Scripture, and Tradition," pp. 51-53.

91. The whole phrase reads as follows: "Sacred Tradition and Sacred Scripture, then, are linked closely together and communicate with each other. For both of them, flowing out from the same divine wellspring, in a certain way come together into a single current and tend toward the same end." *Dei verbum* 9 (*Scripture Documents,* ed. Béchard, p. 23).

92. Before the Council, the neo-Scholastic manuals operating with the perspective of "two sources of divine revelation" (Scripture and Tradition) attempted to link them together perhaps with an at-times too facile use of Scripture as mere *dicta probantia.* Cf. Pontifical Biblical Commission, *The Interpretation of the Bible in the Church,* sec. III.D.4 (*Scripture Documents,* ed. Béchard, p. 302): "[T]heology has often yielded to the temptation to consider the Bible as a store of *dicta probantia* serving to confirm doctrinal theses." It appears that after the Council, however, some Catholic historical-critical scholars in effect have continued operating under the same model of "two sources of revelation," only now they as exegetes are only concerned with the Scripture part, thus leaving to theologians the task of linking Scripture with Tradition.

as the living subject of biblical interpretation. Catholic exegetes who strive
to achieve this task will certainly help their students and others develop an
understanding of Scripture that is integrated with other aspects of the life of
the Church. In this regard, some words of the Pope in *Verbum Domini* that
are directed to seminarians can be adapted and given wider application to
Christians generally: Christians "must learn to love the word of God. Scripture should thus be the soul of their theological formation, and emphasis
must be given to the indispensable interplay of exegesis, theology, spirituality and mission."[93] As the Pope here indicates, the overcoming of the hiatus
between exegesis and theology will thus also contribute to the integration
of biblical studies with scriptural prayer.[94] Indeed, it is helpful to recall that
Scripture is not just a *locus theologicus* but also a *hortus conclusus*.[95] A more
detailed treatment of this other area of needed integration will hopefully be
the subject of a future essay.

93. Benedict XVI, *Verbum Domini* 82, citing *Propositio* 32 of the Synod.

94. Benedict XVI, *Verbum Domini* 82: "The Synod recommended that seminarians be
concretely helped to see *the relationship between biblical studies and scriptural prayer.* . . .
Hence, great care should be taken to ensure that seminarians always cultivate this *reciprocity
between study and prayer* in their lives. This end will be served if candidates are introduced
to the study of Scripture through methods which favour this integral approach."

95. See Henri de Lubac, *Scripture in the Tradition,* trans. Luke O'Neill (New York:
Herder & Herder, 1968; reprint, 2000), p. 49, who cites Jean Châtillon (*Revue du moyenâge
latin* 4 [1948]: 439) writing about twelfth-century mystics, for whom "Scripture is no longer the *locus theologicus* from which the scholar gathers his premises, but is now the *hortus
conclusus* where the soul meets the Spouse, listens to his voice and inhales the fragrance of
his perfumes."

CHAPTER 5

The Catholic Use of the Scriptures in Ecumenical Dialogue

Christian D. Washburn

Since the Second Vatican Council significant ecumenical progress has been made on the journey to what John Paul II called the "full and visible communion in the same faith, the same sacraments and the same apostolic ministry."[1] This progress is due in no small part to an emphasis on our common inheritance of the Sacred Scriptures and the adoption of the historical-critical method as a common methodology in interpreting Scripture. Given its usefulness, this method is repeatedly praised in official documents as the basis for these recent ecumenical breakthroughs.[2] This method, though, has be-

1. John Paul II, Homily at the Vespers Liturgy on the Occasion of the 40th Anniversary of the Promulgation of the conciliar decree, *Unitatis Redintegratio,* Saturday, 13 November 2004. Much of the ecumenical progress is summarized in Walter Kasper, *Harvesting the Fruits: Aspects of Christian Faith in Ecumenical Dialogue* (London: Continuum, 2009). Cardinal Kasper, the former head of the Pontifical Council for the Promotion of Christian Unity, offers insights into the PCPCU's relative success with the Lutheran World Federation, the Anglican churches, the World Methodist Council, and the World Alliance of Reformed Churches. By looking at each dialogue's work on traditionally divisive topics, Cardinal Kasper is able to identify areas where some form of agreement has been achieved and other areas where more discussion is needed.

2. For example, "A remarkable degree of progress has already been achieved. Through the adoption of the same methods and analogous hermeneutical points of view, exegetes of various Christian confessions have arrived at a remarkable level of agreement in the interpretation of Scripture, as is shown by the text and notes of a number of ecumenical translations of the Bible, as well as by other publications." Pontifical Biblical Commission, *The Interpretation of the Bible in the Church* 4. The English text cited here is found in Dean Philip Bechard, ed. and trans., *The Scripture Documents: An Anthology of Official Catholic Teachings* (Collegeville, MN: Liturgical Press, 2002), pp. 312-13. See also Karl Lehmann

come not one tool among many but what Cardinal Dulles has termed the "primary norm" of the various bilateral dialogues.[3] Clearly, the historical-critical method has borne much fruit and is now a permanent fixture in the life of the Church and ecumenism; however, several recent scholars and various ecclesial statements have called for the incorporation of other methods of scriptural interpretation within the context of these dialogues. The purpose of this essay is to examine the role of the Catholic use of Scripture in ecumenical dialogue and to suggest that a more theological, patristic, and ecclesial reading of Scripture will assist in further ecumenical agreement and consensus.

The Role of the Historical-Critical Method in the Lutheran-Catholic Dialogue

The incorporation of methodologies other than the historical-critical method has not always been warmly received. Both Frs. Raymond E. Brown and Joseph A. Fitzmyer have been vigorous defenders of the use of the historical-critical method in ecumenical dialogue as well as circumspect in their discussion of the value of other methodologies.[4] Fr. Brown, an early member of the U.S. Lutheran-Catholic Dialogue (Rounds I-V), wrote an important article in 1964, calling for the use of "modern critical biblical studies" and downplaying the criticisms of "fundamentalists" and "ultraconservatives." Modern critical biblical study, asserts Brown, is useful since it allows one to ascertain "clearly what the Bible has to say for itself, has pinpointed how many of the traditional divisions among Christians really flow from the Bible and how many are the products of post-biblical theological development." He spends most of the article showing the value of form criticism, the study of the Dead Sea Scrolls, and the value of a common Bible.[5]

---

and Wolfhart Pannenberg, *The Condemnations of the Reformation Era: Do They Still Divide?* (Minneapolis: Fortress Press, 1990), pp. 17, 25, 27.

3. Avery Cardinal Dulles, "Saving Ecumenism from Itself," *First Things* 12 (2007): 25.

4. Joseph A. Fitzmyer, *The Interpretation of Scripture: In Defense of the Historical-Critical Method* (New York: Paulist Press, 2008), pp. 73-74. For a Lutheran defense of the historical-critical method, see Gerhard Ebeling, "The Significance of the Critical Historical Method for Church and Theology in Protestantism," in *Word and Faith* (Philadelphia: Fortress Press, 1963), pp. 17-61; John Reumann, "After Historical-Critical Criticism, What? Trends in Biblical Interpretation and Ecumenical, Interfaith Dialogues," *Journal of Ecumenical Studies* 29, no. 1 (Winter 1992): 55-86.

5. Raymond E. Brown, "Ecumenism and New Testament Research," *Journal of Ecumenical Studies* 1 (1964): 299-314.

Twenty-five years later, Fr. Brown delivered a lecture for a conference titled "Biblical Interpretation in Crisis: The Ratzinger Conference on Bible and Church" at which Ratzinger gave the keynote lecture. In his lecture, Brown was still concerned with defending the use of a "moderate biblical criticism" against "fundamentalists" and "ultraconservative Roman Catholics."[6] Brown argues that "most theological apprehensions about historical criticism are focused on something past and are not relevant to the moderate and adapted form of criticism."[7] Ecumenical discussion, Brown continues, profits from "being subject to the control of the written text rather than to speculations that go far beyond the text."[8] All churches, he continues to note, must acknowledge that serious biblical criticism has shown that their "theology, structure, and liturgy" have "gone considerably beyond the New Testament Church with their inchoative diversities." Therefore each church has to examine why it has followed "one line of development rather than another."[9] This, Brown argues, will lead churches to recognize that another church which has followed "a different biblical line of development" has also preserved a biblical value.[10] Most remarkable in Brown's discussion is the absence of the call for any other method for reading the Scriptures to complement the historical-critical method, despite the fact that Cardinal Ratzinger, at this very same conference, called explicitly for the Scriptures to be read within the faith of the Church. Brown is silent on the value of canonical, ecclesial, or patristic methodologies.[11]

Fr. Fitzmyer, also a member of the U.S. Lutheran-Catholic Dialogue

---

6. Raymond E. Brown, "The Contribution of Historical Biblical Criticism to Ecumenical Discussion," in *Biblical Interpretation in Crisis: The Ratzinger Conference on the Bible and the Church,* ed. R. J. Neuhaus (Grand Rapids: Eerdmans, 1989), pp. 24-49.

7. Brown, "The Contribution of Historical Biblical Criticism to Ecumenical Discussion," p. 24.

8. Brown, "The Contribution of Historical Biblical Criticism to Ecumenical Discussion," p. 26.

9. Brown, "The Contribution of Historical Biblical Criticism to Ecumenical Discussion," p. 34.

10. Brown, "The Contribution of Historical Biblical Criticism to Ecumenical Discussion," p. 35.

11. Brown, "The Contribution of Historical Biblical Criticism to Ecumenical Discussion," p. 32. His one mention of a Father allowed him to conclude that "biblical criticism can lend support to the contention that the Nicene definition was faithful to the directions of the New Testament." On this point Lewis Ayres offers some useful reflections that are corrective of Brown's language. Lewis Ayres, *Nicaea and Its Legacy: An Approach to Fourth-Century Trinitarian Theology* (Oxford: Oxford University Press, 2006), pp. 415-17.

(Rounds V-XI) and of the International Dialogue, is no less a stalwart defender of the historical-critical method in ecumenical dialogue. He notes that "such common endeavors have been based in large part on the use of the historical-critical method of biblical interpretation as a tool to arrive at the genuine religious or spiritual sense of the biblical writings that constitute our common heritage."[12] He further notes that when this method is used correctly and not as an end in itself, "it has no peer."[13] From this he seems to conclude that other traditional methodologies are suspect. For example, while Fr. Fitzmyer affirms that "the Fathers thus strove to accomplish what is still a legitimate goal of all biblical interpretation," i.e., to read the Bible "theologically,"[14] he is clear that he is not calling for the reintegration of patristic exegesis as a means of interpreting the Scriptures. One must note that Fr. Fitzmyer has deftly shifted the discussion. He is willing to concede that the end or "goal" of patristic exegesis is acceptable, but not the means the Fathers used to achieve this goal. Thus in one of his more rhetorical moments, he rejects the revival of the use of patristic allegory: "When it comes to the allegorical interpretation of Scripture that the Fathers used, I have only one comment: *'admirandum sed non imitandum,'* to be marveled at but not imitated."[15]

This hegemony of the historical-critical method in ecumenical dialogue has been challenged, most notably by Avery Cardinal Dulles — yet another member of the U.S. Lutheran-Catholic Dialogue (Rounds V-IX).[16]

12. H. George Anderson, T. Austin Murphy, and Joseph A. Burgess, eds., *Justification by Faith* (Minneapolis: Augsburg, 1985), p. 78.

13. Anderson, Murphy, and Burgess, eds., *Justification by Faith,* p. 78. It must be noted that, from a Catholic dogmatic perspective, this is a rather curious claim. It is perhaps more correct to say that the historical-critical method has no peer in the natural order. As we will see below, those interpretations that are considered infallible, either according to the unanimous consent of the Fathers or guaranteed by the magisterium, clearly would be above other interpretations. Since in the historical-critical method there is no necessary guarantee of infallibility, any interpretations provided by its methodology are clearly subordinate.

14. Joseph A. Fitzmyer, *The Biblical Commission's Document "The Interpretation of the Bible in the Church": Text and Commentary* (Rome: Pontificio Istituto Biblico, 1995), pp. 149-50.

15. Thomas H. Stahel, "Scripture, the Soul of Theology: An Interview with Joseph A. Fitzmyer, S.J.," *America,* 6 May 1995, p. 11.

16. Others have also raised questions about this matter. In 1995, a bilateral Study Group of the Faith and Order Commission suggested that ecumenists need to be careful concerning the potential liabilities of the historical-critical method. It then goes on to name two of these liabilities. First, the ecumenical agreements may be far ahead of the churches represented; and second, the use of the historical-critical method may actually be "sewing [sic] the seeds

He is critical of the overreliance on the historical-critical method by various bilateral dialogues, noting that "many of the twentieth-century dialogues have opted to take Scripture, interpreted by the historical-critical method, as their primary norm."[17] Although this method has worked reasonably well for mainline Protestant churches and for the Catholic Church since Vatican II, he notes that there are two basic problems with the exclusive use of modern biblical criticism in ecumenical dialogue. First, Dulles warns that this method is of little use to those "Christians who do not rely on the critical approach to Scripture as normative." There are still significant groups of Christians who are suspicious of this methodology for a variety of reasons. Second, Catholics have historically embraced not only the historical-critical method but have also drawn "on allegorical or spiritual exegesis, authenticated by the sense of the faithful and long-standing theological tradition."[18] I think that one may add to Dulles's critique that this is not only true for Catholics, but as we will see later, it is also true for many of our bilateral partners.

Another critic of the overreliance on the historical-critical method in ecumenical dialogue is the biblical scholar Brevard Childs, who is best known as an advocate of canonical exegesis. Childs is more concerned with the final form of the Scriptures than with the source for any particular text, precisely because he wishes to affirm that there is "a single unified voice in scripture," Jesus Christ.[19] His approach is ultimately concerned with a theological reading of the Scriptures. Consequently, Childs is directly critical of the predominance of the historical-critical method in Lutheran-Catholic dialogue, asserting that it is "naïve and patently erroneous" to think that any major ecumenical advances are "possible" based on the historical-critical method alone.[20] Childs enumerates and then rejects virtually every argument posed in favor of the dominance of the historical-critical method in ecumenical theology. First, he doubts that the good will among contemporary Lutheran and Catholic ecumenists is really due to the common use of

---

of future division." Joseph A. Burgess and Jeffrey Gros, *Growing Consensus: Church Dialogues in the United States, 1962-1991* (New York: Paulist Press, 1995), p. 641.

17. Avery Cardinal Dulles, "Ecumenism and Theological Method," *Journal of Ecumenical Studies* (1980): 40-48.

18. Avery Cardinal Dulles, "Saving Ecumenism from Itself," *First Things* 12 (2007): 25.

19. Gerhard F. Hasel, "Recent Models of Biblical Theology: Three Major Perspectives," *Andrews University Studies* 33, nos. 1-2 (Spring-Summer 1995): 63; Frank C. Senn, *Lutheran Identity: A Classical Understanding* (Minneapolis: Augsburg Fortress, 2008), pp. 33-34.

20. Brevard S. Childs, *Biblical Theology of the Old and New Testaments: Theological Reflection on the Christian Bible* (Minneapolis: Fortress Press, 1993), p. 524.

the method rather than to some other reason.[21] Second, he argues that the treatment of the biblical texts as "a human phenomenon" is "incapable of providing serious positive aid in discerning the true subject matter to which the [scriptural] texts point."[22] In Childs's opinion, historical-critical exegesis "flounders at the crucial junction which must be crossed if one seeks to reflect theologically on what the Bible characterizes as the divine word." In proof of his thesis he penetratingly notes that while a "level of descriptive agreement can be achieved," this descriptive agreement plays little role with these same scholars in "evaluating the classic dogmatic positions." On the important issue of the nature of grace, for example, the serious theological differences in the classic Catholic and Lutheran confessions are "harmonized by appeals to a tension within the New Testament itself."[23] In other words, one set of New Testament texts within the tension serves as a justification for the Catholic position while another set serves for the Protestant.

The hard-fought battles over the historical-critical method's use are not to be undone: recent ecclesiastical documents are all in agreement that its place is secure. As the Pontifical Biblical Commission notes, "The historical-critical method is the indispensable method for the scientific study of the meaning of ancient texts."[24] But neither Dulles nor Childs has called into question either the necessity or utility of employing the historical-critical method; they have only questioned the undue emphasis on this method in ecumenical dialogue and the failure of some to recognize the inherent limitations of the historical-critical method. Besides, Catholic theologians have always recognized the importance of a sound historical approach in theology, even if in the past their tools were rather limited.[25] Theologians such as Cardinals Dulles and Ratzinger have made the same point that both old and recent magisterial documents have continually made: the necessity of incorporating other methodologies into scriptural exegesis.[26] The difficulty

21. Childs, *Biblical Theology of the Old and New Testaments*, pp. 524-25.

22. Childs, *Biblical Theology of the Old and New Testaments*, p. 525.

23. Childs, *Biblical Theology of the Old and New Testaments*, p. 526.

24. Pontifical Biblical Commission, *The Interpretation of the Bible in the Church* 249. See also Joseph G. Prior, *The Historical Critical Method in Catholic Exegesis* (Rome: Pontificia Universita Gregoriana, 1999), pp. 248-53.

25. Some contemporaries treat this assertion as if it is some new insight into theology and biblical studies. Melchior Cano wrote, "Certe quantum historiae cognitione theologus indigeat, vel illi abunde magno argumento sunt, qui ejus ignoratione sunt in varios erroes lapsi. . . ." Melchior Canus, *De locis theologicis libri duodecim: cum indice copiosissimo atque locupletissimo* (Salamanca: Excudebat Mathias Gastius, 1563), XI.2.

26. Ratzinger, both before and after his election, repeatedly pointed out the limita-

with documents such as *The Interpretation of the Bible in the Church* is that they are not entirely clear how these methodologies should be employed in complementary ways.[27]

Theological Reading of the Scriptures

The Scriptures are primarily theological, and all other genres employed in the Bible are ultimately subordinate to the theological. The purpose of the Bible is to speak of God and of creatures in their relation to him. Therefore, the Catholic theologian approaches the Scriptures already with faith in the one true God, who has revealed to us those things necessary for salvation.

---

tions of the historical-critical method. Joseph Cardinal Ratzinger, "Biblical Interpretation in Crisis: On the Question of the Foundations and Approaches of Exegesis Today," in *Biblical Interpretation in Crisis,* pp. 1-24. Thus Benedict XVI states, "The application of the historical method to the Bible as a historical text was a path that had to be taken. If we believe that Christ is real history, and not myth, then the testimony concerning him has to be historically accessible as well. In this sense, the historical method has also given us many gifts. It has brought us back closer to the text and its originality, it has shown us more precisely how it grew, and much more besides. The historical-critical method will always remain one dimension of interpretation. Vatican II made this clear. On the one hand, it presents the essential elements of the historical method as a necessary part of access to the Bible. At the same time, though, it adds that the Bible has to be read in the same Spirit in which it was written. It has to be read in its wholeness, in its unity. And that can be done only when we approach it as a book of the People of God progressively advancing toward Christ. What is needed is not simply a break with the historical method, but a self-critique of the historical method; a self-critique of historical reason that takes cognizance of its limits and recognizes the compatibility of a type of knowledge that derives from faith; in short, we need a synthesis between an exegesis that operates with historical reason and an exegesis that is guided by faith. We have to bring the two things into a proper relationship to each other. That is also a requirement of the basic relationship between faith and reason." Benedict XVI, *Light of the World: The Pope, the Church, and the Signs of the Times* (San Francisco: Ignatius Press, 2010), pp. 171-72.

27. Thus Ayres and Fowl write, "The best that can be said is that *Interpretation* allows traditional methods of reading according to the multiple sense of Scripture to supplement interpretation that discovers the intentions of the human authors. But again, this position cannot be squared with its earlier insistence that no reading that is not the meaning expressed by the human authors in their written text is to be accepted. For example, *Interpretation* allows that Matthew 1:23 provides the fuller sense to Isaiah 7:14, so that the latter text should be interpreted to mean 'a virgin shall conceive.'" Lewis Ayres and Stephen E. Fowl, "(MIS)Reading the Face of God: *The Interpretation of the Bible in the Church,*" *Theological Studies* 60 (1999): 520.

Dei verbum is clear that "Sacred Scripture must be read and interpreted in the light of the same Spirit by whom it was written."[28] The goal of Catholic exegesis is "to see clearly what God wanted to communicate to us," and therefore the Catholic exegete "should carefully investigate what meaning the sacred writers really intended, and what God wanted to manifest by means of their words."[29] The relationship between the two levels of authorship is touched on by *Dei verbum* 11, which acknowledges that these sacred authors are "true authors" who "consigned to writing everything and only those things which He wanted."[30] Thus what the Catholic is principally interested in is what God has intended to say through the human authors. Since the Christian approaches the text attempting to find God's self-revelation, one must affirm that the historical-critical method is methodologically posterior to and merely in the service of a theological reading of the text.

The difficulty with the historical-critical method is that it is, as Brian E. Daley has noted, "methodologically atheistic," and if Daley is correct, there are a number of important ecumenical implications.[31] First, modern historical criticism as such cannot and should not be classified as a theological discipline. It is instead like logic, history, or philology, merely a subordinate tool that the theologian utilizes. After all, "without faith," as Ratzinger has noted, "Scripture itself is not Scripture, but rather an ill-assorted ensemble of bits of literature which cannot claim any normative significance today."[32] Second, a theological reading of Scripture is suited better than the historical-critical method to answer theological questions that underlie the divisions present

28. *Catechism of the Catholic Church* 111; *Dei verbum* 12. See also Avery Cardinal Dulles, S.J., "Vatican II on the Interpretation of Scripture," *Letter & Spirit* 2 (2006): 17-26.

29. *Dei verbum* 12; DH 4217 (= *Enchiridion symbolorum definitionum et declarationum de rebus fidei et morum,* ed. Heinrich Denzinger and Peter Hünermann, bilingual 43rd edition [San Francisco: Ignatius, 2012]).

30. DH 4215.

31. Brian E. Daley, "Is Patristic Exegesis Still Useable? Reflections on Early Christian Interpretations of the Psalms," *Communio* 29 (Spring 2002): 194-204. A shorter version of this essay is available in *The Art of Reading Scripture,* ed. Ellen F. Davis and Richard B. Hays (Grand Rapids: Eerdmans, 2003), pp. 69-88. Ratzinger has made essentially the same observation: "Modern exegesis, as we have seen, completely relegated God to the incomprehensible, the otherworldly, and the inexpressible in order to be able to treat the biblical text itself as an entirely worldly reality according to natural-scientific methods." Joseph Cardinal Ratzinger, "Biblical Interpretation in Crisis," p. 17.

32. Joseph Cardinal Ratzinger, "The Theology of the Liturgy," in *Looking Again at the Question of the Liturgy with Cardinal Ratzinger: Proceedings of the July 2001 Fontgombault Liturgical Conference,* ed. Alcuin Reid (Farnborough: St. Michael's Abbey Press, 2003), p. 19.

in Christianity. The predominant use of the modern critical method is essentially regressive ecumenically since it prescinds from what the bilateral partners already hold in common, e.g., a belief that the Bible is the inspired Word of God. Certainly while one can conceive of a Christian approaching the text as a merely human document by employing the historical-critical method, one must ask why Christians dialoguing with each other would begin with a methodology that is essentially atheistic. Third, it is precisely by our agreement on the Scriptures as God's word that we give common witness to the world of our belief. To utilize an approach whereby we treat the Scriptures as merely a human creation certainly sends an odd message to the world.

In a theological reading there are two distinct but related elements. The first is to read the Scriptures christologically, thereby establishing the fundamental unity between the Old and the New Testaments and interpreting all that is contained in each Testament in the light of who Christ is. This reading has the ecumenical advantage of being accepted, albeit in slightly different respects, by most bilateral partners. In the Lutheran tradition, for example, this was a common way of proceeding. Luther himself was, at least in his early career, not outside of this tradition of reading the Scriptures the way the Fathers and medieval Doctors had, though in a modified way.[33] This christological principle extends not only to the two Testaments but also to all the doctrines contained in them. In Round XI of the U.S. Lutheran-Catholic Dialogue there was an attempt to explain the doctrine of Purgatory in its proper christological context.[34] The dialogue, however, failed to link this christological reading with the scriptural texts on which the doctrine of Purgatory is based.[35] The second aspect of a canonical reading is that one part of the Bible is read in light of other parts of the Bible.

To read the text theologically, one not only considers the totality and unity of the Scriptures; such a reading also serves to find individual theological truths derived from particular passages of the Bible. Here it is helpful to give an example of how a theological reading of Scripture can be sensitive to

33. Jared Wicks, S.J., "The Beginning of Luther's Beginnings in the Psalms," *Lutheran Forum* (Fall 2010): 30-34; Stephen J. Hultgren, "Holy Scripture and the Word of God: Biblical Authority in the Church," in *Seeking New Directions for Lutheranism: Biblical, Theological, and Churchly Perspectives,* ed. and intro. Carl E. Braaten (Delhi, NY: ALPB Books, 2010).

34. *The Hope of Eternal Life — Common Statement of the Eleventh Round of the U.S. Lutheran-Catholic Dialogue,* ed. Lowell G. Almen and Richard J. Sklba (Minneapolis: Lutheran University Press, 2011), pp. 83-85, 132.

35. *The Hope of Eternal Life,* pp. 70-73.

the historical context of particular passages of Scripture and simultaneously derive important theological conclusions from the text. The Scriptures, for example, do not explicitly affirm that Christ has a soul, nor do they state that he is capable of laughing, but they explicitly reveal that Christ has flesh (John 1:14), that he walks and talks, that he is born of a woman, and that he dies (Heb. 2:9). All of these point to the fact, which few today would dispute, that Christ is a *perfectus homo,* i.e., he has that integrity *(integritas)* or wholeness that is common to man. This transition from particular passages of the New Testament to what is essentially an abstract claim about Christ's nature is not a violation of the sacred text and does not "go beyond" what the New Testament affirms. This conclusion can be said to be formally contained in revelation, though not explicitly. We can even take this one step further: if Christ is indeed a *perfectus homo,* he must have all the qualities that are attendant upon such an affirmation. Now the Scriptures never explicitly affirm that Christ has a soul, but if we affirm that he is *perfectus homo,* then he must at least have those things that are necessary to the nature of man. Another classic example concerns Christ's risibility. If Christ is fully man *(perfectus homo),* then it is the case that Christ is capable of laughter *(risibilitas),* even though the Scriptures do not record Christ laughing.[36] Christians engaged in ecumenical dialogue should feel perfectly free to assess the theological import of a passage, since this type of reading does not go "beyond" the meaning of a particular passage.

Patristic Reading of Scripture

As noted above, proponents of the historical-critical method are fairly circumspect in their discussion of the usefulness of patristic exegesis,[37] while

36. St. John Chrysostom points out that none of the evangelists records Christ laughing. Chrysostom, *Homilies on the Gospel of Matthew,* 6.7, Nicene and Post-Nicene Fathers, 1st series, vol. 10, p. 41.

37. In answering the question, "What then is the practical import of patristic exegesis as a guide?," Fr. Brown writes that "the area in which Patristic authority is strongest is that of the dogmatic implications of Scripture, not that of literal exegesis," and he later informs us that in "practical guidance in modern literal exegesis of individual texts, patristic authority is of restricted importance." Here I think we have the fundamental problem. Notice Brown's sleight of hand: the "dogmatic implications" are now divorced from the "modern literal" sense, leading one to wonder what the value of these "dogmatic implications" could possibly then have. Brown and Sandra M. Schneiders, "Hermeneutics," *New Jerome Biblical Commentary,* ed. Raymond E. Brown, Joseph A. Fitzmyer, and Roland E. Murphy (Englewood Cliffs, NJ: Prentice Hall, 1990), p. 1164. Brown goes on to assert that the church wishes us

magisterial documents have repeatedly called for the incorporation of patristic exegesis into the Catholic theologian's interpretation of Scripture.[38] As Patriarch Bartholomew has noted, the Fathers not only show us the way to the past but also to the future;[39] therefore the new attempts to recover patristic exegesis should not be viewed as theological archeologism. Despite the repeated magisterial promotion of patristic exegesis, documents such as *The Interpretation of the Bible in the Church* and *Verbum Domini* remain primarily descriptive and as such do not assist the theologian in how to appropriate patristic exegesis. For the Catholic ecumenist there are three issues related to the role of the Fathers in ecumenical work: the first is theological, the second is dogmatic, and the third is methodological.

The first issue to which Catholic ecumenists must give heed is the fundamentally theological orientation of patristic exegesis. Here the Pontifical Biblical Commission has offered some helpful insight, in part addressing the concerns of Childs and Dulles in noting that "the Fathers look upon the Bible above all as the Book of God, the single work of a single author."[40] Or as Thomas Oden has succinctly put it, the Fathers were more "aware of what was mediated and paid less attention to the mediating author."[41] Moreover, the Fathers were inclined to see Christ as the center of the Scriptures. St. Athanasius, for example, wrote, "Now the scope and character of Holy Scripture, as we have often said, is this — it contains a double account of the Saviour; that He was ever God, and is the Son, being the Father's Word and Radiance and Wisdom; and that afterwards for us He took flesh of a Virgin,

---

"to emulate the success of the Fathers in having the Bible nourish the faith, life, teaching, and preaching of the Christian Community." Thus Brown seems to suggest that the use of the Fathers should be relegated to merely pious concerns. In this Brown makes the teaching of the Council of Trent and Vatican I virtually unintelligible. His primary concern seems to be to demonstrate that "Patristic authority is no restriction on the liberty of the modern Catholic exegesis."

38. See, for example, Trent, DH 1507; *Profession of the Faith of the Council of Trent* (1565), DH 1863; Vatican I, DII 3007; Leo XIII, *Providentissimus Deus* 14, DH 3284; Pius XII, *Divino afflante Spiritu* 24; Pontifical Biblical Commission, *The Historicity of the Gospels* (1964); Congregation for Catholic Education, "Instruction on the Study of the Fathers of the Church in the Formation of Priests," *L'Osservatore Romano,* 15 January 1990, pp. 8-12.

39. *Speaking the Truth in Love: Theological and Spiritual Exhortations of Ecumenical Patriarch Bartholomew,* edited with an introduction by John Chryssavgis (New York: Fordham University Press, 2010), p. 268.

40. *Interpretation of the Bible in the Church,* p. 291.

41. Francis Martin and Thomas C. Oden, *Acts* (Downers Grove, IL: InterVarsity, 2006), p. xxv.

Mary Bearer of God, and was made man. And this scope is to be found throughout inspired Scripture."[42] St. Cyril of Alexandria is no less emphatic: "The goal of inspired Scripture is to signify the mystery of Christ through innumerable objects."[43]

St. Augustine notes that "whenever you hear the voice of the body, do not separate it from the voice of the Head; and whenever you hear the voice of the Head, do not separate Him from the body."[44] In part, this theological sense acknowledges that the truth is to be fundamentally found within the context of a community, a point that is pressed home by both Tertullian and St. Irenaeus. Irenaeus is emphatic that the truth is to be found in the Church:

> Since therefore we have such proofs, it is not necessary to seek the truth among others which it is easy to obtain from the Church; since the apostles, like a rich man [depositing his money] in a bank, lodged in her hands most copiously all things pertaining to the truth: so that every man, whosoever will, can draw from her the water of life (Revelation 22:17). For she is the entrance to life; all others are thieves and robbers. On this account are we bound to avoid them, but to make choice of the thing pertaining to the Church with the utmost diligence, and to lay hold of the tradition of the truth. For how stands the case? Suppose there arise a dispute relative to some important question among us, should we not have recourse to the most ancient Churches with which the apostles held constant intercourse, and learn from them what is certain and clear in regard to the present question? For how should it be if the apostles themselves had not left us writings? Would it not be necessary, [in that case,] to follow the course of the tradition which they handed down to those to whom they did commit the Churches?[45]

This ecclesiological principle of St. Irenaeus is directly linked by St. Augustine to the christological principle.

The Fathers of the Church were not simply early Christian witnesses but were for the most part also members of the magisterium, and as such their

---

42. St. Athanasius, *Four Discourses against the Arians,* 29, Nicene and Post-Nicene Fathers, 2nd series, vol. 4, p. 409; Patrologia Graeca, vol. 26, p. 385.

43. St. Cyril of Alexandria, *Glaphyra,* Patrologia Graeca, vol. 69, p. 308; cited in Bertrand de Margerie, *An Introduction to the History of Exegesis* (Petersham, MA: Saint Bede's Publications, 1991), vol. 1, p. 242.

44. St. Augustine, *Expositions of the Psalms, 33–50,* ed. John E. Rotelle (Hyde Park, NY: New City Press, 2000), pp. 151-52. Patrologia Latina, vol. 36, p. 399.

45. St. Irenaeus, *Against Heresies,* III.4.1, Ante-Nicene Fathers, vol. 1, p. 416.

teaching has dogmatic implications for the ecumenical theologian.[46] The binding character of the Fathers' teaching on both doctrine and scriptural interpretation has a long history and has been repeatedly affirmed by the magisterium.[47] Thus, the Council of Trent and the First Vatican Council are clear that "no one . . . shall dare to interpret the . . . Sacred Scripture . . . contrary to the unanimous consent of the Fathers."[48] The Fathers' interpretation is a theological locus when certain conditions are met.[49] Thus, the Fathers'

---

46. One needs to distinguish between the theological use of the term "Fathers" and the merely historical use of the term. Theologically, Fathers are those who: (a) lived between the first and sixth centuries, (b) lived holy lives, (c) were theologically orthodox, and (d) meet ecclesiastical approval. Thinkers such as Origen, Tertullian, Lactantius, and Eusebius are merely considered ecclesiastical writers.

47. Nevertheless, more recent magisterial texts, such as *Dei verbum, Interpretation of the Bible in the Church, Verbum Domini,* and the *Catechism of the Catholic Church* have all been curiously silent on this issue.

48. Both the Council of Trent (1545-63) and the First Vatican Council are clear concerning the dogmatic content of the Fathers. Trent says: "Furthermore, in order to curb impudent clever persons, the synod decrees that no one who relies on his own judgment in matters of faith and morals, which pertain to the building up of Christian doctrine, and that no one who distorts the Sacred Scripture according to his own opinions, shall dare to interpret the said Sacred Scripture contrary to that sense which is held by holy mother Church, whose duty it is to judge regarding the true sense and interpretation of holy Scriptures, or even contrary to the unanimous consent of the Fathers, even though interpretations of this kind were never intended to be brought to light" (DH 1507). Vatican I likewise decreed: "[The interpretation of Sacred Scripture]. But, since the rules which the holy Synod of Trent salutarily decreed concerning the interpretation of Divine Scripture in order to restrain impetuous minds, are wrongly explained by certain men, We, renewing the same decree, declare this to be its intention: that, in matters of faith and morals pertaining to the instruction of Christian Doctrine, that must be considered as the true sense of Sacred Scripture which Holy Mother Church has held and holds, whose office it is to judge concerning the true understanding and interpretation of the Sacred Scriptures; and, for that reason, no one is permitted to interpret Sacred Scripture itself contrary to this sense, or even contrary to the unanimous agreement of the Fathers" (DH 3007).

49. As to such conditions, Pope Leo XIII writes: "Because the defense of Holy Scripture must be carried on vigorously, all the opinions which the individual Fathers or the recent interpreters have set forth in explaining it need not be maintained equally. For they, in interpreting passages where physical matters are concerned, have made judgments according to the opinions of the age, and thus not always according to truth, so that they have made statements which today are not approved. Therefore, we must carefully discern what they hand down which really pertains to faith or is intimately connected with it, and what they hand down with unanimous consent; for 'in those matters which are not under the obligation of faith, the saints were free to have different opinions, just as we are,' according to the opinion of St. Thomas" (DH 3289).

agreement must be morally (not numerically) unanimous on a biblical interpretation, the interpretation must concern a matter of faith and morals, and the Fathers must consider the doctrine as divinely revealed.[50]

The dogmatic value of patristic exegesis obviously applies to Catholic ecumenists and has a number of rather practical ramifications. First, there is the acknowledgment that these patristic interpretations function differently for Catholics than for the bilateral partners who stem from the magisterial Reformation. Second, Catholic ecumenists will need to exercise special care that they do the essential research to demonstrate whether a particular Scripture passage has a received meaning that is doctrinally binding, even if such passages with a definitive meaning are not numerous.[51] One may note that in the U.S. Lutheran-Catholic Dialogue there has not been a single paper delivered that explicitly attempted to verify the dogmatic values of the Fathers' interpretation of a particular passage.[52] Conversely, if it can be shown that the Fathers do not have unanimous consent on the meaning of a particular passage, then this opens up ecumenical possibilities.

If we are to follow the Fathers in their attentiveness to the word of God, we need to be sure we do so not only in the order of intention but also in the order of execution, which leads us to the use of senses other than the literal sense. While the proponents of the exclusive use of the historical-critical method are vociferous in their warning against the exaggerations inherent in the patristic use of figural interpretation, a point on which even the Pontifical

50. Franc. X. De Abarzuza, O.F.M. Cap., *Manuale Theologiae Dogmaticae,* 2nd ed. (Madrid: Ediciones Studium, 1956), vol. 1, pp. 481-88; R. P. Hermann, *Theologia Generalis,* vol. 1 of *Institutiones Theologiae Dogmaticae,* 7th ed. (Paris, Lyons: Emmanuelem Vitte, 1937), pp. 539-40; J. M. Hervé, *Manuale Theologiae Dogmaticae,* 16th ed. (Westminster, MD: The Newman Bookshop, 1943), vol. 1, pp. 565-75; H. Hurter, S.J., *Theologiae Dogmaticae Compendium,* 12th ed. (Oeniponte: Libraria Academica Wagneriana: 1908), vol. 1, pp. 155-57; Salaverri, *Sacrae Theologiae Summa,* 4th ed. (Matriti: Biblioteca de Autores Cristianos, 1967), vol. 1, p. 765; Adolphe Tanquery, *Manual of Dogmatic Theology,* trans. John J. Byrnes (New York: Desclée, 1959), vol. 1, p. 179, n. 1; Adolphe Tanquery, *Synopsis Theologicae Dogmaticae* (Paris: Desclée et Socii, 1953), vol. 1, pp. 739-48; G. Van Noort, *The Sources of Revelation and Divine Faith,* vol. 3 of *Dogmatic Theology,* trans. John Castelot and William Murphy (Westminster, MD: The Newman Press, 1961), p. 174.

51. Pius XII, *Divino afflante Spiritu* 47.

52. It will do no good to dismiss this topic, as is frequently done, by protesting that the Fathers never agree. In fact, establishing unanimous consent is not impossible, and on many issues, such as prayer for the dead or the divinity of Christ, it is quite simple, albeit time consuming. See, for example, my article: Christian D. Washburn, "The Value of Offering Sacrifice for the Dead in the Thought of the Fathers of the Church," *Antiphon* 16, no. 3 (2012): 154-78.

Biblical Commission agrees,[53] the fact that this sense was sometimes abused is hardly an argument against allegorical readings. While many contemporary biblical scholars shy away from allegory, the Fathers were clear, as Augustine notes, that "no Christian would dare to say that the words of God are not to be taken figuratively."[54] It is, after all, a method used repeatedly by St. Paul in interpreting the Old Testament; in this he was followed by the Fathers. Early on, most of the opposition to an allegorical reading came from Jews and early heretics who insisted on the *sensus historicus*.[55] Against Marcion, for example, allegory was used to establish the fundamental continuity between the Old and New Testaments.[56] It is precisely these considerations that led Newman to write that "it may be almost laid down as an historical fact that the mystical interpretation and orthodoxy stand or fall together."[57] The point here is that there is no reason that Christians, whether Lutheran or Catholic, should fear the judicious use of allegorical readings of the Scriptures.

There are a number of ecumenical advantages to reintroducing patristic exegesis into ecumenical dialogue. First, it is valuable to see how certain biblical texts were received by early Christians before certain medieval developments and the division of the sixteenth century. Moreover, the rediscovery of certain older formulations may be a helpful corrective to theological formulations that were in a later age expressed incompletely (but not falsely) or were expressed in the changeable conceptions of a given epoch.[58] Second,

---

53. Peter Williamson, *Catholic Principles for Interpreting Scripture: A Study of the Pontifical Biblical Commission's "The Interpretation of the Bible in the Church"* (Rome: Pontificio Istituto Biblico, 2001), pp. 145-46.

54. *Literal Commentary on Genesis,* cited by Robert L. Wilken, *The Spirit of Early Christian Thought* (New Haven: Yale University Press, 2003), pp. 70-71. See also Robert L. Wilken, "Interpreting Job Allegorically: The *Moralia* of Gregory the Great," *Pro Ecclesia* 10 (2001): 213-26; R. L. Wilken, "Allegory and the Interpretation of the Old Testament in the 21st Century," *Letter and Spirit* 1 (2005): 11-21.

55. John Henry Newman, *An Essay on the Development of Christian Doctrine* (Westminster, MD: Christian Classics, 1968), p. 343. See also his *The Arians of the Fourth Century* (Westminster, MD: Christian Classics, 1968), pp. 404-7. For the context of Newman's position, see Benjamin John King, *Newman and the Alexandrian Fathers: Shaping Doctrine in Nineteenth-Century England* (Oxford: Oxford University Press, 2009), pp. 253-54; Stanley L. Jaki, *Neo-Arianism as Foreseen by Newman* (Port Huron, MI: Real View Books, 2006), p. 48, 58.

56. Jaroslav Pelikan, *Divine Rhetoric: The Sermon on the Mount as Message and as Model in Augustine, Chrysostom, and Luther* (Crestwood, NY: St. Vladimir's Seminary Press, 2001), p. 74.

57. Newman, *An Essay on the Development of Christian Doctrine,* p. 344.

58. *Mysterium Ecclesiae* 5, DH 4539.

it seems ecumenically imprudent to avoid or deride patristic exegesis as a matter of principle precisely at the time when there is a growing movement among Protestant theologians to rediscover and incorporate the work of the Fathers. The Ancient Christian Commentary on Scripture and the Ancient Christian Doctrine series are excellent examples of such a rediscovery of the Fathers, to which Catholics owe our separated brethren a great deal of debt. Moreover, Catholics who deride the value of the Fathers in exegesis are likely to alienate our Orthodox partners in dialogue.

Ecclesial Reading

The ecclesial nature of theology is simply an extension of all that has been thus far said, and what follows will be of particular concern to the Catholic ecumenist. The Church existed prior to the final determination of the entire canon of the Scriptures, and it is in the Church that the New Testament Scriptures were written and the entire canon is protected. Because of the distinctive promise of Christ to the Church, that the Holy Spirit will guide the Apostles and, by extension, their successors into all the truth (John 16:13), it belongs to the Church to discern those books that make up the Scriptures and, further, to protect the meaning and ensure the correct interpretation of the sacred texts. In this sense the Second Vatican Council has called the magisterium "the servant" of the word of God, a service she fulfills by expounding and protecting God's word. This service was given to the Church as a gift, which explains why the council concluded that "[t]he task of authentically interpreting the word of God, whether written or handed on, has been entrusted *exclusively* to the living teaching office of the Church, whose authority is exercised in the name of Jesus Christ."[59] As Ratzinger has noted, "a churchless theology melts away into caprice."[60]

The Catholic ecumenist must recall that the magisterium has repeatedly defined that it has the authority to interpret infallibly the Scriptures, though the number of such interpretations is generally estimated to be less than twenty.[61] The First Vatican Council was clear that "in matters of faith

---

59. *Dei verbum* 10.

60. Joseph Cardinal Ratzinger, *The Nature and Mission of Theology: Essays to Orient Theology in Today's Debates* (San Francisco: Ignatius Press, 1995), p. 48.

61. E. Mangenot and J. Rivère, "Interprétation de L'Écriture," in *Dictionnaire de théologie catholique* (Paris: Librairie Letouzey et Ané, 1932), vol. 7, p. 2314; Alfred Durand, S.J., "Exégèse," in *Dictionnaire apologétique de la foi catholique, contenant les preuves de la veérité*

and morals pertaining to the instruction of Christian Doctrine, that must be considered as the true sense of Sacred Scripture which Holy Mother Church has held and holds, whose office it is to judge concerning the true understanding and interpretation of the Sacred Scriptures."[62] Later Pope Pius X condemned the following proposition of modernists: "The magisterium of the Church, even by dogmatic definitions, cannot determine the genuine sense of the Sacred Scriptures."[63] There are a number of levels of authentic magisterial interventions on scriptural matters, ranging anywhere from a definitive declaration of revealed truth to a prudential judgment; thus the theologian must be careful in evaluating the precise level of authority exerted by a magisterial intervention on Scripture.

The Church can authentically interpret the word of God in two distinct ways. First, the magisterium can offer at least one authentic meaning of a particular text. Second, the magisterium can prohibit an erroneous interpretation, i.e., the teaching of what a particular biblical text does not mean. A number of the authentic interventions of the magisterium are found in the Council of Trent. Already in the sixteenth century, St. Robert Bellarmine pointed to chapter one of the thirteenth session of the Council of Trent as an example of the magisterium exercising such authority. This particular decree of the Council of Trent determined that the words "This is my Body" are to be understood properly and not merely figuratively.[64] The magisterium

---

de la religion et les réponses aux objections tirées des sciences humaines (Paris: G. Beauchesne, 1911), vol. 1, p. 1838. One popular apologetic text lists fifteen biblical examples on which the magisterium has solemnly issued a decree but without referencing a single magisterial statement. Fr. Leslie Rumble, *Questions People Ask about the Catholic Church* (Kensington, Australia: Chevalier, 1972), pp. 176-77.

62. DH 3007.

63. Pius X, *Lamentabili,* DH 3404.

64. The Council of Trent says: "Ita enim maiores omnes nostri, quotquot in vera Christi ecclesia fuerunt, qui de sanctissimo hoc sacramento disseruerunt, apertissime professi sunt, hoc tam admirabile sacramentum in ultima coena Redemptorem nostrum instituisse, cum post panis vinique benedicitonem se suum ipsius corpus illis praebere ac suum sanguinem disertis et perspicuis verbis testatus est. Quae verba a sanctis evangelistis commemorata et a divo Paulo postea repetita, cum propriam illam et apertissimam significationem prae se ferant, secundum quam a Patribus intellecta sunt, indignissimum sane flagitium est. . . ." In Norman P. Tanner, S.J., *Decrees of the Ecumenical Councils* (London: Sheed & Ward/Washington, DC: Georgetown University Press, 1990), vol. 2, p. 694. For Bellarmine's development of this point, see Bellarmine, *Disputationes Roberti Bellarmini Politiani Societatis Jesu, de Controversiis Christianae Fidei, adversus huius temporis Haereticos* (Paris: Triadelphorum, 1613), X.I.II, vol. 4, pp. 348-52. By the late sixteenth century the number of errors regarding the words of institution alone was immense. In his treatise *De Eucharistia,* Cardinal Bel-

also issues authentic interventions stating explicitly what the Scriptures do not mean.[65] Thus canon two of the seventh session of the Council of Trent teaches, "If anyone shall say that real and natural water is not necessary for baptism, and on that account those words of our Lord Jesus Christ: 'Unless a man be born again of water and the Holy Spirit' (John 3:5), are distorted into some sort of metaphor: let him be anathema."[66]

The Church is not only able to teach on biblical texts in a solemn way; she can also teach on these texts in an ordinary way that can be binding on the Church.[67] This mode of teaching is less simple to analyze since it is exercised

---

larmine reduced these different interpretations into ten groups, four concerning the word *hoc,* two concerning the word *est,* three concerning the word *corpus,* and one concerning the word *meum.* Bellarmine, *De Controversiis,* X.I.X. vol. 4, pp. 376-84. Christoph Rasperger wrote a book on the 200 different interpretations given to the words "This is my body" by Protestants. Christoph Rasperger, *Ducentae paucorum istorum et quidem clarissimorum Christi verborum: Hoc est Corpus meum; interpretationes quibus continentur vocum novitates, deprevationes, errores, haereses, contra dictiones . . . theologorum . . . ex propriis . . . scriptis fideliter collectae* (Ingolstadt: Excudebat A. Weissenhorn cum cohaeredibus suis, 1577). Cano had used this same argument to much effect: "Lutherus ipse clamat illa verba: *Hoc est corpus meum* proprie accipienda; Zuinglius contra figurate. Quis sententiam dicet? Num Scriptura ipsa?" *De locis theologicis,* V.IV, p. 172.

Raymond Brown argues that the Council of Trent "was not settling a historical question about what was in the mind of the author when he wrote the text, but a religious question about the implications of Scripture for the life of the faithful." Raymond E. Brown and Sandra M. Schneiders, "Hermeneutics," in *New Jerome Biblical Commentary,* ed. Raymond E. Brown, Joseph A. Fitzmyer, and Roland E. Murphy (Englewood Cliffs, NJ: Prentice Hall, 1990), p. 1163. Such a distinction is foreign to the mind of the council fathers, who call God the "author" of both the Old and the New Testaments, the contents of which were "received by the Apostles from the mouth of Christ himself, or from the Apostles themselves, the Holy Ghost dictating" (DH 1501). Later, the First Vatican Council was even more insistent on God as the author of Scripture, stating that "the Church holds these books as sacred and canonical, not because, having been put together by human industry alone, they were then approved by its authority; nor because they contain revelation without error; but because, having been written by the inspiration of the Holy Spirit, they have God as their author and, as such, they have been handed down to the Church itself (can. 4)" (DH 3006).

65. Examples of this type of intervention can be found in: DH 443, 1922, 1950, 1975, 1976, 3447.

66. DH 1615.

67. This ecclesial reading should not and cannot be reduced merely to the authentic interventions of the magisterium. An ecclesial reading of the Scriptures also embraces the kergymatic, catechetical, and most importantly the liturgical reading of the sacred text. A liturgical reading is at least twofold. First, the words of Scripture take on a specific meaning as they are used in the liturgy. Second, passages of Scripture receive a particular meaning as they are used in the lectionary, such as particular feast days.

by the ordinary universal magisterium, which does not set forth teaching in a "solemn" or "defining" manner, even if in a "definitive" manner. It is probably the case that there are a significant number of passages, in both the Old and New Testaments, that have a fixed meaning on this basis. While contemporary theologians are frequently inclined to look for these teachings in the area of doctrine, it is likely that they will more easily discover these on moral issues.

When the Church solemnly defines a doctrine or condemns a heresy, moreover, it is offering an interpretation of the Scriptures, even if the meaning of a particular passage is not directly defined. Thus when an ecumenical council, as St. Robert Bellarmine noted, chooses a term to represent the faith of the Church, such as it did at Nicea with the term *homoousios*, it is preserving the meaning of Scripture.[68] Sacred Scripture cannot consequently have a meaning in either the literal sense or the spiritual sense that contradicts the meaning proposed by that term. Ecumenical councils have taught infallibly by choosing the words in which to express revealed truths.[69] The Councils of Nicea and Ephesus, for example, demanded the acceptance of the words *homoousion* and *Theotokos* precisely to explain the correct meaning of revelation.[70] Thus the role of the magisterium regarding the meaning of Scripture can range anywhere from declaring the meaning of a particular passage of revelation to stipulating words that truly express revealed truth.

Conclusion

Recent ecclesiastical documents are all in agreement that the historical-critical method's presence is secure in Catholic theology. Even its critics

68. Bellarmine, *De Controversiis,* IV.II.XII, vol. 2, p. 86.

69. Bellarmine, *De Controversiis,* III.II.II, vol. 2, p. 53.

70. Bellarmine, *De Controversiis,* IV.II.12, vol. 2, p. 87. In response to the objection that Christians should not apply the term "person" to God since the term is not used in either the Old or New Testament, St. Thomas argues that "although the word 'person' is not found applied to God in Scripture, either in the Old or New Testament, nevertheless what the word signifies is found to be affirmed of God in many places of Scripture; as that He is the supreme self-subsisting being, and the most perfectly intelligent being. If we could speak of God only in the very terms themselves of Scripture, it would follow that no one could speak about God in any but the original language of the Old or New Testament. The urgency of confuting heretics made it necessary to find new words to express the ancient faith about God. Nor is such a kind of novelty to be shunned; since it is by no means profane, for it does not lead us astray from the sense of Scripture. The Apostle warns us to avoid 'profane novelties of words' (1 Timothy 6:20)." St. Thomas Aquinas, *Summa Theologiae,* I, q. 29, a. 3, ad 2.

do not challenge its role in ecumenical dialogue. Nonetheless, the limits of the historical-critical method have probably been reached: by itself, it is no longer capable of answering in any meaningful way the theological questions posed in ecumenical dialogue. Therefore, it is incumbent upon Catholic ecumenists to account for the ecclesiological, patristic, and theological readings of the Scriptures in their encounters with our separated brethren. This is true particularly in an age when the value of a theological and patristic reading is being renewed by the children of the Reformation. Moreover, many of our separated brethren are coming to see the value of ecclesial structures that preserve the meaning of the word of God against the forces of a hostile culture. Finally, these three aspects of scriptural interpretation must be seen as part of the organic structure by which divine revelation is handed on. So essential are these aspects that the removal of any one of them can lead to a fundamental disarticulation of the entire Christian message.

PART II

The Word of God in the Formation of Seminarians

CHAPTER 6

Preparing Seminarians for the Ministry of the Word in Light of *Verbum Domini*

Peter S. Williamson

Verbum Domini on Forming Future Priests for the Ministry of the Word

Although Pope Benedict's Apostolic Exhortation *Verbum Domini (VD)* is extremely rich, its length and encyclopedic nature can make it hard to distinguish the essential points. Leaving to others the Pope's important teaching on hermeneutics and the relationship of exegesis to theology, I see five points in the Holy Father's teaching that have practical implications for forming seminarians for the ministry of the word.

First, the Holy Father prioritizes the ministry of the word in the life of a priest, quoting St. John Paul II's teaching in *Pastores dabo vobis (PDV)*:

> The priest is first of all a *minister of the word of God,* consecrated and sent to announce the Good News of the Kingdom to all, calling every person to the obedience of faith and leading believers to an ever increasing knowledge of and communion in the mystery of God. (emphasis original, *PDV* 26, scc *VD* 80)

The priority of the ministry of the word in the life of a priest underscores the critical importance of Scripture courses in preparing seminarians for priesthood.

Second, the Holy Father emphasizes the "decisive role that the word of God must play in the spiritual life of candidates for the ministerial priesthood." He says, "Those aspiring to the ministerial priesthood are called to a profound personal relationship with God's word . . . so that this relationship will in turn nurture their vocation. . . . [They] must learn to love the word of God" (82).[1] This relationship with God's word depends on the action of the Holy Spirit: "[W]ithout the efficacious working of the 'Spirit of truth' (John 14:16), the words of the Lord cannot be understood" (16).

Third, lectio divina *is the privileged means of growing in this relationship of love with God's word.* After becoming Pope, Benedict XVI repeatedly called for the revival of this traditional Christian practice. He mentions it ten times in this document and devotes a section to a step-by-step instruction on it.[2]

Fourth, the Holy Father urges that seminarians cultivate a "reciprocity between study and prayer" *in their lives* (82, emphasis original). He is particularly concerned that formation avoid a "dichotomy between prayerful reading and exegetical studies" and desires that "candidates are introduced to the study of Scripture through methods that favor this integral approach" (82).[3] In other words, the Pope excludes both a secular academic approach to teaching Scripture *and* an exclusively spiritual approach: both faith and reason must be engaged in a seminarian's study of Scripture.

This is a good point at which to pause and consider the biblical training that we as Scripture professors received in our graduate studies. To what degree was it an "integral approach" characterized by a "reciprocity between study and prayer"? More common, I think, is an educational experience characterized by a "dichotomy between prayerful reading and exegetical studies." If so, we professors must learn to teach Scripture in a very different way than we learned it — something that is not so easy to do.

Finally, in Verbum Domini *Pope Benedict offers specific instruction about three forms of ministry of the word: preaching homilies, catechesis, and "the biblical apostolate."*

In regard to homilies, the Pope underscores the duty of ordained ministers to "expound the word of God" (59, quoting *Ordo lectionum missae* 8),

1. Unless otherwise noted, reference numbers are to the numbered sections of *Verbum Domini.*
2. The Pope offers a distinctive emphasis in his treatment of *contemplatio,* the fourth in the traditional description of the elements: "Contemplation aims at creating within us a truly wise and discerning vision of reality, as God sees it, and at forming within us 'the mind of Christ' (1 Cor. 2:16). The word of God appears here as a criterion for discernment . . .'" (86-87). The Holy Father considers this a major way that Scripture should mark the life of a priest, touching on this idea in paragraphs 80 and 82 and citing Hebrews 4:12.
3. This is echoed in section 35, where the Pope warns against "the danger of dualism and a secularized hermeneutic."

by which he means to explain the Scriptures rather than saying whatever is on their minds. In regard to preaching, the Pope says,

> The homily is a means of bringing the scriptural message to life in a way that helps the faithful to realize that God's word is present and at work in their everyday lives. . . . Generic and abstract homilies which obscure the directness of God's word should be avoided, as well as useless digressions. . . . For this reason preachers need to be in close and constant contact with the sacred text [*DV* 25]; they should prepare for the homily by meditation and prayer, so as to preach with conviction and passion. . . . (59)

To bridge the gap between ancient text and contemporary life, Pope Benedict recommends a few questions to preachers as they prepare:

> What are the Scriptures being proclaimed saying? What do they say to me personally? What should I say to the community in the light of its concrete situation? The preacher "should be the first to hear the word of God which he proclaims." (59)

Regarding catechesis, the Pope teaches that Jesus' conversation with his disciples on the road to Emmaus provides "the model of a catechesis centered on 'the explanation of the Scriptures'" (74). The Pope recommends the *General Catechetical Directory*

> for its valuable guidelines for a biblically inspired catechesis . . . [which] must be permeated by the mindset, the spirit and the outlook of the Bible and the Gospels through assiduous contact with the texts themselves.
>
> A knowledge of biblical personages, events and well-known sayings should thus be encouraged; this can also be promoted by the judicious *memorization* of some passages [emphasis original].
>
> Catechesis should communicate in a lively way the history of salvation and the content of the Church's faith, and so enable every member of the faithful to realize that this history is also a part of his or her own life. (74)

Finally, referring to the goal set by the Synod of "an increased emphasis on the Bible in the Church's pastoral activity" (78), the Pope speaks of the biblical apostolate, not so much as a separate project but as "making the Bible the inspiration of every ordinary and extraordinary pastoral outreach" (73). He believes this is the best solution to the pastoral problems mentioned at the Synod, especially "the *proliferation of sects*. . . . Where the faithful are not helped to know the Bible . . . this pastoral vacuum becomes fertile ground" for the sects. In other words, if Catholics are well nourished on Scripture in the Church, they will not go elsewhere to be fed.

Biblical Roots of the "Ministry of the Word"

The teaching of Benedict XVI and John Paul II about the *priority* of the ministry of the word among the duties of a priest is rooted biblically in the account of the appointment of the Seven in Acts 6. When an oversight in the apostles' distribution of food to the Church's needy is pointed out, the Twelve respond, "It is not right for us to neglect the word of God to serve at table" (Acts 6:2). Their solution is to appoint other ministers to oversee the care of the needy, leaving the apostles free to devote themselves "to prayer and to the ministry of the word" (Acts 6:4).[4]

In Acts, "the word" which the apostles communicate usually refers to the gospel of Jesus Christ to those who have not heard it (e.g., Acts 4:4, 31; 8:4), although it is sometimes used to refer to instruction given to those who are already believers (Acts 2:42; 18:11).

What is interesting about the apostles' statement of their priorities is that the ministry of the word comes second to their responsibility to pray. Apparently, adoring God in worship, interceding for his people, and listening to the Holy Spirit are means, alongside reading and study, through which the apostles receive what they communicate to others.[5]

4. In these verses there is a play on words and an underlying metaphor that does not come through in English translations. The apostles are criticized for a failure in their daily *diakonia* (translated "distribution"). They respond that it is not right for them to neglect the word of God to serve *(diakoneō)* tables. Instead they will devote themselves to prayer and the ministry *(diakonia)* of the word. The metaphor is that of servants, *diakonoi,* who serve at a meal (Luke 12:41-48). Those they serve are the guests. The food they provide is not their own, but the master's, on whose behalf the servants perform their ministry *(diakonia)*.

5. Although the phrase "ministry of the word" is not found elsewhere in the New Testament, the rest of Acts and the Pauline letters illustrate what this phrase entailed for the first generation of Christians. A partial list would include Acts 20:20-21, 27, 31-32; 1 Cor. 1:17, 22-24; 2:1-7, 13; Eph. 3:7-9; 4:11-16; 6:17-20; Col. 1:28; 4:3-4; 1 Tim. 4:13; 2 Tim. 2:2, 15, 24-25; 3:14-17; 4:5; Titus 1:7-9; 2:1, 15; Heb. 4:12.

Foundational Scriptural Formation: Practical Proposals

In light of Pope Benedict's Apostolic Exhortation *Verbum Domini* and in light of the example of the apostles' ministry of the word depicted in the New Testament, how concretely should seminarians be prepared for the ministry of the word? Here I will offer some practical proposals drawn from my own reflection and experience as well as that of colleagues who teach Scripture at Sacred Heart Major Seminary (Detroit) and elsewhere. I do not aim or claim to be comprehensive (e.g., biblical preaching is not treated). This is a work in progress, and I look forward to the feedback of others.

I distinguish two stages in the formation of ministers of the word: (1) foundational scriptural formation, entailing evangelization and biblical catechesis, which ought to occur prior to someone entering seminary or at the undergraduate level; and (2) professional scriptural formation (defined below), the goal proper to graduate theology.

Foundational preparation for the ministry of the word includes both spiritual and cognitive elements.

At the very beginning of formation, seminarians need to develop a "profound personal relationship with God's word . . . so that this relationship will in turn nurture their vocation" (82). This is essential because of the "decisive role that the word of God must play in the spiritual life of candidates for the ministerial priesthood" (82). The first phase of formation thus entails leading the seminarian to a deeper conversion to Christ and into an experiential relationship with the Holy Spirit. Programs aimed at conversion, such as Cursillo, the Life in the Spirit Seminar, St. Philip's course, and Ignatian retreats are some of the instruments that have been found effective to lead seminarians into the kind of personal relationship with the Father, Son, and Holy Spirit that motivates and makes them capable of deriving nourishment from Scripture.

Next, it is essential that seminarians be instructed and formed in *lectio divina,* the habit that will enable them to grow in a love relationship with Scripture. Since the Bible and this practice of spiritual reading is new to most seminarians, the effort necessary to form them in it should not be underestimated.

Cognitively, at this stage the seminarian must become acquainted with the Bible. This begins with the elementary biblical catechesis that many seminarians never received prior to entering seminary — "a knowledge of biblical personages, events and well-known sayings" (*VD* 74), and basic instruction in what the Church believes about the Bible (*Catechism* 101-41). From an introductory acquaintance the seminarian must progress to a solid familiarity with the Bible's grand narrative, the history of salvation, as well as its stories, principal theological themes, variety of genre and books, structure, etc.[6]

The best way to acquire familiarity with the Bible is a program of spiritual reading that covers substantial portions, if not all, of the Bible over the course of a year or two at the outset of seminary formation (and is hopefully repeated once or twice during the seminary years). A prayerful *lectio continua* provides an important complement to introductory Scripture courses, which also should focus primarily on introducing students to the *contents* of the Bible, rather than to scholarship about it.[7]

A good example of this approach is the Scripture formation employed during the spiritual year before philosophy studies at St. John Vianney Seminary in Denver. Professor Timothy Gray, who has been responsible for the Scripture formation of the spiritual-year students, shared his experience with me in a telephone interview.[8]

Gray's students are expected to read through the entire Bible in the course of a year according to a reading plan that he supplies. Each week Gray meets with the students for two hours and gives lectures that explain what is going on in the biblical texts they are reading. He also draws them out to discover what is happening in their reading. The focus is not academic but spiritual.

The goal is to get them to do *lectio divina*. According to Gray, it takes the whole year for the spiritual-year students to learn to do this well. Typically, most do not have any significant familiarity with the Bible. The challenge is that the students are both learning about Scripture for the first time *and* seeking to read it prayerfully. It takes work to get the students to move from the head to the heart in their reading, to read slowly and carefully enough, and to apply it to themselves.[9]

---

6. Books that can help students grasp Scripture's grand narrative include Craig Bartholomew and Michael Goheen, *The Drama of Scripture* (Grand Rapids: Baker, 2004), and Tim Gray and Jeff Cavins, *Walking with God: A Journey Through the Bible* (West Chester, PA: Ascension, 2010). Timothy Beal's *Biblical Literacy* (New York: HarperCollins, 2009) provides a useful selection of Bible stories and key texts, although with an individualistic and relativistic approach to interpretation.

7. The presentation of critical issues should be saved for more advanced courses, although it is important to respond to questions along the way. Since the goal of these courses is to facilitate reading, acquaintance, and initial reflection, they need not require as many classroom hours as more advanced courses.

8. Telephone interview with Timothy Gray on October 12, 2010.

9. Besides the Bible, Gray uses two of his own books with his students: *Praying Scrip-*

Since experience indicates that one of the best ways of learning something is to teach it, an additional way of deepening this biblical foundation of undergraduate seminarians might be to have them facilitate a Bible study as part of their pastoral formation (providing them with suitable guidance and materials, of course).

Unfortunately, at the present moment serious obstacles stand in the way of laying a solid foundation in Scripture for undergraduate seminarians. On the one hand, the increase in required philosophy credit hours resulting from the Vatican Congregation on Education's reform of the seminary philosophy curriculum has had the unintended effect of leaving virtually no room in the undergraduate curriculum for Scripture. On the other hand, most North American bishops do not favor adding a spiritual year to what is already a lengthy seminary formation. Often the result is that seminarians enter graduate theology without the foundations of love for Scripture, a habit of *lectio divina,* and a basic familiarity with the whole Bible having been laid. The sad consequence is seminarians who regard Scripture courses as academic hoops to jump through whose relation to life and priestly ministry they do not understand. When ordained, they remain relatively ignorant of Scripture. Failure to lay the foundation well bodes ill for the stability and longevity of any building. To avoid this outcome, seminary Scripture professors who discover that some of their students lack the foundation should do their best to remediate the problem, even if it means turning back to teach at a more basic level. Obviously, a better solution is urgently needed.

Professional Scriptural Formation

By "professional Scripture formation," I mean that which is specific to preparing seminarians for their ministry of the word as priests.

Over the last couple years the faculty at Sacred Heart Major Seminary has given considerable attention to teaching Scripture across the curriculum, a topic I presented at the 2009 conference of the Quinn Institute.[10] In April of 2013, the Sacred Heart Major Seminary (SHMS) graduate faculty adopted

---

ture for a Change: An Introduction to Lectio Divina (West Chester, PA: Ascension, 2009), and *Walking with God: A Journey Through the Bible,* coauthored with Jeff Cavins (West Chester, PA: Ascension, 2010).

10. Available at http://www.stthomas.edu/spssod/pdf/articles/williamson.pdf.

a ten-page "Guiding Document" as a first major step. Meanwhile, my colleagues and I who teach Scripture at Sacred Heart have begun to discuss how to teach our Scripture courses in a more effective and unified manner.[11] What follows is a combination of our common views and my perspectives.

The Tasks Entailed in a Priest's Ministry of the Word

We started by asking ourselves what precisely we are preparing men to do, i.e., what are the specific ministry-of-the-word tasks priests must fulfill? If we are clear on these, teaching and formation can be more precisely targeted.

1. Every priest needs to be able to explain the gospel, the *kerygma,* and to lead people in making the necessary response of faith, repentance, and baptism, helping them to attain salvation in Jesus Christ. While obvious and vital for the New Evangelization, this skill is often overlooked. The content of the *kerygma* is straightforward and expressed in many places in Acts, Paul's letters, and the liturgy.[12] Priests need to know how to explain the message and its importance, relating it to people's lives, sometimes through telling their own story.

2. A priest should be able to preach a homily on the Scripture readings given in the Lectionary, explaining the message of one or more of the texts, explaining the relation of the texts to one another (the OT reading to the Gospel) or to the season or feast, and "applying [the readings] to the lives of the Christian faithful."[13]

3. A priest should be able to give biblical catechetical teaching, that is, to explain Catholic doctrine from Scripture; or if a doctrine is not explicitly taught in Scripture, to be able to explain its relationship with Scripture.

4. A priest should be able to use Scripture in pastoral counseling, in spir-

---

11. The colleagues participating in this discussion included Richard Cassidy, Bishop Michael Byrnes, Mary Healy, Daniel Keating, and myself. We reflected on the biblical formation that ministry of the word requires of future priests, deacons, and lay ministers.

12. It is the proclamation of Jesus as Savior, Son of God, and Lord, who saved us by atoning for our sins through his death and resurrection, who gives us the Holy Spirit, and who will return in glory to judge every person according to his or her deeds and to establish the eternal kingdom of God in its fullness. See Acts 2:14-40; 4:8-12; 13:15-41; Rom. 10:4-17; 1 Cor. 15:1-8; 2 Cor. 5:10-21; Eph. 2:1-10.

13. United States Council of Catholic Bishops, *Program of Priestly Formation* (Washington, DC, 2006), p. 200.

itual direction, and in the confessional. He should be familiar with the texts most pertinent to these forms of individual pastoral ministry.[14]

5. A priest should be able to teach the Bible, whether a Scripture study on a particular book or on a biblical theme.

6. A priest should be able to answer apologetic questions related to Scripture, including its inspiration, truthfulness, credibility, historical basis, morality, canonicity, and its proper method of interpretation. He should also be able to answer the questions raised by Protestants about the relation of Catholic doctrine to Scripture.

A Practical Method of Pastoral Exegesis

Our Scripture faculty agreed that it is not reasonable to expect seminarians to utilize the sophisticated methods described in textbooks on exegesis (or in the Pontifical Biblical Commission's *Interpretation of the Bible in the Church*) because of unfamiliarity with the biblical languages on the part of most, inadequate time to acquire proficiency in technical methods, and the time constraints of their future pastoral ministry.[15]

Instead, future priests should be trained in a practical method of Scripture study that they can use in the limited time they will have for preparing homilies and catechetical teaching and that they can incorporate in a lifelong program of personal study. The exegetical method intended for future clergy should be as simple as possible and should be guided by sound principles of Catholic interpretation.

So far we have not adopted a common method. However, I have developed a three-step method of pastoral exegesis based on *Dei verbum* 12 that I have refined in light of discussions with my colleagues. This "Three-Step Pastoral Exegesis" method aims at unpacking three dimensions of meaning in the biblical text: the literal sense, the theological significance, and the meaning for Christian life today (contemporary application).

---

14. A priest will be better equipped to do this if Scripture played a significant role in his priestly formation. See the article by Sacred Heart Major Seminary professor Fr. Daniel Jones, "Scripture-based Human Formation," in *Homiletic and Pastoral Review,* August/September 2011, pp. 82-83.

15. It *is* important, however, that they have enough familiarity with these methods to profit from commentaries that utilize them and to be able to respond to parishioners' questions.

STEP 1: To discover the literal sense, the meaning "expressed directly by the inspired human authors," by analyzing texts *in their literary and historical contexts*[16] — the task set forth in the first part of *Dei verbum* 12.

(a) Here the pastoral interpreter[17] takes into account the genre of a passage, considers its immediate context, outlines it while paying close attention to connecting words that indicate its logic, and looks up its key terms and references to earlier biblical events or texts. If it is a narrative, the interpreter reflects on the characters, the action, and the outcome, noting any explicit or implicit evaluation present in the narration.

(b) The interpreter considers how the historical situation, customs, and way of thinking and communicating at the time the text was written shed light on its meaning.

(c) On these bases the student expresses as precisely as possible, in his own words, what the biblical author was saying, or — if the passage reports the words of Jesus, a prophet, or an apostle — what that authoritative person is saying.

STEP 2: To discover the theological significance of the text with the help of the Holy Spirit, i.e., to understand what the divine author is saying by interpreting the text in light of the content and unity of the whole of Scripture, the living tradition, and the analogy of faith. This simply follows the principles of interpretation indicated in the second part of *Dei verbum* 12.

(a) First, the pastoral interpreter studies the text in the context of the canon of Scripture and considers how other biblical texts confirm, complete, or balance the passage at hand, giving special consideration to the light shed on the text by the teaching of Christ and the paschal mystery.

(b) Then, he reflects on the text in the context of the Church's faith,[18] including the writings of the Church Fathers, the liturgy's use of the text,

---

16. As defined by the Pontifical Biblical Commission in *The Interpretation of the Bible in the Church* II.B.1.

17. Besides seminarians, I use this method to teach future deacons and lay ecclesial ministers.

18. I am indebted to my colleague Daniel A. Keating for the presentation of biblical interpretation as reading Scripture in a series of contexts, which can be illustrated by a diagram of concentric circles: (1) the passage in its own context; (2) the passage in the wider biblical context; (3) the passage in the context of the Church and Tradition: the "rule of faith" (i.e., the creed and the faith of the Church), the liturgy, and Christian life and experience; (4) the passage as God's address to me/us.

and the way the text fits with the rest of Christian doctrine (the creeds, the *Catechism*) and Church tradition.
(c) On these bases, the seminarian seeks to articulate what the divine author wants the Church to understand through this passage, its perennial message.

STEP 3: To apply the biblical word to oneself and to one's community[19] by considering the text's meaning in *the context of Christian faith and life today*, a step that the Biblical Commission calls "actualization" (Pontifical Biblical Commission, *The Interpretation of the Bible in the Church* IV.A).
(a) The pastoral interpreter reflects on what the Holy Spirit is drawing to his attention in the text.
(b) The seminarian considers what contemporary problems or questions of his community are addressed by the text. If something in the present is analogous to what the passage depicts, what are the similarities and differences?
(c) What response does this text call for? Is there a warning to heed, an example to follow, an instruction to obey, a promise to trust, wisdom to ponder, or a truth to believe? Does this text lead to self-examination and repentance, to prayer or praise?
(d) How do the Church Fathers, the saints, the liturgy, or the *Catechism* apply this text to Christian life?[20]

Ideally, the seminarian can study a text with this method before consulting commentaries. Sometimes, however, a student may prefer to consult a commentary or study Bible as he works through Step 1. An advantage of this approach to the text is that in Steps 2 and 3 the method leads the student to consider essential dimensions of meaning that many commentaries neglect.

19. Second Vatican Council, *Optatum totius* [*Decree on Priestly Training*] 16: "They should learn to seek the solutions to human problems under the light of revelation, to apply the eternal truths of revelation to the changeable conditions of human affairs and to communicate them in a way suited to men of our day."

20. Note that the tradition of the Church plays a role in both the second and third levels of meaning. In some cases, papal teaching, the liturgy, or Church Fathers articulate with authority the theological significance of the text, the intention of the divine Author — for example, in expressing the doctrine of the Trinity. In other cases, interpretations from these sources belong to the category of pastoral actualization rather than to authoritative theological interpretation. Examples include some allegorical interpretations of the Fathers, biblical language re-used out of context in liturgical prayers, or lectionary selections for feasts that apply texts analogously (e.g., Eph. 1:3-6, 11-12, for the Immaculate Conception).

This method is flexible, able to be expanded or contracted according to the time available and the expertise of the one using it. I have developed an exercise template based on it and assign seminarians to do a couple of brief (1000-word) exegetical studies of texts in each Scripture class.[21] The hope is that by being taught as a method and assigned as an exercise, this method will become a habitual way in which seminarians think about and interpret Scripture.

Prerequisite Knowledge, Skills, and Resources

Our Scripture faculty also considered what future priests ought to *know,* the *interpretive skills* they ought to acquire, and the *Scripture resources* with which they ought to be familiar in order to carry out the ministry of the word.

As regards *knowledge,* a competent minister of the word needs a solid familiarity with the whole Bible, a knowledge drawn both from seminary courses that cover the whole Bible[22] and from personal reading and study. By the time he graduates, a seminarian ought to know the relationship of a particular passage or biblical book to the broader body of biblical literature in which it occurs. For example, he should be able to say how a particular passage fits within Pauline literature or how a prophetic text fits within the prophetic corpus.

In particular, a seminarian must have an overview of Scripture's grand narrative, the history of salvation. He should know how "the New Testament lies hidden in the Old and the Old Testament is unveiled in the New," including the most important OT types of Christ, the Church, and the sacraments (*Catechism* 128-30). This knowledge of the relationships of the Testaments and of the themes that run through the Bible will enable priests to explain

---

21. The exercise template and assignments for specific courses are posted on the Sacred Heart Major Seminary website, www.shms.edu, on my faculty page under the heading "Course Resources."

22. *Program of Priestly Formation,* p. 199: "In Scripture, the core should include the study of the Pentateuch, the historical, prophetic and wisdom (especially the Psalms) books of the Old Testament, the Synoptic Gospels and Acts, Pauline and Johannine literature, and the Catholic epistles." It seems that the whole Bible is intended (assuming Hebrews is implied in the Pauline literature and Revelation in the Johannine). Regrettably, in practice, the number of credit hours available for Scripture courses often makes it necessary to omit parts of the canon or include them in theory but not in practice.

the relationship between the Old Testament reading and the Gospel and the relationship of the readings to the season or feast.

If at all possible, the seminarian should know enough Greek and Hebrew to look beyond the English translation he is using to consult the original.

As regards *interpretive skills,* ministers of the word should know how to study biblical words and themes; they should at least grasp that words have different meanings in different contexts and that the meanings of words bear different connotations in different time periods. If the seminarian is unfamiliar with the biblical languages, he should be able to compensate by consulting more than one English translation and by knowing how to use reference works that explain the various meanings of the Greek and Hebrew words in his text.

Seminarians should know how to read a story, how to get inside it, and how to use imagination in retelling and expounding it.

Above all, a future priest must acquire skill in actualization, i.e., in applying Scripture to life, both for preaching and teaching and for ministry to individuals. A personal habit of *lectio divina* is necessary, but it is not sufficient. Both training and pastoral experience are needed. Often the beginner tends toward a moralizing approach, not knowing how to teach God's requirements in the context of the good news of salvation in Christ. Then there is the challenge of speaking to people in ordinary language, rather than with theological or exegetical terms that they do not understand, and of speaking to the needs and challenges they are experiencing. Forming future priests in effective pastoral actualization of Scripture is a topic deserving attention in its own right.[23]

As regards *Scripture resources,* seminarians should acquire familiarity during the course of their assignments with the following tools: study Bibles, cross-references, Bible dictionaries, analytical concordances, online resources or Bible software that enables them to study the usage of Greek or Hebrew words, theological word books and dictionaries, and a synopsis of the Gospels. They should be familiar with Scripture commentaries that are useful for pastoral ministry,[24] including those that make ancient interpretations available (i.e., commentaries from the Christian tradition or *catenae* such as the Ancient Christian Commentary on Scripture series).

---

23. I have developed a handout and an exercise on actualization that is posted on my SHMS faculty web page under "Course Resources."

24. I mean those that consider the theology and relevance of texts to Christian faith and life today. The Catholic Commentary on Sacred Scripture series, of which I am one of the general editors, aims to do this.

Implications for the Classroom

At SHMS we are working on a plan to introduce seminarians to basic skills and reference works early on in their Scripture course work, with the expectation that they will use them throughout their studies and gradually become proficient.

Most of the time in teaching should be spent on helping future pastoral ministers master the content of the Bible rather than on scholarship about it. Emphasis should be placed on the text's theological and pastoral implications (by "pastoral" I mean its application to Christian life), i.e., what the Lord teaches us to believe and to do through his word. Personal examples from our experience of applying Scripture to life can be particularly effective.

In assignments, it helps to give seminarians plenty of practice in explaining texts and their theological implications for Christian faith and life, both in written and oral presentations. Although occasional lengthy exegetical papers are helpful to teach seminarians to plumb the depths of texts, more frequent short papers or exercises in biblical interpretation may prepare them better for their future ministry.

Since the aim of our work is to produce "doers of the word, and not hearers only" (James 1:22), Scripture professors must strive to teach, by word and example, an authentic biblical piety that emphasizes faith and obedience as well as delight in God's word. The Torah piety of the Old Testament, expressed in Deuteronomy and many of the Psalms (e.g., Pss. 1, 19B, 119, etc.), provides a model; so does Mary's faith and docility to the word of God. Other practices can reinforce this example, such as beginning and ending with prayer and encouraging meditation upon and memorization of texts.

Realistic Goals for Lifelong Learning and Continuing Education

Finally, our Scripture faculty considered what habits of lifelong Scripture learning we would like to encourage and inculcate in seminarians for the sake of their future ministry of the word, and we came up with the following:

1. to engage in daily or at least regular continuous reading of Scripture according to a reading plan that enables them to read through the whole Bible every two to four years;
2. to study biblical books with the help of a commentary; to read books, attend conferences, or listen to audio recordings on Scripture;

3. to maintain Scripture notes, whether in notebooks or computer files, that will help them retain and use the fruits of their study and reflection.

Conclusion

I would like to recall a few words regarding the role of exegesis in the Church from the conclusion of the Pontifical Biblical Commission's *The Interpretation of the Bible in the Church* (1993):

> Through fidelity to the great Tradition, of which the Bible itself is a witness, Catholic exegesis should . . . maintain its identity as a theological discipline, the principal aim of which is the deepening of faith. . . . [The] task [of Catholic exegesis] is to fulfill, in the Church and in the world, a vital function, that of contributing to an ever more authentic transmission of the content of the inspired Scriptures.

This applies in a very particular way to us who have been entrusted with forming future priests for the ministry of the word.

CHAPTER 7

Searching for the Obvious: Toward a Catholic Hermeneutic of Scripture with Seminarians Especially in Mind

James Swetnam, S.J.

Some Preliminary Considerations

In the past two hundred years or more a massive quantity of information about Scripture and the world that saw the writing of Scripture has been produced.[1] All of this information is precious and, obviously, none of it should be discarded but should be considered useful, potentially if not actually, for helping make Scripture a vital force in the lives of believers. But just how and to what extent this information should be used at the present time in approaching the Scriptures when seminarians are in mind — that is the question. More exactly, how should the study of Scripture be framed and hence how should Scripture be presented to those interested in making the Scripture and its message an integral part of their lives? Specifically, an attempt will be made here explicitly to frame the study and presentation of Scripture as it was implicitly framed and presented to the first generation of Christian believers. Hence the first part of the title, "Searching for the Obvious." But this orientation based on the first generation of Christian believers will be guided by the goal of framing and presenting the material to contemporary seminarians who presumably wish to make Scripture a part of their lives and to help others do the same. Hence the second part of the title, "Toward a Catholic Hermeneutic of Scripture with Seminarians Especially in Mind."

---

1. What follows in this section is a deliberate simplification of a complex problem, which of course merits extended treatment in its own right. It is hoped that the simplification has not led to distortion.

The first-generation Christians approached the Scriptures with faith, believing instinctively that Scripture was written by people of faith, about people of faith, and for people of faith. They approached it with their Christian worship already firmly in place — the Eucharist, which came into existence through the words of Jesus at the Last Supper and was brought to fulfillment with his death and resurrection. This was the nucleus of the tradition that existed before any New Testament writing existed and provided the basis for the eventual writing of the Gospels. The belief of these Christians, as they were well aware, came about as a gift of God through the resurrection and was centered on the Eucharist; it was a faith that the Gospels would be designed to deepen and illumine. There was no "hermeneutic of suspicion" to cloud their reception of what their leaders wrote for their guidance. For their Scripture they relied at first on what is now known as the Old Testament. But the guidance they needed in interpreting this written word was given ultimately by Jesus and what he said and did — and what happened to him at the resurrection. It was ultimately the Father acting through Jesus and the Spirit whom Jesus bestowed on the Church he founded that gave the first Christians the orientation they needed for living their lives based on a faith they had taken as legitimated by God at the resurrection.

Given this approach, then, two basic needs are evident:

(1) the need to enable the contemporary Catholic to be placed in contact with the original meaning of the text of Scripture as closely as possible to the way the first-generation Christians used in approaching it;

(2) the need to enable the contemporary Catholic to grasp the relevance of this original meaning for his/her own life as the first-generation Christians did.

Put succinctly, the contemporary Catholic must be helped to go backward in time to the world of the first Christians in order to grasp the meaning of the Scriptures as they did, and then must be helped to return to the present from the world of the first Christians to see and apply the relevance of that original meaning for his or her life in the contemporary world.[2]

2. When approaching a text — any text — we are entitled to interpret it any way that we think appropriate. Naturally this results in some interpretations that are as a matter of fact more appropriate than others. In the twenty-first century, where science is so uncritically accepted as the ultimate arbiter of knowing things as they really are, it is not surprising that even some believers choose science as the prime analogate for their study of the Bible. Inasmuch as science is popularly accepted as the embodiment of reason at its most successful

Underlying this process are several factors that make the endeavor feasible:

(1) the same shared faith of the Church among the first Christians and among the Catholics of today;

(2) the same shared Eucharist among the first Christians and among the Catholics of today;

(3) the same shared gift of the Spirit for both understanding the original meaning and then applying it to everyday living among the first Christians and among the Catholics of today;

(4) the same shared virtues (in addition to faith) on the part of the first Christians and on the part of the Catholics of today.

The above approach, it should be noted, is not the approach of the many scholars who choose to examine the text of Scripture from points of view in accord with their own goals of amassing information or of influencing/ enriching others in various ways. Further, it is not the approach of other Christian communities who do not share in the Eucharist and in membership in the Catholic Church the way Catholics do. Their approaches are not necessarily wrong as far as they go, but they are different and, from the Catholic standpoint, limited. The results of such approaches can be helpful at times to the Catholic approach, but only if in conjunction with them the integrity of the Catholic approach is maintained.

---

in understanding the real world (the hard sciences of physics, chemistry, and biology and their handmaid, technology), an approach to Scripture based on this approach would seem at first sight the best chance for understanding Scripture as it really should be understood. And since part of this success is attributed to science's prescinding from God, it would seem that the study of Scripture should also prescind from God, i.e., faith. But this approach is really an acceptance of scientism, not science, i.e., an approach to reality that arrogates to itself all knowledge, claiming that beyond the scientific method lies only the unknowable. Further, this approach of prescinding from faith ignores the whole question of Scripture as literature: the prime analogate for understanding Scripture should be the art of reading, for literature is basically what Scripture is — not the object of the hard sciences, which are divorced from persons. Just as great literature inevitably involves the reader in a unique mix of objective meaning and subjective relevance in the context of persons, so Scripture inevitably involves the reader in a unique mix of objective meaning and subjective relevance in the context of persons, even on the level of unaided reason. But for those gifted with faith, this unique mix of objective meaning and subjective relevance is ever so much more profound because the persons involved are ever so much more meaningful. But it is a profundity and meaning known only through faith, and this, it would seem, is unacceptable even to some believers — for whom reason and reason alone is the bottom line of all knowledge.

The Basic Principles of a Catholic Hermeneutic of Scripture

The Basic Principles of a Catholic Hermeneutic of Scripture Involving the Original Meaning

In the context of the approach to Scripture outlined above, it is useful to review the instructions for interpreting the original meaning of Scripture given by the Second Vatican Council as schematized in the *Catechism of the Catholic Church* (CCC). The unspoken understanding is that these instructions are intended for believing Catholics who want to make Scripture a meaningful part of their lives.

The first principle is that the meaning of Scripture cannot be divorced from the meaning intended by the human author, and that the discovery of this meaning requires awareness of all the purely human factors that went into the composition of the text (CCC, §§109-10).

The second principle is that Scripture must be interpreted in accordance with the Spirit who inspired it (CCC, §111). Thus, implicitly, a second, divine, author enters the picture. Three criteria are proposed by the Council for interpreting Scripture according to the second principle, i.e., interpreting Scripture according to the Spirit who inspired it, i.e., according to the second, divine author (CCC, §§111-14):

1. attention to the unity and content of the whole of Scripture;
2. attention to the living Tradition of the Church;
3. attention to the analogy of faith.

Each of these three directives needs clarification.

1. The Council explains that the unity and content of the whole of Scripture is based on Jesus Christ who is the center of God's purposes in inspiring the sacred text (CCC, §112). This implies that all of Scripture, even the Old Testament, is to be interpreted in the light of Jesus Christ. Given the supposition that faith should be involved in reading every part of Scripture, this consideration about the centrality of Jesus Christ indicates that reading the Old Testament with (Christian) faith needs elucidation, for the original human authors of the Old Testament were Israelites, Old Testament persons of faith, writing for Old Testament persons of faith, and about Old Testament persons of faith. But this Old Testament faith, genuine though it was (and is), did not (and does not) have the view of Jesus Christ that Christians have, i.e., that he rose from the dead and that he was divine. The inference would thus

seem to be that there are two ways in which faith can come into play in the reading of the Old Testament, one from the standpoint of the Old Testament human authors and one from the standpoint of the New Testament human authors. But God speaks through the human authors, and so the christological meaning of the Old Testament is ultimately based on the Old Testament meaning, which was the work of authors who did not have the awareness of the Messiah that New Testament authors did. Understandably so, for the New Testament is in continuity with the Old Testament but also in discontinuity — and in a definitive way. This definitive discontinuity is to be understood in the context of New Testament faith in the resurrection and all that this implies about the resurrection as the foundation for Christian belief (CCC, §112). But the belief that the human authors of the Old Testament wrote texts that objectively speak of Christ even though these human authors were unaware of this dimension implies the existence of the second, divine author speaking through them. This understanding of the Old Testament is available only to those who believe in the resurrection, i.e., as Christians, and are thus open to the action of the Spirit, as the following directive explains.

2. The Council declares that the Church carries in her Tradition the living memorial of God's Word, and it is the Holy Spirit who empowers the Church to give a spiritual interpretation of Scripture (CCC, §113). That is to say, the Spirit's guidance enables the Church to retain in her nonscriptural identity what the written Word — Scripture — essentially represents. Hence her teaching can serve as a guide to what Scripture means, again with the Spirit as guarantor of truth.

3. The Council explains the analogy of faith as "the coherence of the truths of faith among themselves and within the whole plan of Revelation" (CCC, §114).

Perhaps an example would help bring home what would seem to be an illustration of what the Council intended. It is quite doubtful if the authors of the Old Testament ever thought that the Messiah they spoke about would be fully divine in the sense held by Catholic belief. But in the light of the risen Christ one can see that certain Old Testament expressions can be understood in this sense, for example, "son of God." An Old Testament author would have understood this expression as referring to an extraordinary person. And even in the New Testament, the phrase, e.g., as originally uttered by Peter at the giving of the keys, would seem to have been understood in this sense, even if the words in some special sense applicable to Jesus are seen to come from an inspiration of God. But after the resurrection, the apostles and the other early Christians would have understood the phrase in the sense that

Christ is fully divine. Assent to this truth is a gift of God, a gift given to the first Christians, for it was implied in the gift of assent to the resurrection. Further, it was enshrined in the Tradition of the Church, as is indicated by the First Council of Nicea, in 325. Finally, the truth of Christ's divinity gives a coherence to the entire body of Scripture, Old Testament as well as New, as one would expect according to the analogy of faith.

Faith and reason are involved in all interpretation of the original meaning(s) of Scripture. But faith would seem to be the determining element, so that faith is the "form" of the intellectual virtues just as charity is the "form" of all the moral virtues (cf. Aquinas's *Summa Theologica* II-II.23.8). Thus faith "informs" reason without eliminating reason. Reason would prompt the interpreter to realize that an interpretation of Scripture that distorts the text instead of illumining it is not a way to arrive at the truth of what the Scripture says or what faith implies. This role of reason in interpreting should be neither overemphasized nor underemphasized if fideism and rationalism are to be avoided. It should not be in favor of an interpretation that takes a positive view of the Church and her teaching without an objective grounding in a text, nor should it be in favor of an interpretation that takes a negative view without such a grounding.

The Basic Principles of a Catholic Hermeneutic of Scripture Involving the Contemporary Relevance of Scripture

Under section 2.A. the first step in the interpretation of Scripture was presented, i.e., the interpretation of the meaning of the text according to the intention of the human and divine authors. The second step has to do with the determination of the relevance of that original meaning for the life of the person doing the interpreting. And just as the Holy Spirit has a crucial role in the determination of the meaning of the text according to the mind of the original authors, human and divine, so the Holy Spirit has a crucial role in the determination of the relevance of that meaning for the life of the one doing the exegesis. That is to say, the Spirit acts as guide in applying the meaning of the inspired text to the believer's life (CCC, §1101). Here, too, perhaps, it would not be inappropriate to speak of two "authors" of the life of each person: (1) the person himself/herself and (2) the Spirit. For each believer, just like any other person born into the world, is writing the story of his or her life, that is, he or she is responsible for what he or she does and needs the Spirit for those actions insofar as they are good. Insofar as the individual believer's actions are good, the Holy Spirit is a true "coauthor."

In other words, the Catholic hermeneutic of Scripture is intrinsically vertical in its twin aspects, both as regards the objective meaning of the text and as regards the subjective application of the text: Catholic hermeneutic has an explicit relation to the Transcendent. The fact that the second step involves individual application of Scripture will not result in the chaos of the private interpretation of Scripture that characterized and continues to characterize Protestant Christianity, for the second step has to proceed through the first step if it is to be in agreement with what the Spirit has objectively inspired. The link between the original meaning of the text and the relevance of that original meaning for anyone not constituting the original audience is vital for assuring continuity between the two steps.

Reflections

It is clear that the Catholics of today cannot return to the first century and become the believers of the first Christian generation. But it is also clear, from a comparison between the suggestions made in the Section 1 above ("Some Preliminary Considerations") and the norms outlined in Section 2 above ("The Basic Principles of a Catholic Hermeneutic of Scripture") that the essentials of the approach of the Christians of the first generation can be translated into the contemporary world in a meaningful way because of the common elements involved in the lives of both generations.

Basic to the approaches in both eras is primacy of the implied authority of the Church with regard to Scripture. This approach does not mean that the Church is "over" Scripture; but it does mean that the Church's teaching authority judges the interpretation of Scripture: the Holy Spirit living in the magisterium of the Church has the ultimate say as regards the meaning of the same Holy Spirit who inspired Scripture. But Catholics, in interpreting the original meaning of Scripture, should be reflexively aware of the need to look at a given text in the context of all of Scripture and in the context of the analogy of faith, and, above all, in the context of the authorship of the Holy Spirit. And this, not only for access to the original meaning of the text as intended by both the human and divine authors, but also for ascertaining the relevance of that meaning in their own lives.

Nowhere does the Church seek to "prove" her authority, though she does explain it as she asserts it. Everything is based on faith as a "given," an attribute of the Mystical Body of Christ which constitutes the essence of the Church and is based ultimately on the divine Christ's gift to the Church of his Spirit. Individual participants of that Mystical Body which is the Church are capable of rejecting that faith but not capable of acquiring it: faith is a gift from God, freely given and freely to be kept.

Seminarians Especially in Mind

The Goal of a Seminary Teacher of Scripture in the Catholic Tradition

A seminary teacher in the Catholic tradition should review the above material at the beginning of each course and, in addition, make clear his or her own position. That is to say, he should make clear that he is teaching in the Catholic tradition or, if he is not, what tradition he is teaching in — for example, the Lutheran tradition, the Calvinist tradition, the secularist tradition, etc. He should specify how this affects his teaching in a Catholic seminary. Further, it is the prerogative of the teacher to make known his understanding of the relevance of the objective meaning for his own life, though he should not be required to do so. But nothing prevents him from giving examples of how various individuals view such relevance, provided that the rights of privacy be honored. The professor of Scripture should be aware of how Scripture can fit in as the soul of theology, and should be ready to expatiate on the relationship at will.

In general it should be emphasized that Scripture is the soul of theology because Scripture is centered on Christ, and theology in the Catholic tradition should be centered on Christ. This of course is a challenge to professors of theology as well as to professors of Scripture.

In this connection it would be useful to point out how much Western civilization owes to the Catholic Church with regard to the unique value of the human person. This heritage is, of course, being challenged today by many -isms such as secularism, paganism, hedonism, evolutionism, etc. The basic dignity of the human person consists in his or her capacity to transcend himself or herself. Many if not all contemporary challenges to the Church's view of the person propose a diametrically opposite approach, advocating self-centered self-satisfaction as the means of human fulfillment, self-satisfaction guided by norms determined by principles established independently of any transcendent guide. The Bible, especially the New Testament, is replete with examples of how human beings transcended themselves as part of the mystery of how Jesus Christ transcended himself in becoming man. And behind the self-transcendence of Christ is the self-transcendence of the Father. One of the advantages of the approach to Scripture that has characterized the best of the Church's use of Scripture down the centuries is the immediate contact it fosters between the believing persons of the Church and the believing persons of the Bible. It is such immediate contact that has enabled the Church to be aware that the human person is primarily a mystery to contemplate and respect, not simply a puzzle to analyze and decipher. And the reason for this is the link that a faith-filled approach to Scripture senses between the human person and the divine persons. For the latter are above all mysteries to contemplate and adore.

What a Seminarian Should Look for in a Course on Scripture

The seminarian should be fully conversant with the basic reason for the explicit choice of faith as a principle of interpretation, with a firm grasp of the principles involved in the interpretation of Scripture in both the interpretation of the text and the application of this interpretation to his own life, as outlined above. Further, he should be aware of what tradition the professor of any given course is working in.

The seminarian should look for the following three things (among others):

(1) a deepening of his knowledge of Jesus Christ and how Jesus Christ entered the world of time;
(2) a deepening of his respect for all persons, human and divine;
(3) a deepening of his awareness of the gift of faith as a member of the Catholic Church.

But the seminarian also has an obligation to prepare himself for the study of Scripture well before formal coursework begins. In particular he should do his courses in philosophy and literature as well as he is able, so that he has the ability to think abstractly about the human person in the context of the universe (philosophy) as well as concretely (literature). Not any philosophy will do — Thomism is recommended above all. Not any literature will do — the great classics of the Western world are recommended: Homer, Virgil, Augustine, Dante, Shakespeare, Jane Austen, Tolstoy, for example. With this background, contact with the persons of the Bible, both human and divine, will be facilitated so that the Holy Spirit can work as profoundly and meaningfully as he wishes.

CHAPTER 8

Verbum Domini and the Renewal of Biblical Preaching

Mary Healy

*Is not my word like fire, declares the Lord, and like a hammer that
breaks the rock in pieces?*

JEREMIAH 23:29

*Our gospel came to you not only in word, but also in power and in the
Holy Spirit and with full conviction.*

1 THESSALONIANS 1:5

It is difficult to exaggerate the importance of good preaching in the life of
the Church. All the great waves of revival in Church history can be traced
at least in part to exceptional preaching — preaching that broke open the
bread of the word of God, proclaimed the gospel in its simplicity and life-
changing power, shattered hearts of stone and moved the listeners to repentance, faith, and conversion. As recent popes have repeatedly emphasized,
the Church's most urgent priority today is the mobilization of the laity for
the New Evangelization and the revitalization of faith in the post-Christian
West. Although many interrelated factors are entailed, such a revitalization
will *begin* with good preaching or it will not begin at all. "Faith comes from
what is heard, and what is heard comes by the preaching of Christ" (Rom.
10:17). Pope John Paul II affirmed this principle in his Apostolic Exhortation
on priestly formation: "The priest is *first of all* a minister of the word of God.
He is consecrated and sent forth to proclaim the good news of the kingdom

to all, calling every person to the obedience of faith. . . ."[1] People will be interiorly converted, avail themselves of the full power of the sacraments, and pursue a fervent countercultural life of holiness and mission only if their hearts are stirred to do so by preaching that brings them into an encounter with Christ.

Nearly all agree that there is room for improvement in Catholic preaching today. In his 2010 Apostolic Exhortation *Verbum Domini,* Pope Benedict was delicately candid in noting certain weaknesses in contemporary homilies, especially in their relationship with Sacred Scripture. The gulf that has arisen between biblical exegesis and faith, he said, "can give rise to a lack of clarity in the preparation of homilies" (no. 35). Further,

> given the importance of the word of God, the quality of homilies needs to be improved. . . . Generic and abstract homilies which obscure the directness of God's word should be avoided, as well as useless digressions which risk drawing greater attention to the preacher than to the heart of the Gospel message. The faithful should be able to perceive clearly that the preacher has a compelling desire to present Christ, who must stand at the centre of every homily. (no. 59)

Many Catholics who have left the Church for evangelical churches claim (whether fairly or not) that at Sunday Mass they never heard the gospel kerygma or had the Bible explained to them in a way that made clear its relevance to their life. Common experience suggests that the majority of homilies are connected to the lectionary readings only loosely if at all, and often use the readings as a springboard for a moral or devotional exhortation rather than explaining the meaning of the texts themselves. Many homilies begin with an anecdote or joke that distances the audience from the Gospel passage just heard. Few offer an in-depth exposition of one or more of the readings.

If one compares homilies today — even those of high quality — to patristic homilies, the difference is striking. The preaching of the Fathers was virtually saturated with Scripture, often drawing theological insight from the linkage of seemingly unrelated parts of the biblical canon, and making abundant reference to the spiritual sense — the way Christ is mysteriously prefigured in the persons, events, and institutions of the Old Testament. Preachers today are less familiar with the content of the Bible and gener-

1. John Paul II, *Pastores dabo vobis* 26; emphasis added. See also Vatican II, *Presbyterorum Ordinis* 4.

ally limit themselves to a few texts that helpfully illustrate their point. They usually avoid expounding on the spiritual sense, despite the fact that the lectionary lends itself to this manner of interpretation.

Where preaching is anemic, Christian life is anemic and God's people are not awakened to their call to discipleship and their mission to bring the gospel into every sector of society. "If the bugle gives an indistinct sound, who will get ready for battle?" (1 Cor. 14:8). Where preaching is not deeply biblical, the faithful fail to experience the power of God's word to renew their minds and liberate them from captivity to the ideologies of the age. St. Thomas Aquinas makes a striking remark concerning the result of effective preaching. Commenting on the "sword of the Spirit, which is the word of God" (Eph. 6:17), he writes, "We have weapons to assault the demons. . . . This happens frequently during sermons when the word of God, penetrating into the hearts of sinners, thrusts out the chaos of sins and demons."[2] One might ask: Does it happen frequently in sermons today?

The present essay will explore two ways in which *Verbum Domini,* the most important ecclesial document on Scripture since Vatican II, points the way toward such a renewal of biblical preaching: first, through a deeper appreciation for the unique authority of Scripture, and second, through the rediscovery of Scripture's spiritual sense. A specific lectionary text will then be used as an example to illustrate how these two principles might be applied in homily preparation.

Biblical Inspiration and Authority

One reason for the lack of biblical engagement in homilies today is not difficult to identify, at least for most priests and deacons in the U.S. They are essentially carrying out what they were taught to do by the bishops' 1982 instruction on homiletics, *Fulfilled in Your Hearing.* This document was the foundational text for seminary homiletics courses for a generation, although it was replaced in 2012 by new guidelines.[3] According to *Fulfilled,* "The homily is not so much *on* the Scriptures as *from* and *through* them" (*Fulfilled,* 20;

2. Aquinas, *Commentary on St. Paul's Epistle to the Ephesians,* trans. Matthew Lamb, Aquinas Scripture Series (Albany, NY: Magi Books, 1966), p. 243.

3. The vastly improved 2012 instruction, *Preaching the Mystery of Faith,* makes clear that preaching is "from the Scriptures themselves" and that the Sunday homily should center on Christ and "typically involve the bringing together, in mutual illumination, of the Old Testament and the New Testament."

emphasis in the original). In fact, the document cautions, a preacher who begins by explaining the lectionary readings "gives the impression that [his] principal purpose is to interpret scriptural texts rather than communicate with real people, and that he interprets these texts primarily to extract ethical demands to impose on a congregation" (*Fulfilled*, 24). This advice is obviously intended to caution against dry, exegetical homilies that simply collate information gleaned from biblical commentaries and that have little relevance to contemporary Christian life. But perhaps inadvertently, it implies a dichotomy between interpreting Scripture and communicating with real people. To reach real people, the document says, a homilist should "begin with a description of a contemporary human situation which is evoked by the scriptural texts, rather than with an interpretation or reiteration of the text. After the human situation has been addressed, the homilist can turn to the Scriptures to interpret the situation, showing how the God described therein is also present and active in our lives today" (*Fulfilled*, 24). The homilist is to use Scripture to interpret contemporary human experience, rather than interpreting Scripture itself.

Although *Fulfilled* was published nearly thirty years ago, its de-emphasis on biblical interpretation continues to guide homilists today. An official commentary on *Fulfilled* published by the Catholic Association of Teachers of Homiletics (CATH) in 2010 (the same year that *Verbum Domini* was promulgated) actually takes this distancing from Scripture a step further:

> In some respects [*Fulfilled's*] overemphasis [!] on preaching the Scriptures is a result of the somewhat confused state of other church documents at the time. In the conciliar eagerness to embrace the Word of God and place it back at the center of church teaching and worship, [*Sacrosanctum concilium*] unfortunately described the liturgy of the Word as the moment in which the readings are proclaimed and "explained in the homily," an image repeated in the 1981 *Introduction to the Lectionary*. Echoes of this perspective are yet found in the 2002 *General Instruction of the Roman Missal* which speaks of the homily as "a living commentary on the word" and employs the unfortunate phrase that the readings are "explained by the homily."[4]

4. Edward Foley, O.F.M.Cap., Guerric DeBona, O.S.B., and Mary Margaret Pazdan, O.P., "The Homily," in *Preaching in the Sunday Assembly: A Pastoral Commentary on "Fulfilled in Your Hearing,"* ed. James A. Wallace (Collegeville, MN: Liturgical Press, 2010), p. 35. The authors hold that "the emphasis on preaching 'from and through' the Scriptures" in *Fulfilled* is "commendable" but is a "one-sided emphasis" because it does not take into

The CATH commentary thus portrays every significant conciliar and post-conciliar document relevant to liturgical preaching as misguided in its insistence on preaching the Scriptures. If this is the official position of those who teach homiletics in U.S. seminaries, it partly explains why the faithful are biblically impoverished.

There are two factors in *Fulfilled* that may underlie the CATH commentary's attempt to divorce liturgical preaching from biblical exposition. First, there seems to be an assumption that Scripture is just one mode in which God speaks, on a par with other modes including daily human experience and preaching itself (cf. *Fulfilled,* 10). The task of the homily, then, is to bring these different modes of revelation into "dialogue," rather than to call forth obedient faith in response to the supreme authority of God's word. Second, contemporary works of biblical scholarship — not to mention seminary Scripture courses — are still largely dominated by historical criticism and other approaches that are in themselves insufficient for biblical interpretation. *Fulfilled* shows an awareness of the difficulty of translating such works into pastorally useful explanations of the text as God's living word addressed to his people today. The document rightly advises homilists not to consult exegetical resources without first praying and meditating personally on the word. But it goes further in relegating the discernment of the text's original meaning to the domain of biblical professionals who alone have all the necessary tools. The homilist consults biblical scholarship only as a secondary, fine-tuning step. "We are our own interpreters first of all, and then when we do turn to the professional exegetes, we do so for the purpose of checking out the accuracy of our own interpretation" (*Fulfilled,* 32). The premise seems to be that the text's literal sense — the meaning conveyed by the words of Scripture, which is discovered by the tools and methods of exegesis[5] — is only marginally relevant to whatever use the homilist might want to make of it. This minimalist view of the value of exegesis is undeniably due in part to deficiencies in biblical scholarship itself. Much contemporary biblical scholarship, including that taught in seminaries, has been characterized by a methodological exclusion of faith, which not only leads to theologically questionable results but weakens the relevance of such research for Christian faith and life.[6] The hermeneutic of

---

account the appropriateness of preaching on other texts in the liturgy or on the liturgical rites and actions themselves ("The Homily," pp. 35-36).

5. See the *Catechism of the Catholic Church* 116.

6. As theologian Brian Daley notes, "Modern historical criticism — including the criticism of biblical texts — is methodologically atheistic, even if what it studies is some form or

suspicion characterizing many biblical resources undermines confidence that Scripture reliably communicates truth about Jesus Christ and about God's will for his people, which in turn impairs a preacher's ability to preach on it with confidence and conviction.

When we turn to *Verbum Domini*, we find a very different valuation of the authority and function of Scripture. Pope Benedict emphasizes that "Word of God" (capitalized) refers first and foremost to the Person of Jesus Christ, and then analogously to divine revelation in all its modes — through creation itself, through salvation history, through the preaching of the prophets and apostles, and as handed down in the Church's Scripture and living Tradition. But he makes clear that Sacred Scripture, as inspired by God, contains the divine word "in an altogether singular way" (*Verbum Domini* 17), and he underlines this singularity by using "word of God" (lowercase) and "Scripture" interchangeably. To explain the unique status of Scripture, Benedict draws an analogy between Christ's Eucharistic presence and his presence in the biblical word. "Christ, truly present under the species of bread and wine, is analogously present in the word proclaimed in the liturgy. A deeper understanding of the sacramentality of God's word can thus lead us to a more unified understanding of the mystery of revelation" (no. 56). He illustrates the point with an arresting quotation from St. Jerome:

> For me, the Gospel is the Body of Christ; for me, the holy Scriptures are his teaching. And when he says: *whoever does not eat my flesh and drink my blood* (Jn 6:53), even though these words can also be understood of the [Eucharistic] Mystery, Christ's body and blood are really the word of Scripture, God's teaching. When we approach the [Eucharistic] Mystery, if a crumb falls to the ground we are troubled. Yet when we are listening to the word of God, and God's Word and Christ's flesh and blood are being poured into our ears yet we pay no heed, what great peril should we not feel? (no. 56)

Benedict clearly has a high view of the authority and uniqueness of Sacred Scripture, one more in harmony with patristic thought than with some currents of contemporary homiletics. This view is of course founded in Scripture itself. The Old Testament, especially the Psalter, is replete with

---

facet of religious belief, and even if it is practiced by believers. Only 'natural,' inner-worldly explanations of why or how things happen, explanations that could be acceptable to believers and unbelievers alike, are taken as historically admissible. . . ." Daley, "Is Patristic Exegesis Still Usable?" *Communio* 29 (2002): 185-216; here 191.

expressions of reverence for and devotion to God's word, a devotion that motivates one to meditate on it "day and night" (Ps. 1:2; cf. 19:7-11; 119:1-176). Jeremiah exemplifies this attitude: "When I found your words, I devoured them; they became my joy and the happiness of my heart, Because I bore your name, O Lord, God of hosts" (Jer. 15:16). In Isaiah God declares his approval of one who "trembles at my word" (Isa. 66:2). The New Testament likewise calls for reverence toward God's written word as having supreme authority: Scripture is "God-breathed" (2 Tim. 3:16); it was composed "in the Spirit" (Mark 12:36; cf. 2 Pet. 1:21) and therefore it "cannot be broken" (John 10:35). Catholic tradition has expressed this truth by affirming that Scripture alone is divinely inspired (*Verbum Domini* 19).[7]

If there is to be a renaissance in Catholic preaching, seminary formation needs to inculcate a profound veneration and love for the biblical word, following the example of Pope Benedict himself. Only if the preacher himself has "devoured" the word and lives under its authority will he be a credible witness to the word's power to bring the faithful into living contact with Christ, to teach, reprove, correct, train in righteousness, and equip people for every good work (cf. 2 Tim. 3:16-17).

Despite the protestations of the CATH commentary, *Verbum Domini* leaves no doubt that the function of the homily is indeed to explain the lectionary readings (no. 95, quoting *Sacrosanctum concilium*). Benedict reiterates his earlier exhortation in *Sacramentum Caritatis* that the homily "is meant to foster a deeper understanding of the word of God" (no. 107). To that end, *Verbum Domini* specifically enjoins a new approach to seminary Scripture courses that will better prepare priests and deacons for expository preaching. Scripture courses must teach a hermeneutic of faith rather than "a notion of scholarly research that would consider itself neutral with regard to Scripture" (no. 47). Besides learning the content of the Bible, the Bible's original languages, and sound exegetical methods, future preachers must learn that "we cannot come to an understanding of Scripture without the assistance of the Holy Spirit who inspired it" (no. 16). Citing Richard of Saint Victor, the Pope writes that "we need 'the eyes of doves,' enlightened and

---

7. See also the Second Council of Lyons, Profession of Faith of Michael Paleologus (1274); Council of Florence, *Cantate Domino* (1442); Council of Trent, *Decretum de libris sacris et de traditionibus recipiendis* (1546); First Vatican Council, *Dei Filius* (1870), 2; Second Vatican Council, *Dei verbum* (1965), 11. The Congregation for the Doctrine of the Faith, in *Dominus Iesus* (2000), notes that "The Church's tradition . . . reserves the designation of inspired texts to the canonical books of the Old and New Testaments, since these are inspired by the Holy Spirit" (no. 8).

MARY HEALY

taught by the Spirit, in order to understand the sacred text" (no. 16). This in turn requires an integration between biblical studies and prayer (no. 82) that is not yet the norm in most biblical courses and publications.

The Rediscovery of the Fourfold Sense

The second significant new emphasis in *Verbum Domini* is its insistence on recovering Scripture's fourfold sense. For most of Christian history, the doctrine that Scripture has not only a literal sense but also a (threefold) hidden spiritual sense was considered a basic datum of faith. All Scripture, the Old Testament as well as the New, was understood as finding its fulfillment and ultimate intelligibility in Christ and the new covenant established in him. In Augustine's famous dictum, "The New Testament is hidden in the Old, and the Old is made plain in the New."

This conviction forms the foundation of the Church's lectionary cycle. On Sundays, feast days, and most weekdays in the special seasons, the Old Testament reading is selected to coordinate with the Gospel so as to display prophecy and fulfillment, a type and its antitype, or a theme amplified and brought to completion in Christ.[8] The lectionary thus presupposes and teaches a christological reading of the Old Testament — what tradition calls the "spiritual sense" — which is itself rooted in a christocentric vision of the economy of salvation.[9] Yet oddly enough, the spiritual sense is rarely taught today in Catholic colleges or even in seminaries preparing priests to preach on these very readings. The result is a disjuncture between the Church's traditional manner of interpreting the word and contemporary preaching and teaching. Homilists today often find difficulty connecting the first reading with the Gospel, and are unprepared to expound on old covenant events and persons as figures pointing forward to the new covenant in Christ. The principle that "All sacred Scripture is but one book, and this one book is Christ, 'because all divine Scripture speaks of Christ, and all divine Scripture is fulfilled in Christ,' "[10] is affirmed in theory but largely ignored in practice.

8. This coordination was also evident in the *Roman Missal* prior to Vatican II, although far fewer Old Testament readings were included.
9. In a broader way the New Testament also has a "spiritual sense," in that it has a capacity to lead us into the mystery of Jesus' divine sonship and saving mission (see *Catechism of the Catholic Church*, 515). The events in the life of Jesus narrated in the Gospels, in particular, can be interpreted as figures of our life in Christ and of the life to come.
10. Hugh of St. Victor, quoted in the *Catechism of the Catholic Church* 134.

116

This state of affairs is partly due to modern scholarship's almost exclusive focus on the literal sense of Scripture. Modern biblical criticism has emphasized that the primary meaning of a text is to be found in the meaning intended by the original author(s) and the historical circumstances that gave rise to the text. Spiritual interpretation as practiced in ancient and medieval Christianity, even where admired for its inspirational appeal, has come to be regarded as eisegesis, an arbitrary and subjective imposition of meaning on the texts. Critics point out that the spiritual sense was often used to justify artificial, accommodated readings not rooted in the text. But recent years have witnessed a new interest in the spiritual sense, spurred in part by the renewal in patristic studies and in part by the postmodern rejection of the hegemony of the historical-critical approach.

Is it necessary, or even possible, to rehabilitate this ancient approach to Scripture that has borne such rich fruit theologically and spiritually? *Verbum Domini* answers with a resounding yes. Pope Benedict calls for "renewed attention to the Fathers of the Church and their exegetical approach," while at the same time availing ourselves of the philological and historical resources at our disposal for discerning the literal sense (no. 37). He quotes the medieval couplet:

The letter speaks of deeds; allegory about the faith;
The moral about our actions; anagogy about our destiny.[11]

For Christian tradition, the four senses are not so much four different "meanings" as four different ways the mystery of Christ pervades history. The literal sense of the events of the old covenant is Jesus' coming in prophecy; the allegorical, his coming in the flesh; the moral, his coming in the life of the believer; the anagogical, his coming in glory. The senses are, then, "a single reality: the mystery of Christ lived at various levels."[12] Christ, the Word made flesh, was *already present* in a hidden way in the words and deeds of the former covenant — and even in all human history. As Mark Shea illustrates,

---

11. It is important to note that the terms used here are technical terms in Christian biblical interpretation. "Allegory" is not allegory in the ancient Greek sense, in which narratives are figures for atemporal ideas, but rather historical analogy in which biblical events point forward to the event of Christ. Likewise the moral sense (also called the tropological sense) does not refer to Scripture's straightforward moral teaching, such as the Decalogue, but to the way biblical *events* foreshadow life in Christ.

12. Mariano Magrassi, *Praying the Bible: An Introduction to Lectio Divina,* trans. Edward Hagman (Collegeville, MN: Liturgical Press, 1998), p. 9.

"When John said, 'Behold the Lamb of God,' he did not mean, '"Lamb" is an interesting literary motif that I think I'll apply to Jesus,' but rather, 'All those lambs who have been slain on all altars for all time are images, shadows, and copies of this Lamb, the real Lamb.' "[13]

To understand the events of the old covenant as figures for the new has immense implications for Christian life, and thus for preaching. To live the Christian life is to allow the Holy Spirit to reproduce in us the life of Christ, who himself mysteriously recapitulates all salvation history (cf. Eph. 1:10). As Henri de Lubac notes, that means that the Christian life consists of a "daily reenactment" of the events of biblical history.

> Each day, in the depths of our being, Israel leaves Egypt, each day it is nourished with the manna, each day it fulfills the Law, each day it must engage in combat, each day the promises that were made to this people in a carnal way are realized spiritually in us. . . . Each day the Lord comes, each day he approaches Jerusalem.[14]

Pope Benedict rightly insists, then, that the discernment of the spiritual sense is not merely a matter of cataloguing verbal correspondences. Rather, it is a spiritual process that requires letting oneself be drawn into the text's own movement. In words reminiscent of de Lubac, the Pope states that "the *passage from letter to spirit* . . . is not an automatic, spontaneous passage; rather, the letter needs to be transcended" (*Verbum Domini* 38; emphasis in the original).[15] Biblical interpretation "is never purely an intellectual process but also a lived one, demanding full engagement in the life of the Church, which is life 'according to the Spirit' (Gal. 5:16). . . . There is an inner drama in this process, since the passage that takes place in the power of the Spirit inevitably engages each person's freedom" (no. 38). Part of the task of the homilist is to help the faithful enter into that drama.

---

13. Mark Shea, "Making Senses Out of Scripture" (Conference presentation, Minneapolis, July 9, 2005).

14. Henri de Lubac, *Exégèse Médiévale,* vol. 2, p. 138; translation from the French by George Montague in *Understanding the Bible: A Basic Introduction to Biblical Interpretation,* rev. ed. (Mahwah, NJ: Paulist, 2007), p. 54.

15. Cf. de Lubac, *Scripture in the Tradition,* trans. Luke O'Neill (New York: Herder & Herder, 2000), pp. 20-23.

An Example: Numbers 13–14

How might the two principles mentioned above — recognition of the supreme authority of Scripture and engagement with the spiritual sense — be concretely applied to homily preparation? As an illustration let us consider the story of Israel at Kadesh (Numbers 13–14), selections of which are read on Wednesday of the Eighteenth Week in Ordinary Time.[16] In this narrative, the Israelites arrive at the border of the promised land after having escaped Egypt and journeyed across the Sinai desert. Christian tradition regards the desert journey as a figure of our earthly pilgrimage of faith. Likewise the entry into the promised land foreshadows our entrance into life in Christ, both sacramentally through baptism (the moral or tropological sense) and ultimately in the life to come (the anagogical sense). Such a reading is based on numerous typological clues in the Gospels[17] as well as explicit typological linkages in 1 Corinthians 10 and Hebrews 3–4.

Since in this case the lectionary provides only snippets (Num. 13:1-2, 25; 14:1, 26a-29a, 34-35) of a narrative that would be too long to include in its entirety,[18] it would be helpful for the homilist to begin with a recap of the story. In this pivotal episode, the Israelites have arrived at a crossroads. Having experienced miraculous deliverance from slavery in Egypt and received the covenant at Mount Sinai, they are about to enter the land that God promised Abraham centuries earlier. But before granting the fulfillment of the promise God first tests his people, seeking from them a concrete act of faith. He does so by instructing them to send twelve scouts to reconnoiter the land and report on their findings. His purpose is to bring Israel to a crisis, a point of decision: Will they trust God or not?

The scouts explore the land for forty days (a number that in Scripture often signifies a period of testing) and return to report, in effect: "True, the land is lush and prosperous. However, God neglected to tell us that the inhabitants are giants, and compared to them we look like grasshoppers. We're

---

16. The interpretation below was inspired in part by a talk given by Curtis Martin, "Kingdom Crossroads" (Applied Biblical Studies Conference, Franciscan University, July 2006).

17. For a thorough examination of such clues in one of the Gospels, see Rikki E. Watts, *Isaiah's New Exodus in Mark,* Biblical Studies Library (Grand Rapids: Baker Academic, 1997).

18. This unfortunate expedient, not uncommon in the lectionary, underscores the importance of Catholics' personal reading of Scripture outside of Mass, as Pope Benedict urges (*Verbum Domini* 87).

outnumbered, out-fortified, and out-gunned. There is no way we can enter and conquer the land." Their assessment is a direct contradiction to God's promise and a denial of the whole goal of the exodus! As the story unfolds, the people panic in response to this faithless report and ignore the "minority report" of two scouts, Joshua and Caleb, who urge them to trust God. This is the generation that has seen God's interventions on a scale unheard-of in history (cf. Deut. 4:34) — the plagues visited on Egypt, the Red Sea divided in two, manna given from heaven, water gushing from a split rock. Yet on the threshold of fulfillment of the promise they plead, in effect, "O God, please do not make us enter the land." God's response is to answer their prayer and decree that indeed, none of that generation will see the land of Canaan. Rather they will wander in the wilderness for forty years until they have all perished, leaving their children to enter the land (Num. 14:22-24).

Having explicated the literal sense of the passage, the preacher could then draw out the spiritual sense, first by showing how Jesus relived the story of Israel in his own earthly life. Subjected to his own trial in the desert, Jesus resisted temptation and offered to God the perfect response of faithful, obedient sonship that Israel was incapable of offering on its own. Jesus' baptism in the Jordan was, in a particular way, the moment of his unconditional acceptance of the Father's will for his messianic mission. He submitted to a "baptism of repentance" as a sign of his total solidarity with sinful humanity — a solidarity that would lead inexorably to the cross. Throughout his public ministry Jesus, in his human nature, radically trusted the Father even in the face of human and demonic opposition, hostility, mockery, and ultimately imprisonment and agonizing death. Because of his fidelity, not only he but all those joined to him through faith and baptism can enter into the true promised land — the share in God's own life and love that is our inheritance in Christ, not only in the age to come but even here and now.

The christological sense of the passage leads directly to the moral or tropological sense. St. Paul affirms that the biblical account of Israel's trials in the desert was "written down for our instruction, upon whom the end of the ages has come" (1 Cor. 10:11). Like the Israelites, we are pilgrims who have experienced a stupendous divine act of deliverance but are being tested prior to entering into the full consummation of the gift. The land promised to them was only a pale shadow of the far more wonderful gift we have been given in Christ (cf. Heb. 4:6-11). But before we can receive this gift in its fullness, God invites us to an act of faith: Will you trust me? Will you surrender your life fully to me and believe in my word more than in the conclusions you draw from your human reasoning and the daily challenges you face? This is the decision of faith in Christ that accompanies baptism and must be renewed daily. The Israelites, within sight of their goal, got cold feet, afraid that God would abandon them. They even professed they would rather return to slavery than receive God's promise! We too can get fearful and want to "return to Egypt" — to living apart from Christ and pursuing the false gods that this world tells us will bring happiness and security. But God calls us out of our comfort zones and into deeper faith. He also calls us to battle — not against human enemies but against the "powers and principalities," the evil spirits that would deceive us into seeking life on our own terms. He promises us that he will protect, guide, and lead us to victory if we trust in him. Those who dodge the battle will miss out on the victory!

The homilist could conclude by inviting his listeners to make a renewed act of faith in the Lord, especially as they are about to receive him in the Eucharist: "Jesus, my King, I believe in you, I trust you, and I will follow wherever you lead. I set my hand to the plow and will not turn back. Even when I feel like a grasshopper in the face of the struggles and temptations in my life, I will remember that 'he who is in me is greater than he who is in the world' (cf. 1 John 4:4). Jesus, give me victory in the spiritual battle this week. Bring your promises to fulfillment in my life!" As we take up the call to discipleship with radical fidelity, we will begin to experience the freedom, peace, joy, and fullness of life that God intends for his children (cf. Gal. 5:22-23; John 15:8).

This is, of course, only one way of explicating the spiritual sense of Numbers 13–14, but such examples of spiritual interpretation rooted in the New Testament's own reading of the Old Testament need to be offered both in seminary homiletics courses and (in a more restrained way) in Scripture courses. This example illustrates how such interpretation does not eclipse the literal sense, but rather depends on it. It also illustrates the inseparable connection, emphasized by Pope Benedict, between spiritual interpretation and the spiritual life. It goes without saying that this insistence is challenging to contemporary biblical scholarship as well as to preachers. But the recovery of such a deeply Christian perspective is crucial to rediscovering the power of God's word to edify, challenge, convict, and guide the faithful.

Conclusion

Besides the two principles discussed in this article — reverence for Scripture's unique authority and the rediscovery of the spiritual sense — *Verbum*

Domini touches on several other crucial elements to a renewal of biblical preaching, including the following:

- Homilies must be christocentric. "The faithful should be able to perceive clearly that the preacher has a compelling desire to present Christ, who must stand at the centre of every homily" (no. 59).
- Homilies must be primarily kerygmatic, and only secondarily hortatory. "At the dawn of the third millennium not only are there still many peoples who have not come to know the Good News, but also a great many Christians who need to have the word of God once more persuasively proclaimed to them, so that they can concretely experience the power of the Gospel" (no. 96). As Raniero Cantalamessa observes, "Every religion or religious philosophy begins by telling people what they must do to be saved, be it ascetic renunciations or intellectual speculations. Christianity doesn't begin by telling people what they must do, but what God has done for them. Gift comes before duty."[19]
- Preachers "need to be in close and constant contact with the sacred text" (no. 59). That is, they need to develop an intense familiarity with Scripture and an understanding of the "grand narrative" of salvation history. Realistically, this requires years of continuous reading of the Bible, along with regular in-depth study of key portions.
- Preachers must display a profound unity between what they preach and what they live. "The preacher 'should be the first to hear the word of God which he proclaims' since, as Saint Augustine says: 'He is undoubtedly barren who preaches outwardly the word of God without hearing it inwardly'" (no. 59). A homilist who lives under the authority of the word is able to not only teach but model the fact that Scripture contains a divine power enabling one to put into practice that which it teaches.

Already a renewed attention to these principles is helping the Catholic faithful once again to hear God's word "in power and in the Holy Spirit and with full conviction," and *Verbum Domini* promises to give fresh momentum to that renewal.

---

19. Address to Caritas general assembly, May 27, 2011, available at http://www.zenit .org/article-32700?l=english; accessed Oct. 17, 2011. *Fulfilled in Your Hearing* rightly emphasizes this point, urging preachers not to give the impression that their primary goal is to enjoin certain forms of behavior (p. 24). See also *Preaching the Mystery of Faith*, p. 11.

CHAPTER 9

The Word of God and the Textual Pluriformity of the Old Testament

Stephen Ryan, O.P.

This essay considers the question of the original texts of the Old Testament, textual pluriformity, and the doctrine of biblical inspiration. Modern readers of the Old Testament in translation will increasingly in the future be faced with the phenomenon of parallel translations of the same biblical book presenting different forms of the text.[1] These may be long and short forms of the text, as in Jeremiah or Tobit, or divergent Hebrew and Greek forms of the text, as in Daniel or Esther. The pluriform nature of the text of the Old Testament, the theory that a significant portion of the Old Testament has been transmitted in two or three different and irreducible versions, is widely accepted in the field of textual criticism. But this theory raises many questions about the text to be preferred, something that will only increase as new translations choose to present more than one form of the text. I will

---

1. The École Biblique's new translation, *La Bible en ses Traditions/The Bible in Its Traditions,* is described this way: "*The Bible in Its Traditions* will present significant differences between different versions of the text of the Bible in the text itself, rather than in footnotes." From the description at www.bibest.org. Over forty years ago an agreement between the United Bible Societies and the Vatican Secretariat for Promoting Christian Unity allowed for the Book of Esther to be translated twice, based on both the Hebrew and the Greek. See the article "Guiding Principles for Interconfessional Cooperation in Translating the Bible," *The Bible Translator* 19 (1968): 103. The editors of the new Oxford Hebrew Bible, a critical edition of the Hebrew text, intend to print parallel Hebrew texts in some chapters of the Hebrew Bible, and the editors of the new *Biblia Hebraica Quinta* speak of "the earliest attainable form(s) of the text based on the available evidence." From the General Introduction, *Biblia Hebraica Quinta, Fascicle 18: General Introduction and Megilloth* (Stuttgart: Deutsche Bibelgesellschaft, 2004), p. xv.

argue here that the Catholic theological tradition is ideally situated to answer such questions, while maintaining a high and traditional doctrine of biblical inspiration. Catholic scholars such as Adrian Schenker and Maurice Gilbert have in fact already begun to offer a reasoned account of how it is that the Word of God revealed to the Prophets and Apostles is received by the Church in several authentic forms.

I have been thinking about this topic for about twenty years, and wrote my S.T.L. thesis on the texts of the Book of Tobit in 1994. What started me thinking was noting the great difference between the translations of that book in the RSV and the NRSV, the latter being based on Codex Sinaiticus, which is longer by some 1,300 words.[2] Recently Michael Magee has published an excellent article titled "From the Bible to the Lectionary of the Holy Mass: Norms and Principles."[3] It touches on the topic of textual pluriformity, treating the matter from a biblical, liturgical, and canonical perspective in an exemplary way. In the present essay I intend to take a similar approach, focusing more narrowly on textual pluriformity, and to offer further examples and a theoretical perspective, relying on the Church Fathers and on the work of Adrian Schenker.[4] Schenker's contribution to this question is particularly valuable in that it is both theologically informed and fully cognizant of the emerging picture of the origins and transmission of the texts of the Old Testament. As such, Schenker's work nicely complements Denis Farkasfalvy's recent book on biblical inspiration, especially the distinction Farkasfalvy makes between inspired authors (subjective inspiration) and inspired texts (objective inspiration).[5]

2. For valuable reflections on the textual pluriformity of the Book of Tobit and on the feasibility of reconstructing an *Urtext* (deemed impossible in this case), see T. Nicklas and C. Wagner, "Thesen zur textlichen Vielfalt im Tobitbuch," *Journal for the Study of Judaism in the Persian, Hellenistic, and Roman Periods* 34 (2003): 141-59.

3. Michael K. Magee, "From the Bible to the Lectionary of the Holy Mass: Norms and Principles," *Notitiae* 47 (2010): 53-64; available online in *Adoremus Bulletin* 16, no. 8 (November 2010).

4. Adrian Schenker is a Swiss Dominican, a former member of the Pontifical Biblical Commission, and the general editor of the *Quinta*, a new edition of the Masoretic text. His work on the plurality of the canonical forms of the Old Testament was cited in the footnotes to the Regensburg Lecture by Pope Benedict XVI, in conjunction with the Holy Father's comments on the importance of the Septuagint. Schenker's most recent book offers a good introduction to his work: *Anfänge der Textgeschichte des Alten Testaments: Studien zu Entstehung und Verhältnis der frühesten Textformen* (Stuttgart: Kohlhammer, 2011).

5. Denis Farkasfalvy, O.Cist., *Inspiration & Interpretation: A Theological Introduction to Sacred Scripture* (Washington, DC: Catholic University of America Press), pp. 54, 61,

Part two of the essay will offer a brief, bird's-eye view of the transmission of the text of the Old Testament as understood in recent research. My intention here is to show that several Old Testament biblical books have been transmitted in whole or in part in more than one literary edition. This is the distinction common in contemporary textual criticism between textual and literary variants.[6] Often it does not seem possible to definitively declare one edition of the text to be earlier or more original. This discussion thus moves beyond the question of individual readings and textual variants properly so-called; and it complicates traditional understandings of an original text. Part three will review Origen's ecclesiological argument on the basis of Divine Providence for the authenticity of the Septuagint. Part four will root this discussion in concrete texts by offering several brief examples of pluriform texts received in the Church. Part five will summarize the topic in the form of several brief theses that are intended to help clarify the arguments and underlying assumptions in this essay.

The Transmission of the Text of the Old Testament

The evidence of the Dead Sea Scrolls has, generally speaking, led to both a heightened appreciation for the fidelity of the transmission of the Hebrew text of the Old Testament, and at the same time, a growing awareness of the textual pluriformity of certain Old Testament books. By textual pluriformity I mean simply that some verses and chapters of Old Testament books have been preserved and transmitted in more than one form, more than one edition.[7] At times we might describe these, for the sake of simplicity, as long

---

238. "Subjective" is not used pejoratively here. Farkasfalvy writes (p. 54, n. 1): "I keep the distinction of 'subjective' vs. 'objective' inspiration as two sides of one salvific action."

6. See the chapter titled "Textual Criticism and Literary Criticism: Glosses and Doublets," in J. Trebolle Barrera, *The Jewish Bible and the Christian Bible: An Introduction to the History of the Bible* (Leiden: Brill and Grand Rapids: Eerdmans, 1998), pp. 390-404.

7. See in general the works of E. Tov (e.g., "The Nature of the Large-Scale Differences between the LXX and MT S T V, Compared with Similar Evidence in Other Sources," in *The Earliest Text of the Hebrew Bible*, ed. Adrian Schenker, Society of Biblical Literature Septuagint and Cognitive Studies 52 [Leiden and Boston: Brill, 2003], pp. 121-43; *Hebrew Bible, Greek Bible, and Qumran: Collected Essays* [Tübingen: Mohr Siebeck, 2008], pp. 155-70) and E. Ulrich (e.g., "Double Literary Editions of Biblical Narratives and Reflections on Determining the Form to Be Translated," in *The Dead Sea Scrolls and the Origins of the Bible,* ed. E. Ulrich, Studies in the Dead Sea Scrolls and Related Literature [Leiden: Brill and Grand Rapids: Eerdmans, 1999], pp. 34-50).

and short forms of a book. The Book of Tobit is a case in point. The King James and the Revised Standard Version follow the short form of the Greek text (GI), considering it to be the earlier text. Recent translations, such as the New American Bible, in both its original and revised (New American Bible Revised Edition [NABRE]) editions, and the New Revised Standard Version, follow the Greek text of Sinaiticus (GII), which is longer by some 1,300 words. These newer translations maintain correctly, and partly on the basis of new evidence from Qumran, that the longer form is a closer approximation of the original Aramaic or Hebrew form of the book.

When the evidence suggests that multiple literary editions of a given book have been transmitted, it is sometimes hard to determine which edition is chronologically prior. Consider the Book of the Prophet Jeremiah. It seems that we have both a shorter form of the book, as witnessed by the Old Greek and Vetus Latina, and a longer form preserved in the Masoretic text and the Vulgate. I hold with the majority that view the shorter text, that found in the Greek, to represent, in general, an earlier form of the book, one closer to the Prophet Jeremiah and his circle of disciples. The longer form of the book, the one preserved in the Masoretic text, would then represent a later edition of the text. This view is of course contested, and some major recent commentaries argue for the priority of the Hebrew text.[8] Almost all modern translations are based on this later and longer form of the book, even if the editors indicate that the Greek text is a witness to an earlier Hebrew form of the book.

Given the teaching of *Divino afflante Spiritu* (DAS) that scholars should "explain the original text which, having been written by the inspired author himself, has more authority and greater weight than even the very best translation, whether ancient or modern" (DAS 16),[9] one might well wonder whether the ancient translations such as the Septuagint, the Vulgate, and the Peshitta have any place in the life of the contemporary Church. I will argue here that they do, and suggest how this might be realized in practice. In short, what I argue is that the Church does not choose one textual form

8. I would note here the commentaries by Lundbom (Anchor Bible) and Fischer (Herders theologischer Kommentar zum Alten Testament), which hold (on dubious grounds) for the priority of the longer Hebrew text.

9. The translation is that published on the Vatican website. The Latin text of DAS 16, which speaks of the sacred author instead of the inspired author (the French has "l'auteur sacré"), reads: "Eadem igitur ratione primigenium illum textum explanari oportet, qui ab ipso sacro auctore conscriptus maiorem auctoritatem maiusque pondus habet, quam quaelibet, utut optima, sive antiqua sive recentior conversio."

of the Old Testament over and against others, but has historically accepted several authentic witnesses to the books of the Old Testament, to the written Word of God. As the Praenotanda of the Nova Vulgata says of the Book of Esther, "Liber Esther in Ecclesia legitur secundum duas formas canonicas."[10]

The essentially pluriform nature of the Bible is enshrined visually in the great polyglot Bibles, a point made by the Spanish textual critic N. Fernández Marcos, who writes: "The procedure adopted by the Polyglot Bibles has something to teach us today: to edit the different ancient texts that circulated among the distinct communities and which constitute sensu pleno the Books, ta biblia."[11]

While my remarks are focused on the Old Testament, analogies with the transmission of the New Testament can be made. Pope Benedict's 2010 Christmas homily at Midnight Mass, for example, made reference to two divergent forms of the angelic salutation in Luke 2:14, "peace to men of good will" according to the Latin and "peace among men with whom he is pleased" according to the Greek. "But which is the correct translation?" the Holy Father asked. He concluded that the Church must not choose one over the other, but rather "we must read both texts together; only in this way do we truly understand the angels' song."[12]

Origen's Ecclesiological Argument

Adrian Schenker has articulated a theological vision of the place of the Septuagint in the Church that can both account for its importance in Christian history, and at the same time, provide a rationale for modern Catholic translations to be based on the original languages of composition. Schenker's article, "Septuaginta und christliche Bibel,"[13] offers a description of Origen's

10. "The book of Esther is read in the Church in two canonical forms." *Nova Vulgata Biblia Sacrorum, editio typica altera* (Vatican City: Libreria Editrice Vaticana, 1986), p. xvii. For this reference I am indebted to Magee, "From the Bible to the Lectionary of the Holy Mass," p. 64.

11. F. Marcos, "The Use of the Septuagint in the Criticism of the Hebrew Bible," *Sefarad* 47 (1987): 59-72.

12. Homily of His Holiness Benedict XVI, Saint Peter's Basilica, Friday, 24 December 2010, cited from the Vatican website. In context the Holy Father refers not precisely to two forms of the text, but to the realities they mediate, those of divine grace and human freedom. It is these two that must be held together.

13. A. Schenker, "Septuaginta und christliche Bibel," *Theologische Revue* 91 (1995): 459-64.

ecclesiological argument that the churches that used the Septuagint had access thereby to the authentic Word of God, access provided by God in his Divine Providence. Origen's thinking on this topic is most clearly expressed in his response to Julius Africanus, who had doubts that the story of Susanna is a translation from Hebrew or Aramaic, and thus wondered if it is an authentic part of the Book of Daniel. Origen's Letter to Africanus 8 reads, in part:

> And indeed, when we notice such things, are we then to suppress the copies in use in the churches, and to order the community to reject the sacred books in use among them? . . . Are we to suppose that Providence (Πρόνοια) which has given in the Sacred Scriptures edification for all the churches of Christ, had no thought for those bought with a price (1 Cor. 6:20; 7:23), for whom Christ died (Rom. 14:15); whom, although his Son, God who is love (1 John 4:9-16) spared not, but gave him up for us all, that with him he might freely give us all things (Rom. 8:32)? In this case consider whether it would not be well to remember the words, "You shall not remove the ancient landmarks which your predecessors have set" (Deut. 19:14).[14]

From the beginning of the Church to Origen's own day there had been authentic Christian churches that had no access to the Hebrew Bible, but used only the Greek Scriptures.[15] For Origen it was unthinkable that God would have established Christian churches without giving them access at the same time to the Word of God in an authentic form. Hearing the Word of God in the Scriptures is a constitutive element of the Church.

Pierre Benoit and Dominique Barthélemy have seen in this passage a

---

14. Origen, *La Lettre à Africanus sur l'Histoire de Suzanne,* Sources Chrétiennes 302, ed. Nicholas de Lange (Paris: Cerf, 1983), p. 532.

15. In this section I will be summarizing Schenker's article "L'Ecriture sainte subsiste en plusieurs formes canoniques simultanées," in *L'interpretazione della Bibbia nella Chiesa. Atti del Simposio promosso dalla Congregazione per la Dottrina della Fede* (Vatican City, 2001), pp. 178-86 (the article cited by Pope Benedict in notes to his Regensburg Lecture; see note 9), and the revised and expanded German form of that article, "Die Heilige Schrift subsistiert gleichzeitig in mehreren kanonischen Formen," in *Studien zu Propheten und Religionsgeschichte,* ed. A. Schenker (Stuttgart: Katholisches Bibelwerk, 2003), pp. 192-200. Schenker's most recent discussion of this topic is found in A. Schenker, "L'apport durable des Hexaples d'Origène. Bilan de la Lettre à Africanus, bilan aujourd'hui," in *Eukarpa, Études sur la Bible et ses exégètes, en hommage à Gilles Dorival,* ed. M. Loubet and D. Pralon (Paris: Cerf, 2011), pp. 385-94.

very important patristic witness to the belief that the Septuagint used in the churches was an authentic form of the Bible given by God in his divine providence.[16] This argument for the Septuagint is not one based on usage and tradition alone. It is an ecclesiological argument touching on questions of God's providence and the ecclesiological authenticity of the early Greek-speaking churches. It differs then from the argument for the Septuagint developed by Mogens Müller in his 1996 book, *The First Bible of the Church: A Plea for the Septuagint.*[17] Müller's argument is largely based on tradition, centering on the notion that the Septuagint was often used by the writers of the New Testament and widely used in the early church.

Schenker's 2003 article, titled "Holy Scripture Exists Simultaneously in Several Canonical Forms," notes that in discussing the canon of Scripture one can refer not only to lists of books but also to the question of the textual form of individual books.[18] As examples of the latter he cites passages from each of the four parts of the Old Testament in which the Hebrew and Greek witnesses reveal divergent textual forms of certain sections of biblical books; in other words, sections of the Bible where we have two literary editions of a biblical book. Schenker then cites Origen, Augustine, and Jerome and

---

16. Origen's argument from providence for the status of the Septuagint as the authentic Word of God in its own right was noted already by Paul Wendland in 1900: "Zur ältesten Geschichte der Bibel in der Kirche," *Zeitschrift für die Neutestamentliche Wissenschaft* 1 (1900): 267-90, esp. 273-74. Pierre Benoit discussed the argument in the 1950s and 1960s, and it was treated more extensively by Dominique Barthélemy. See Barthélemy: "L'Ancien Testament a mûri à Alexandrie," *Theologische Zeischrift* 21 (1965): 358-70; D. Barthélemy, *Études d'histoire du texte de l'Ancien Testament,* Orbis biblicus et orientalis 21 (Fribourg: Éditions Universitaires, 1978), pp. 127-39; "La place de la Septante dans l'Église," in *Aux grands carrefours de la révélation et de l'exégèse de l'Ancien Testament* (Paris: De Brouwer, 1967), pp. 13-28 = Barthélemy, *Études d'histoire du texte de l'Ancien Testament,* pp. 111-26. A helpful recent discussion of Origen's argument, with bibliography, is found in J. N. B. Paget, "The Christian Exegesis of the Old Testament in the Alexandrian Tradition," in M. Sæbø, *Hebrew Bible /Old Testament,* vol. 1: *From the Beginnings to the Middle Ages (Until 1300)* (Göttingen: Vandenhoeck & Ruprecht, 1996), I/1, p. 506.

17. M. Müller, *The First Bible of the Church: A Plea for the Septuagint,* Journal for the Study of the Old Testament: Supplement 206 (Sheffield: Sheffield Academic, 1996). His most recent contribution provides a useful summary of his position, with a focus on canonical interpretation: "Die Septuaginta als Teil des christlichen Kanons," in *Die Septuaginta — Texte, Kontexte, Lebenswelten,* pp. 708-27. A recent Festschrift in Müller's honor contains several contributions relating to this topic: *Kanon: Bibelens tilblivelse og normative status: Festskrift til Mogens Müller,* ed. N. P. Lemche et al. (Copenhagen: Museum Tusculanum, 2006).

18. Schenker, "Die Heilige Schrift subsistiert," p. 192.

argues that in the thought of these patristic authors the Sacred Scriptures subsist simultaneously in several canonical forms.[19]

With regard to Augustine, Schenker argues that though Augustine knows and cites the legend of the divine inspiration of the Septuagint translators, he does so against the background of a belief similar to Origen's about the providential nature of the Greek Scriptures used in the Church. Augustine does not base his notion of the authority of the Septuagint ultimately on the Letter of Aristeas, but rather on the Apostles, who cite the prophetic witness of both the Septuagint and the Hebrew.[20] Under the influence of Jerome, Augustine argued that the Hebrew original was also the true Word of God for the Church, and not merely a text to be used in polemics with the Jewish community. In this way he developed a notion of the textual plurality of the Bible that is true to what we now know about the complex realities of the transmission of the biblical text. At times it is the Hebrew text that witnesses to the earliest form, what might be called the original text, and at times it is the Septuagint or the Vetus Latina. The Church uses them all.

Jerome too recognizes the textual plurality of the Old Testament. Schenker notes Jerome's practice of citing and commenting on both the Hebrew and Greek texts of the Old Testament in his biblical commentaries.[21] For Jerome it is largely apostolic precedent and Church usage that give both the Hebrew and the Greek texts a place in the life of the Church. For Origen, Augustine, and Jerome, the use of the Greek and Hebrew forms of the Old Testament by Jesus, the Apostles, and the early churches is normative. Origen's deeper insight is that the hearing of the Word of God is a constitutive element of any church and that in the Septuagint the early churches, through God's providence, had access to the Word of God in an authentic form.

Schenker raises the question about the canonicity of other early transla-

---

19. Dirk Kurt Kranz has published a book (*Ist die griechische Übersetzung der Heiligen Schrift der LXX inspiriert?* Studi e ricerche 3 [Rome: Ateneo Pontificio Regina Apostolorum, 2005]) and three articles on the topic of patristic attitudes toward the Septuagint and the contemporary discussion of the inspiration of the Septuagint.

20. Augustine, *De civitate Dei* XVIII 44 (Corpus Christianorum: Series Latina 48:641): "Wherefore I, too, in my small measure follow in the footsteps of the apostles who themselves quoted prophetic testimonies from the Hebrew and from the Septuagint alike, and have concluded that both ought to be treated as authorities, since both the one and the other are divine and form a unity."

21. Schenker ("Septuaginta und christliche Bibel," p. 461) writes: "Vergessen wir nicht: In allen seinen Bibelkommentaren bietet Hieronymus stets zwei Lemmata, zuerst die Übersetzung des hebr. Textes, dann jene der LXX. Warum? Weil er auch hier Origenes folgt: die LXX ist die Bibel der Kirche."

tions such as the Peshitta, the Vulgate, the Ethiopic, Coptic, and Armenian. He suggests that Origen's ecclesiological principle also applies to these translations, that is, that in these translations these early churches had access to the authentic Word of God. By this he means a form of the Bible in which the Word of God is truly transmitted, even if many nuances of the biblical text in its original languages may have been lost.[22] Following Origen's principle, one can extend the quality of canonicity to the translations of the other early churches who knew the Word of God in the daughter versions of the Septuagint or in the Vulgate. As the pioneering Catholic biblical scholar Richard Simon wrote in 1699 of the ancient biblical versions: "The Roman Church receives all of these nations with their Bibles."[23]

In fact, Simon was merely summarizing the positions of the Council of Trent and of Robert Bellarmine. Trent's famous decree *Insuper* of the fourth session, April 8, 1546, dealing with the authenticity of the Vulgate, designated one of the many Latin biblical texts in use at the time as authentic for public use.[24] This version, and no other Latin version, was to be used in

22. Origen at times recognizes that a reading in the Hebrew is correct but goes on to offer a commentary on both the correct text and the text read in the churches, arguing that the secondary readings are the work of providence. On this practice, see Paget, "The Christian Exegesis of the Old Testament in the Alexandrian Tradition," p. 506, and M. Harl, "La Septante et la Pluralité textuelle des Écritures: Le Témoignage des Pères Grecs," in *Naissance de la Méthode critique* (Paris: Cerf, 1992), pp. 231-43; M. Harl, *La langue de Japhet. Quinze études sur la Septante et le grec des chrétiens* (Paris: Cerf, 1992), pp. 253-66. Harl shows that the Fathers, who were largely preachers and teachers, were well aware of textual diversity and errors in the texts of the Bible, but generally welcomed any reading that could be used to advance the Gospel, whether it was an original reading or clearly secondary.

23. "L'Eglise Romaine reçoit toutes ces nations avec leurs Bibles." R. Simon, *Réponse au livre intitulé Défense des Sentiments de quelques Théologiens de Hollande sur l'Histoire Critique du Vieux Testament* (Rotterdam: Reinier Leers, 1699), as quoted in D. Barthélemy, "L'enchevêtrement de l'histoire textuelle et de l'histoire littéraire dans les relations entre la Septante et le texte massorétique," in *De Septuaginta: Studies in Honor of John William Wevers on His Sixty-fifth Birthday,* ed. A. Pietersma and C. Cox (Mississauga, ON: Benben Publications, 1984), p. 37.

24. I rely heavily in what follows on the article by J. M. Vosté, "The Vulgate at the Council of Trent," *Catholic Biblical Quarterly* 9 (1947): 9-25. The relevant section of the decree of April 8, 1546, reads: "[N]ot a little advantage will accrue to the Church of God if it be made known which of all the Latin editions of the sacred books now in circulation is to be regarded as authentic (pro authentica habenda), [the same holy council] ordains and declares that the old Latin Vulgate (vetus et Vulgata) edition, which, in use for so many hundred years, has been approved by the Church, be in public lectures, disputations, sermons and expositions held as authentic (pro authentica habeature), and that no one dare or presume under any pretext whatsoever to reject it."

public reading. This was a great practical service to local churches in the West. It was intended to assure the faithful that the Vulgate, though a translation, is truly a Bible, the Word of God guaranteed by the Church. In using this Bible the Church will not be led astray.

Trent decreed that the Latin Vulgate, with all its parts *(integros cum omnibus suis partibus),* is sacred and canonical *(sacris et canonicis),* and therefore "authentic" *(authentica).* When used in public lectures, disputations, sermons, and expositions, it is so to be held. The term "authentic" here means "authoritative in the public sphere of the Church."[25]

As Dominique Barthélemy has argued, when the Church recognized the authenticity of the Vulgate for the Latin Church, it in no way declared previous forms of the Bible, or the Bibles in circulation in the other churches, to be inauthentic. It was rather a recognition of one particular form without prejudice to others. The limits of the juridical authority or authenticity of the Vulgate were clearly defined in Pope Pius XII's encyclical *Divino afflante Spiritu,* which affirmed that the Vulgate, while "free from any error whatsoever in matters of faith and morals," has an authority based primarily on its long-continued use, not for scientific reasons. The special authority, or

> authenticity of the Vulgate was not affirmed by the Council [of Trent] particularly for critical reasons, but rather because of its legitimate use in the Churches throughout so many centuries . . . and so its authenticity is not specified primarily as critical, but rather as juridical. (DAS 21)[26]

In the practical order this means that matters of doctrine in the Latin Church should be determined not only on the basis of the Vulgate, but also with recourse to "the original texts." The scope of the decree is limited to the Latin Church, and it is juridical and disciplinary in character. That it is not a dogmatic decree can be seen in the language it uses. It speaks neither of teaching nor of defining, but rather commands *(statuit et declarat).* It was

25. A. Dulles comments on the sense of the Latin word *authentica* in a different context, that of the "authentic interpretation" mentioned in *Dei verbum* 10, in his article "Vatican II on the Interpretation of Scripture," *Letter & Spirit* 2 (2006): 23-24. There Dulles indicates that the word means authoritative rather than genuine. For an important discussion of the various meanings of "authentic" in Church documents relating to the Vulgate, see K. Raedy, "What Happened to the Vulgate? An Analysis of *Divino afflante Spiritu* and *Dei verbum,*" *Nova et Vetera* 11 (2013): 123-46, esp. 124-29.

26. The Latin text of DAS reads: "atque adeo eiusmodi authentia non primario nomine critica, sed iuridica potius vocatur." Both the Latin and the English translation cited here are taken from the Vatican website.

not intended in any way to detract from the Hebrew, Aramaic, and Greek texts, which continue to be recognized as the privileged original languages of Scripture. It rather commands the sole use of one recognized translation for public occasions.

In declaring the Vulgate authentic and authoritative, the Council did not base its action on an assertion that its text was identical to the original texts. The council fathers knew that it was not, even if it represented the original in a substantial manner. Trent appealed rather to its continuous use for centuries in the Church, which is guided by the Holy Spirit. To say that for centuries the Western Church had been deprived of the authentic Word of God would, Vosté argues, "be equivalent to denying the infallibility of the Church, and to depriving its doctrinal teaching of the assistance of the Holy Spirit."[27]

The Second Vatican Council's Constitution on Divine Revelation, *Dei verbum* 22, speaks of honoring the ancient translations in the context of making the Word of God accessible to the faithful in translations based on the original texts:

> Easy access to Sacred Scripture should be provided for all the Christian faithful. That is why the Church from the very beginning accepted as her own that very ancient Greek translation of the Old Testament which is called the Septuagint; and she has always given a place of honor to other Eastern translations and Latin ones especially the Latin translation known as the Vulgate. But since the word of God should be accessible at all times, the Church by her authority and with maternal concern sees to it that suitable and correct translations are made into different languages, especially from the original texts of the sacred books.[28]

The 2001 instruction of the Vatican's Congregation for Divine Worship titled *Liturgiam authenticam* suggests a similar concern for honoring the ancient biblical versions when preparing liturgical translations:

> [O]ther ancient versions of the Sacred Scriptures should also be consulted, such as the Greek version of the Old Testament commonly known as the "Septuagint," which has been used by the Christian faithful from the earliest days of the Church. . . . Finally, translators are strongly encouraged to pay close attention to the history of interpretation that may

---

27. Vosté, "The Vulgate," p. 19.
28. Translation from the Vatican website.

be drawn from citations of biblical texts in the writings of the Fathers of the Church. . . .[29]

Schenker has spoken of the status of the Septuagint in terms of inspiration only rarely, though this language has been used by Catholic authors.[30] He tends to follow the language of Trent and that used by Dominique Barthélemy in speaking about "authentic" texts of Scripture. It is not possible to enter into the complicated theological questions of canonicity and inspiration here, but a few observations may help to set Schenker's contribution in a larger context. Both Conleth Kearns and Maurice Gilbert have argued that both the Hebrew and the Greek forms of Sirach are to be considered canonical and inspired.[31] In words that could serve as a summary of part

29. *Liturgiam authenticam* 41, cited from the Vatican website. Helpful remarks on this document are found in the article cited above by Magee, "From the Bible to the Lectionary of the Holy Mass," and in Dieter Böhler, S.J., "Some Remarks from an Exegete on the Instruction Liturgiam authenticam," *Antiphon* 8, no. 2 (2003): 2-11. One of the practical effects of this line of thinking about the importance and dignity of the Septuagint is the tendency, noticeable in the work of James Sanders, Dominique Barthélemy, and Adrian Schenker, and thus in the new *Biblia Hebraica Quinta,* to preserve the distinctive Hebrew and Greek textual traditions and to avoid mixing the two into a tertium quid. This is in marked contrast to the approach of the editors of the forthcoming Oxford Hebrew Bible (on which see the article by Williamson, "Do We Need a New Bible? Reflections on the Proposed Oxford Hebrew Bible," *Biblica* 90 [2009]: 153-75, and J. Sanders, "The Hebrew University Bible and Biblia Hebraica Quinta," *Journal of Biblical Literature* 118 [1999]: 518-26).

30. A. Schenker, *Das Neue am neuen Bund und das Alte am alten: Jer 31 in der hebräischen und griechischen Bibel, von der Textgeschichte zu Theologie, Synagoge und Kirche,* Forschungen zur Religion und Literatur des Alten und Neuen Testaments 212 (Göttingen: Vandenhoeck & Ruprecht, 2006), p. 94. Pierre-Maurice Bogaert has argued that is impossible to speak of biblical inspiration in a Christian sense without including the Septuagint. See his article "Les études sur la Septante: Bilan et perspectives," *Revue théologique de Louvain* 16 (1985): 174-200, esp. 195, n. 96. Another work by the same author that is also of interest in this regard is "La Septante, passage obligé entre l'exégèse biblique et les autres disciplines de la théologie," *Revue de l'Institut catholique de Paris* 29 (1989): 63-78. Bogaert's studies are among those surveyed by C. Perrot, "L'Inspiration des Septante et le Pouvoir scripturaire," in *Kata Tous O', Selon les Septante: Trente études sur la Bible grecque des Septante, en hommage à Marguerite Harl* (Paris: Cerf, 1995), pp. 169-83.

31. Conleth Kearns, *The Expanded Text of Ecclesiasticus: Its Teaching on the Future Life as a Clue to Its Origin,* ed. P. C. Beentjes, Deuterocanonical and Cognate Literature Series 11 (Berlin: De Gruyter, 2011), pp. 302-10. Kearns treats the question of inspiration in an appendix titled "The Divine Inspiration of the Added Passages," in which he argues that many of the secondary glosses enjoy inspiration. This is a recent edition of a dissertation defended (successfully) before the Pontifical Biblical Commission in 1951 (!). Kearns's commentaries on Sirach in the *Catholic Commentary on Holy Scripture* and the *New Catholic Commentary*

of the argument advanced in this essay, the German Jesuit Dieter Böhler writes:

> Since the Church has always included books in the Canon rather than particular versions of them, both versions are, in principle, authentic editions of the canonical book. When Jerome, on Pope Damasus' instructions, was preparing a uniform Latin version of the Bible, he departed from this four-hundred-year-old practice of the whole Church and went back to the proto-Masoretic text. And so, despite Augustine's initial objection, yet another tradition of the biblical text was recognized and accepted as inspired. Augustine holds, like the Evangelists before him, that both traditions of the text are inspired and canonical. And so too does the Catholic Church.[32]

Just as the Church preserved four Gospels and not one, so, analogously, with regard to the biblical canon as a whole. The tradition seems quite at home with a plurality of witness to the Word of God. St. Leo the Great, in the preface to the Moralia on Job, describes his use of both the Vetus Latina and the new translation — the Vulgate, in these words:

> I base my discussion on the new translation, but when the need to prove something demands it, I take sometimes the new, sometimes the old as witnesses; because the Apostolic See, over which I preside by God's design, uses both, and also the labor of my study is supported by both.

Schenker's approach to biblical canonicity and inspiration outlined above seems consonant with this tradition of irreducible plurality. Maurice Gilbert

---

on Holy Scripture give a synopsis of his ideas about the canonicity and inspiration of the longer form of the book. See also M. Gilbert, "L'Ecclésiastique: Quel texte? Quelle autorité?" *Revue biblique* 94 (1987): 233-50. Gilbert contends that both the long and short forms of the text are canonical and inspired. L. Hartman ("Sirach in Hebrew and Greek," *Catholic Biblical Quarterly* 23 [1961]: 444) seems to take a different view when he says that "the only 'inspired' text as such is the original manuscript of the inspired author." But Hartman also argues that translations share in inspiration in as far as they reproduce what the original, inspired author wrote. At times Hartman speaks of canonicity, at times of inspiration, and the two related concepts are often difficult to delineate. Hartman seems elsewhere to share the general Catholic tradition of speaking of inspired authors rather than inspired texts. The topic of biblical inspiration, long neglected by biblical scholars and theologians, has recently received new attention. Outstanding in this regard are Farkasfalvy, *Inspiration & Interpretation,* and the entire sixth volume of *Letter & Spirit* (2010).

32. Böhler, "Some Remarks from an Exegete," p. 4.

estimates that some 30 percent of the Catholic Old Testament is found in two or three different, irreducible versions.[33] This presents a problem for Christian traditions that place undue emphasis on the inspiration of only a single original text, something that seems increasingly to recede from view as we learn more about the history of the transmission of the Old Testament.

Unlike the ancient and medieval churches, all contemporary churches have access to the Hebrew, Aramaic, and Greek texts of the Bible through the work of competent scholars who can read, interpret, and translate these texts. The function of translations is thus in one sense more limited in the modern period. They do not have the dignity and honor of the ancient Oriental translations that were used for centuries by the churches as their sole access to the Word of God. Nor are translations the only source from which the vast majority of contemporary churches can know the Word of God in an authentic form. Nonetheless, as Vosté argues, in that these modern translations are made from the original languages, they are preferable to translations made from the Vulgate.[34] Insofar as they represent the original texts, they share, by analogy and to a lesser degree, in the canonicity, inspiration, authority, and authenticity of the original texts. In the conclusion I will suggest ways that the ancient versions can and should play a role in the contemporary Church, even if preference is to be given for liturgical and ecclesial use to translations made from the original languages.[35]

Examples of the Pluriform Nature of the Old Testament

In this section I will briefly present five examples designed to illustrate the issues raised above. These are intended to complement the examples of textual variants offered by Denis Farkasfalvy, and so will include both textual and literary variants.[36]

---

33. Olivier-Thomas Venard, "La Bible en ses Traditions: The new project of the École biblique et archéologique française de Jérusalem presented as a 'fourth generation' enterprise," *Nova et Vetera* 4 (2006): 142-58, here 149. See also, in general, M. Gilbert, "Textes exclus, textes inclus: Les enjeux," in *L'autorité de l'Écriture,* ed. Jean-Michel Poffet (Paris: Cerf, 2002), pp. 51-70, and "L'Ecclésiastique: Quel texte? Quelle autorité?" in *L'autorité de l'Écriture.*

34. Vosté, "The Vulgate," p. 24.

35. K. Raedy, "What Happened to the Vulgate?" pp. 145-46, offers helpful comments about roles the Vulgate could play in contemporary biblical translation and annotation.

36. Farkasfalvy, *Inspiration & Interpretation,* pp. 142-44.

Pentateuch: Genesis 3:15 — The Protoevangelium
"She shall crush your head"

In Genesis 3:15 God addresses the serpent and foretells not only conflict between the offspring of Eve and the serpent, but victory over the serpent (or the devil) as well. The *Catechism of the Catholic Church* (410) teaches that the verse heralds the coming victory over evil and man's restoration from his fall. In this text we find "the first announcement of the Messiah and Redeemer, of a battle between the serpent and the Woman, and of the final victory of a descendant of hers" (410). There are three traditional Christian interpretations of this famous passage: a christological interpretation, depending largely on the Hebrew and Greek texts, and ecclesiological and mariological interpretations, which depend largely on the Vulgate.[37]

Let's begin with the Hebrew text: "Enmity I will put between you and the woman, between your seed (masculine noun) and her seed, he (or they) will strike your head and you will strike his (or their) heel." The Hebrew Masoretic text of 3:15c thus reads: "He (seed is a masculine singular/collective noun) will strike your head." The NABRE translation, "They will strike at your head, while you strike at their heel," uses the plural to render the sense of the collective seed.[38] The "he" of the Hebrew text has been understood to refer to Christ and his victory over Satan.

The Greek text of 3:15c reads: "He will watch your head." As Scott Hahn and Curtis Mitch have noted, this earliest Jewish interpretation of the Hebrew text "takes the offspring of the woman to be an individual man."[39] The Greek might have been expected to have said "it" rather than "he," since Greek *sperma,* seed, is neuter. Its lexical choice of "he" helped the Greek

---

37. The *Catechism of the Catholic Church* (411) mentions the christological and mariological interpretations: "The Christian tradition sees in this passage an announcement of the 'New Adam' who, because he 'became obedient unto death, even death on a cross,' makes amends superabundantly for the disobedience of Adam. Furthermore, many Fathers and Doctors of the Church have seen the woman announced in the Protoevangelium as Mary, the mother of Christ, the 'new Eve.' Mary benefited first of all and uniquely from Christ's victory over sin: she was preserved from all stain of original sin and by a special grace of God committed no sin of any kind during her whole earthly life."

38. Comparing the texts and notes of the NAB and NABRE on this verse is interesting. The NABRE note retains much of the original note but adds to it as well, citing evidence of the Church Fathers in a fuller way and explaining the Vulgate reading that is the basis of the mariological interpretation, something the original note does not do.

39. S. Hahn and C. Mitch, *Genesis: The Ignatius Study Bible* (San Francisco: Ignatius, 2010), p. 23.

Fathers also to see a reference to Christ's victory over sin and death in this verse. The use of the Greek verb τηρέω, which can mean "to watch (so as to attack at an opportune moment)," led some Greek Fathers to see here a reference to the Devil watching Jesus, testing him so as to see his true identity.[40] The Old Latin translation follows the Greek and reads: "He will strike your head." The NABRE notes that Irenaeus of Lyon and several other Fathers interpreted the verse as referring to Christ.

The Vulgate text reads: "She *(ipsa)* shall crush your head." This reading in the Vulgate seems to stem from St. Ambrose, who appears to have gotten it from Philo. Both Ambrose and Philo understood the "she" referred to as Eve, but Christians have often seen a mariological reference here. Mary, through her Son, will crush evil and win a great victory for humanity.

In 1909 the Biblical Commission referred to this verse as a Reparatoris futuri promissio (June 30, 1909, EnchB 3.38). *Ineffabilis Deus* (1854) of Blessed Pius IX, which defined the Immaculate Conception, and *Munificentissimus Deus* (1950; "as foretold in the protoevangelium") of Pius XII, which defined the Assumption, both make use of these christological and mariological interpretations of Genesis 3:15.[41]

The Nova Vulgata departs from the Vulgate in this verse and follows the Masoretic text: "Inimicitias ponam inter te et mulierem et semen tuum et semen illius; ipsum conteret caput tuum, et tu conteres calcaneum eius" (I will put enmities between you and the woman and your seed and her seed; it will crush your head and you will bruise his heel). Dieter Böhler, S.J., comments on the significance of this change: "And so the reading for the Feast of the Immaculate Conception loses a textual variant that was not insignificant for the liturgical choice of the reading. But it would have been arbitrary, from the point of view of scholarly text criticism, to have departed from the Masoretic text on just this one point. The *Nova Vulgata* itself at times has to sacrifice variant readings that have been important in the history of liturgy."[42] I will return to the Nova Vulgata and its authority toward the end of the essay.

This first example shows how small variations between the received Hebrew, Greek, and Latin texts have helped shape traditions of interpretation

40. T. Muracka, *A Greek-English Lexicon of the Septuagint* (Leuven/Paris/Walpole, MA: Peeters, 2009), p. 678. I am grateful to Father Eugen Pentiuc for his comments on the texts and patristic interpretation of Genesis 3:15.

41. See W. Wilfall, "Gen. 3:15: A Protevangelium?" *Catholic Biblical Quarterly* 36 (1974): 361-65.

42. See Böhler, "Some Remarks from an Exegete."

and theological tradition. In order to correctly understand patristic commentary and preaching on this verse it would seem necessary for seminary students to know that the Fathers were basing their comments on authentic texts of Scripture, not textual errors or spurious translations. Even if current English translations have readings based on differing canonical forms of the text, this does not mean that patristic interpretation of a differing text is rendered obsolete or invalid. The written Word of God in Scripture is not limited to one canonical form.

Prophets: Jeremiah 1:6 "A, a, a, Domine Deus"

The prophet Jeremiah's response to the theophany recorded in Jeremiah 1:6 begins with the short Hebrew interjection: "Ah, Lord God!" (NABRE), an expression of the awe or fear that the prophet experienced before the Lord. This awe is captured famously in the Vulgate's stammering: "A, a, a, (Domine Deus)." The Septuagint reads quite differently: ὁ ὤν (δέσποτα κύριε), "You That Are, (Sovereign, Lord)" (New English Translation of the Septuagint).[43] This distinctive Greek text of Jeremiah was seen by the Church Fathers to be an allusion to the divine title revealed to Moses in the Greek text of Exodus 3:14: Ἐγώ εἰμι ὁ ὤν. The phrase ὁ ὤν, qui est, occurs some thirteen times in the New Testament, and has entered into the liturgy of the Orthodox churches, being cited in the opening of the Anaphora of St. Basil the Great. Andrew Louth uses this example in arguing that the Septuagint, having been received by the Orthodox Church in her liturgy, is *the* authoritative text of the Old Testament.[44]

Louth is critical of the *editio minor* of Rahlfs for emending the text of Jeremiah to read the interjection Ὦ, rather than the participle ὤν, thereby giving a reading lacking in Greek manuscripts, but which conforms more closely to the Hebrew. This emendation by Rahlfs is certainly defensible, even if it produces a text that was never received by the Orthodox churches. The Nova Vulgata makes a similar move and departs from the Vulgate, reading "Heu" instead of "A, a, a," a slightly more literal rendition of the Hebrew "Ah."

---

43. A. Pietersma and M. Saunders, "Ieremias," in *A New English Translation of the Septuagint* (New York: Oxford University Press, 2007), p. 881. The LXX.D translation (*Septuaginta Deutsch* [Deutsche Bibelgesellschaft, 2009] 1290) has: "*Seiender, Gebieter,* Herr," which reflects a traditional Orthodox liturgical rendering of this verse.

44. Andrew Louth, "Inspiration of the Scriptures," *Sobornost* (2009): 29-44, here 41, n. 8.

In a recent review article on the Oxford Hebrew Bible project, Hugh Williamson makes an observation about method in textual criticism of the Hebrew Bible that is relevant here:

> In evaluating the evidence, preference should not be afforded against better evidence to the Masoretic Text, the Septuagint, or the Vulgate ... each of which has paramount authority in one religious circle or another.[45]

Williamson is quite correct to maintain that the integrity and autonomy of this field of academic research should be preserved and respected, free from any religiously motivated preferences. But once scholars have established critical editions of the principal biblical versions, important juridical, theological, and pastoral questions remain about the place and use of the various ancient texts of the Old Testament in the life of the Church.[46] The conclusion drawn by Louth, that the Septuagint is the only authoritative form of the Old Testament, while certainly an understandable conclusion from the perspective of Greek Orthodox tradition, is not one that Catholics could accept.

Wisdom Books: Sirach 24:24-25(18) "I am the mother of fair love"

The Douay-Rheims translation of Sirach 24:24-25 reads as follows: "(24) I am the mother of fair love, and of fear, and of knowledge, and of holy hope. (25) In me is all grace of the way and of the truth, in me is all hope of life and of virtue." This is a faithful translation of the standard text found in the Vulgate: "Ego mater pulchrae dilectionis et timoris et agnitionis et sanctae spei. In me gratia omnis viae et veritatis in me omnis spes vitae et virtutis."

Verse 24 is found in the longer Greek text of Sirach known as GII and in the Vetus Latina. Verse 25 is found only in the Latin. Both verses have been transmitted in the Vulgate and retained in the Nova Vulgata, which often follows the Vetus Latina in this book.

Neither of these verses is included in the New American Bible (NAB), though the first, verse 24, in now added in an annotation as Sirach 24:18 in the NABRE. That note reads: "Other ancient authorities read as v. 18: I am

---

45. H. G. M. Williamson, "Do We Need a New Bible? Reflections on the Proposed Oxford Hebrew Bible," *Biblica* 90 (2009): 153-75, here 163.

46. These questions are addressed from a Catholic perspective in a clear and concise way in the article cited above by Magee, "From the Bible to the Lectionary of the Holy Mass."

the mother of fair love, of reverence, of knowledge, and of holy hope; To all my children I give to be everlasting: to those named by Him." The approach to this verse in the NABRE is similar to that taken in Rahlfs's Septuagint, which gives the first verse above (v. 18) in Greek only in the critical apparatus, and omits entirely the following verse, 24:25 of the Vulgate.[47]

This example raises several issues. The first has to do with textual criticism and canonicity. The editors of the NABRE relegate Sirach 24:18 to the footnotes because it is not in the short Greek text, GI, but only in the longer Greek text, GII. This is a defensible position, since the NABRE is a text intended for personal use, not an official liturgical text. The decision to include a translation of the verse in the footnote is to be commended. In the original NAB no such note is to be found, and the existence of the verse is not signaled in any way. Both the NAB and NABRE omit any reference to the following verse, Vulgate 24:25, which is not found in Greek but only in the Vetus Latina. The Irish Dominican Conleth Kearns states that 24:25 "is probably a Christian gloss based on Jn 14:6."[48] This seems plausible, since it is not found in Hebrew or Greek, and the references to the way, the truth, and the life of 24:25 are strongly reminiscent of John 14:6, which reads, in part, "ego sum via et veritas et vita." Kearns contends, however, that this verse and many of the texts in the longer form of Sirach are sacred and canonical, and may be considered inspired glosses. He uses a series of arguments to develop this point, including the decrees of Trent and decrees of the Pontifical Biblical Commission from the early decades of the twentieth century with regard to glosses to the Pentateuch made posterior to the time of Moses, liturgical usage, and patristic usage.[49] His conclusion, in his own words, is that "the additions of Sir. II represented in Lat, can be regarded as sacred and canonical."[50] In the Vulgate, verses 24 and 25 of Sirach 24 match this description, since both are found in Latin. For texts found *only* in the expanded Greek text (GII) or *only* in the Syriac text, Kearns concludes that "the arguments

<hr/>

47. The New English Translation of the Septuagint includes the first of these two verses (Vg. v. 24) as verse 18, placing it in brackets and italics, but omits the second entirely. The Septuaginta Deutsch is similar, using inset spacing and a vertical line rather than brackets and italics to mark the first verse as secondary and omitting the second.

48. Kearns, *The Expanded Text,* p. 174.

49. Kearns, *The Expanded Text,* pp. 303-10.

50. Kearns, *The Expanded Text,* p. 306. Sir II refers to the revised and enlarged text of Sirach that is attested to by texts preserved largely in Greek, Syriac, and Latin. LA refers to the Vetus Latina. For these terms, see the introductory essay by Maurice Gilbert, S.J., in Kearns, *The Expanded Text,* pp. 12-13.

adduced are of much less probative value, and our conclusions in this regard must be accordingly more reserved."[51]

The second issue has to do with the text and the status of the Nova Vulgata, which includes both verses. In the Praenotanda to that edition there are detailed textual notes indicating the manuscript traditions followed. For this book the Vetus Latina tradition is given a certain priority, but the Hebrew, Greek, and Syriac evidence has been used as well. The editors have corrected what appear to be errors of the traditional Latin text. Since *Liturgiam authenticam* #37 indicates that translations made for the purposes of liturgical use are generally to follow the textual decisions reflected in the Nova Vulgata, it would seem that were the NABRE to be approved for liturgical use, both our verses would need to be included.[52]

The third issue has to do with the traditional Marian understanding of this chapter reflected in the liturgy, an understanding based largely, though not exclusively, on these verses.[53] A note to the NAB recalls this tradition: "In the liturgy this chapter is applied to the Blessed Virgin because of her

---

51. Kearns, *The Expanded Text*, p. 310.

52. These verses do not seem to be used very often in the current Roman liturgy, except for one instance (Office of Readings, Wednesday of Week One of Ordinary Time, Sir. 24:1-22). Although some verses from Sirach 24 are used in the current lectionary for Holy Mass on a few occasions, such as the Second Sunday after Christmas (on this see Magee, "From the Bible to the Lectionary"), verses 24-25 are not included among the prescribed verses. In the current Dominican Latin breviary (perhaps elsewhere as well) Sirach 24:23-26 is the *lectio brevis* for Matins for the votive office of Holy Mary Mother of Grace, and the text given is the Nova Vulgata. LA 37 reads, in part: "If the biblical translation from which the Lectionary is composed exhibits readings that differ from those set forth in the Latin liturgical text, it should be borne in mind that the Nova Vulgata Editio is the point of reference as regards the delineation of the canonical text. Thus, in the translation of the deuterocanonical books and wherever else there may exist varying manuscript traditions, the liturgical translation must be prepared in accordance with the same manuscript tradition that the Nova Vulgata has followed. If a previously prepared translation reflects a choice that departs from that which is found in the Nova Vulgata Editio as regards the underlying textual tradition, the order of verses, or similar factors, the discrepancy needs to be remedied in the preparation of any Lectionary so that conformity with the Latin liturgical text may be maintained." LA 38, however, notes the permissibility of using variant readings, by which the Instruction would appear to mean readings of a verse that differ from the Nova Vulgata, since it refers to readings followed "on the basis of critical editions."

53. There are numerous references to these verses in the works of such scholars as St. Louis de Montfort, Matthias Joseph Scheeben, and Réginald Garrigou-Lagrange, O.P. For references to Sirach 24:24-25 (Vg.) in these works see E. Catta, "Sedes Sapientia," in *Maria: Études sur la Sainte Vierge,* ed. H. Du Manoir (Paris: Beauchesne, 1961), vol. 6, pp. 828-31, 860-61.

constant and intimate association with Christ, the incarnate Wisdom." This note, which is omitted in the NABRE, tells only part of the story. It was especially verse 24 of the Vulgate, with its explicit reference to a mother ("I am the mother of fair love"), which fostered this tradition of interpretation and gave rise to several Marian titles (Mother of Fair/Fairest Love, Mother of Holy Hope).[54] These verses are used in the Roman Breviary on the feast of the Most Holy Rosary of the Blessed Virgin Mary because of the patristic and medieval Marian application facilitated by the Latin text of Sirach 24:24-25.

Historical Books

Judith as Exemplum, Judith 15:11 and 16:26

St. Jerome's translation of Judith was made in 407, and is largely a revision of the Vetus Latina based on a "Chaldean" text, a term that may refer to a Syriac version. The Vulgate has a number of pluses not attested elsewhere. Pierre Bogaert, O.S.B., has observed that the addition to the Vulgate in 15:11 about Judith's love of chastity *(quod castitatem amaveris)* and her refusal to remarry, prepares for a similar addition in 16:26, where Judith is again said to join chastity to her virtue *(virtuti castitatis adiuncta)* and to have remained a widow *(non cognosceret virum)* after the death of her husband.[55]

These Vulgate glosses contributed to the patristic development of Judith as a moral example and helped shape a Christian reading of the book. In his preface, Jerome gives his readers a key to this understanding:

> Receive the widow Judith, example of chastity *(casitatis exemplum)* . . . for not only for women, but even for men, she has been given as a model by the one who rewards her chastity, who has ascribed to her such virtue that she conquered the unconquered among humanity, and surmounted the insurmountable.

St. Jerome, in these Vulgate pluses, whether they stem from him or his sources, and in his preface, has developed, clarified, and expanded upon

---

54. There are numerous references to these titles and the text of Sirach 24 in Church documents. One recent example is found in Blessed Pope John Paul II's 1994 *Letter to Families* 13, which reads: ". . . the truth, and only the truth, will prepare you for a love which can be called 'fairest love' (cf. Sir. 24:24, Vulg.)."

55. P.-M. Bogaert, "Judith," *Reallexikon für Antike und Christentum* 19 (1998): 245-58, here 247.

one aspect of the divinely given exemplarity of Judith, helping his readers to see the spiritual meaning of the book. The Nova Vulgata has followed the Vetus Latina tradition, which does not include these Vulgate pluses, thus bearing witness to the critical sense of the Church.[56]

Tobit 8:4 (Vg.) Tobias Nights

There is a Vulgate plus in Tobit 8:4, which reads, in the Douay-Rheims translation: "Then Tobias exhorted the virgin, and said to her: Sara, arise, and let us pray to God today, and tomorrow, and the next day: because for these three nights we are joined to God: and when the third night is over, we will be in our own wedlock." The NABRE, following the longer Greek text of Sinaiticus and the Aramaic and Hebrew texts from Qumran, is much different: "When Sarah's parents left the bedroom and closed the door behind them, Tobiah rose from bed and said to his wife, 'My sister, come, let us pray and beg our Lord to grant us mercy and protection." Both texts agree on prayer, but the Vulgate is distinctive in its description of three days of prayer before consummation of the marriage. The Nova Vulgata follows the Vetus Latina tradition (Vercellensis XXII, tenth century), which is close to the text of Sinaiticus, and thus these verses are not included.

The story behind the making of the Vulgate text of Tobit is interesting. St. Jerome had a Jewish scholar translate an Aramaic text into Hebrew, which Jerome then rendered into Latin (". . . whatever he rendered for me in Hebrew, I expressed in Latin, relying on a secretary").[57] The material unique to the Vulgate in this verse, the reference to the three days and nights of prayer and abstinence, has been prepared for earlier, in the Vulgate text of Tobit 6:18, which also refers to three days of prayer and abstinence. This material is usually attributed to either Jerome's sources or considered to be his own addition.[58]

56. Cf. Gilbert, "Textes exclus, textes inclus: Les enjeux," p. 66. On the texts of Judith and the distinctive elements of the Vulgate version, see S. Ryan, "The Ancient Versions of Judith and the Place of the Septuagint in the Catholic Church," in *A Pious Seductress, Studies in the Book of Judith,* Deuterocanonical and Cognate Literature Series 14, ed. G. Xeravits (Berlin: Walter de Gruyter, 2012), pp. 1-21; and B. Schmitz, "ΙΟΥΔΙΘ und *IUDITH:* Überlegungen zum Verhältnis der Judit-Erzählung in der LXX und der Vulgata," in *Text-Critical and Hermeneutical Studies in the Septuagint,* ed. J. Cook and H-J. Stipp, Vetus Testamentum Supplements 157 (Leiden: Brill, 2012), pp. 359-80.

57. Translation of the preface to the Vulgate from V. Skemp, *The Vulgate Text of Tobit Compared with Other Ancient Witnesses,* Society of Biblical Literature Dissertation Series 180 (Atlanta: SBL, 2000), p. 16.

58. See Skemp, *The Vulgate Text of Tobit,* pp. 229, 463-70.

The Catholic tradition of prayer and abstinence before consummation of a marriage, a custom referred to as Tobias Nights (in German *Tobiasnächte*), stems from these pluses in the Vulgate of Tobit. Joseph Fitzmyer, S.J., refers in this connection to legislation from the Fourth Council of Carthage (398) calling for one night of abstinence, and a ninth-century collection by Benedict Levita of Mainz (*Capitularium Collectio* 463) prescribes chastity for two or three days.[59] In both instances dependence on the Book of Tobit can be supposed. Meinrad Schumpp, O.P., cites a larger number of texts that connect the Book of Tobit with periods of three days of prayer and abstinence before receiving the sacraments either of Marriage or the Holy Eucharist.[60] This example indicates ways that the Vulgate text of Tobit has been received in the liturgical life of the Church, in her preaching and teaching. The decrees of the Council of Trent referring to the authenticity of the Vulgate and all its parts assure us that these verses are part of the canonical and inspired Book of Tobit, even if they are lacking in the earlier Aramaic, Hebrew, Greek, and Latin texts of the book.

The Texts of the Old Testament and the Teaching of Scripture in the Seminary

Hebrew and Greek

The Hebrew text of the Old Testament, and the Masoretic text in particular, will remain central to scholarly study of the Bible and to modern translations based on the original languages of the Bible. Schenker articulates a rationale for contemporary use of translations based on the original languages, fully recognizing that changed historical circumstances allow access to these texts in excellent critical editions, something that was not possible for the early or even the medieval Church. Schenker thus does not advocate a return to an exclusive use of the Septuagint, or a modern translation of it for the contemporary Western Church. It was given to the Christian community in God's providence as part of the pluriform Bible of the Church, and continues to have an important place alongside of the *Hebraica veritas.*

The study of the Septuagint as a literary and theological work in its own

---

59. Joseph Fitzmyer, *Tobit,* Commentaries on Early Jewish Literature (Berlin: De Gruyter, 2003), p. 220.

60. Meinrad M. Schumpp, *Das Buch Tobias,* Exegetisches Handbuch zum Alten Testament 11 (Münster: Aschendorff, 1933), pp. 144-46.

right is alive and well, and there have been a spate of excellent new translations of the Septuagint into English, French, German, and Spanish. Many of these translations are accompanied by commentary on the reception history of the Septuagint. Notable in this regard is the excellent *La Bible d'Alexandrie,* a project inspired by Dominique Barthélemy and directed by Marguerite Harl. The presence of the Septuagint in popular biblical translations in the sense of references to it or complete parallel translations of Masoretic text and Septuagint is something that seems to be on the increase, if *La Bible en ses Traditions,* the new translation project from l'École Biblique, is any indication. New commentary series such as The Church's Bible (Eerdmans) and The Septuagint Commentary Series (Brill) will make a substantive contribution in this regard and will help Christians to appreciate the text that has so profoundly shaped Christian liturgy, teaching, and preaching. These projects will surely help to make what Raija Sollamo has called the "mother of all Bible translations" known to a wider audience.[61]

To hold a place of honor in the Church for the Septuagint is at the same time to honor that encounter between Greek and Jewish cultures which Benedict XVI has called a "distinct and important step in the history of revelation,"[62] one that has joined the tents of Shem to the tents of Japheth,

61. R. Sollamo, "The Significance of the Septuagint," in *Studies in the Hebrew Bible, Qumran, and the Septuagint Presented to Eugene Ulrich,* ed. P. Flint et al. (Leiden and Boston: Brill, 2006), p. 512.

62. In his 2006 lecture at Regensburg, Pope Benedict described the Septuagint as "a distinct and important step in the history of revelation, one which brought about this encounter ['between the Biblical message and Greek thought'] in a way that was decisive for the birth and spread of Christianity. A profound encounter of faith and reason is taking place here, an encounter between genuine enlightenment and religion." English translation from the Vatican website. The German original in a fuller context reads: "Heute wissen wir, daß die in Alexandrien entstandene griechische Übersetzung des Alten Testaments — die Septuaginta — mehr als eine bloße (vielleicht sogar wenig positiv zu beurteilende) Übersetzung des hebräischen Textes, nämlich ein selbständiger Textzeuge und ein eigener wichtiger Schritt der Offenbarungsgeschichte ist, in dem sich diese Begegnung auf eine Weise realisiert hat, die für die Entstehung des Christentums und seine Verbreitung entscheidende Bedeutung gewann.[9] [9-Vgl. A. Schenker, 'L'Ecriture sainte subsiste en plusieurs formes canoniques simultanées,' in: *L'interpretazione della Bibbia nella Chiesa. Atti del Simposio promosso dalla Congregazione per la Dottrina della Fede* (Città del Vaticano, 2001) S. 178-86.] Zutiefst geht es dabei um die Begegnung zwischen Glaube und Vernunft, zwischen rechter Aufklärung und Religion." *Ansprache von Benedikt XVI, Universität Regensburg, Treffen mit den Vertretern aus dem Bereich der Wissenschaften, 12 September, 2006.* Adrian Schenker is the only biblical scholar cited in the footnotes to the Regensburg lecture, and Benedict XVI points to Schenker's work on the textual pluriformity of Sacred Scripture.

and the Old Testament to the New. Schenker's articulation of a theology of the Septuagint and the other early biblical translations, the fruit of long years of work with these versions, seems to me to be an important first step and a lasting and substantive contribution to the field.

The Vulgate and the Nova Vulgata

The Vulgate and the Nova Vulgata will always play a very significant role in the life of the Church. The decrees of Trent on the Vulgate and the continuing magisterial teaching on the Vulgate attest to its abiding importance. The Nova Vulgata is a modern revision of the Vulgate that serves as a Latin typical edition for use in the Roman Rite.[63] Critics of the Nova Vulgata, and of the 2001 Vatican instruction *Liturgiam authenticam,* notably the chant historian Peter Jeffery, have lamented the decision to purge the Vulgate of its distinctive readings, citing the resultant loss of connection with the rich liturgical and artistic tradition based on the Vulgate, and what some regard as the unnecessary harmonization of the received biblical versions. To my mind, however, the Nova Vulgata and *Liturgiam authenticam* provide useful and necessary guidelines for the preparation of liturgical texts for a universal Church, and are actually extremely helpful, and appropriately flexible, in their approach to the complicated textual problems of many of the deuterocanonical books. More importantly, the Nova Vulgata bears witness to the critical sense of the Church, her desire to make full use of the human sciences, and full use of faith and reason. The Church serves the Word of God, making every effort to use the best texts and vigilance to remove errors introduced in the process of transmission — all of this so as to better hear the Word in the words of Sacred Scripture with greater fidelity. St. Jerome, it has been argued, to my mind correctly, would certainly welcome corrections to the Vulgate based on better access to the original texts that modern science affords.

Conclusion

By way of conclusion I will review the arguments advanced above in the form of brief theses about inspiration and textual pluriformity. It is my hope

---

63. For a brief treatment of the history of the Latin texts of the Bible and place of the Nova Vulgata in that history, see Raedy, "What Happened to the Vulgate?" p. 144.

that these theses may clarify my position and reveal its underlying assumptions, its strengths and its weaknesses, more clearly.

1. The Church speaks of both inspired authors (subjective inspiration) and inspired texts (objective inspiration), but seems to have a preference for the former.[64] God inspired Prophets and Apostles, members of the People of God and of the Church, who transmitted the sacred books to the Church. It is indeed correct to speak of inspired texts or inspired books, but there is a danger that such language may lead to erroneous thinking about single, original, inspired manuscripts.[65] Protestant traditions occasionally speak of inspired autographs, of original inspired texts in the sense of specific scrolls. Karen Jobes, in a review of a book by the Wassersteins (father and son) about the origins of the traditional legend about the inspiration of the Septuagint, writes that "Christians who stand in the heritage of the Protestant Reformation will not be disturbed by Wasserstein's conclusion, because Protestant doctrine locates divine inspiration in the autographs of Scripture rather than in any translation of it."[66] Catholic teaching on canonicity and inspiration can account for both the divine and human authorship of Scripture without resorting to a theory of inspired autographs or positing word-for-word dictation (cf. *Verbum Domini* 44).

2. The Church locates objective inspiration primarily at the level of the book or of the entire canon, as transmitted within its ecclesial context. It is the Book of Jeremiah that is sacred and canonical, not the Masoretic text of the book, nor the earliest Qumran fragment of it. And it is the entire Bible which is inspired, with all its books — not one manuscript, one version, or one translation.

3. The Word of God is an expression used analogously (*Verbum Domini*

---

64. On subjective and objective inspiration, see Farkasfalvy, *Inspiration & Interpretation,* pp. 54, 61, 238. My own sense, from reading Church documents, is that the Church refers more typically to inspired sacred authors than she does to inspired texts, though both expressions are indeed found.

65. On this question of inspired authors and inspired texts, see M. Levering, "The Inspiration of Scripture: A Status Quaestionis," *Letter & Spirit* 6 (2010): 304, 306-9, 312-13.

66. K. Jobes, "Review of A. and D. Wasserstein, *The Legend of the Septuagint: From Classical Antiquity to Today," Journal of the Evangelical Theological Society* 49 (2006): 842. See my review of the Wasserstein book: "Review of Abraham Wasserstein and David J. Wasserstein, *The Legend of the Septuagint: From Classical Antiquity to Today," Theological Studies* 69 (2008): 438-39. Jobes seems essentially to accept Wasserstein's argument that the authority of the Septuagint in Christianity is based on an ancient legend (ignoring Origen's argument, and Jerome's rejection of the legend), and suggests that this is an issue only for the Catholic and Orthodox churches.

7). It is a larger reality than the text of Scripture. It is in the first instance used of God, then of the preached word. Scripture is the privileged written expression of the Word of God, but is not coextensive with the Word of God in this larger sense. The Word of God is first of all a person, not a book, and the written form of the Word of God comes to us in a varied, pluriform library that can never be reduced to one single formulation. Just as there is one gospel of our Lord Jesus Christ but four Gospels written by four Evangelists, so analogously there is one Old Testament, received by the Church in three languages and two major forms.

4. The inspired and canonical books of the Old and New Testaments are transmitted in the Church in several forms: Hebrew (and Aramaic), Greek, and Latin. The Praenotanda of the Nova Vulgata says of the Book of Esther that it is read in the Church in two canonical forms. It is the Book of Esther that is canonical and inspired, not one text. It is read in more than one authentic form, even if these differ in their wording, their order, or their content.

5. Hearing the Word of God in the Scriptures is a constitutive element of the Church. Early translations such as the Septuagint were provided by God in his divine providence so that the Greek-speaking churches would have access thereby to the Word of God in an authentic form. Today Christians around the world have access to translations made from the original languages and using the best critical editions.

6. The Church has a critical sense and teaches that translations of Scripture for liturgical and ecclesial use are to be made from the original languages. Errors in manuscripts are to be corrected, making use of the science of textual criticism, and the best critical editions are to be used.

7. The Vulgate and the Nova Vulgata play important roles in the life of the Church. The decrees of Trent on the Vulgate, *Liturgiam authenticam,* the Apostolic Constitution "Scripturarum Thesaurus," and the Praenotanda to the Nova Vulgata are valuable resources to help scholars learn to think with the Church in regard to the place of the Latin tradition among the texts and translations of the Old Testament.[67]

---

67. Especially helpful are Schenker's article "L'Écriture sainte subsiste en plusieurs formes canoniques simultanées," in *L'interpretazione della Bibbia nella Chiesa. Atti del Simposio promosso dalla Congregazione per la Dottrina della Fede* (Vatican City, 2001), pp. 178-86; A. Schenker, "Die Heilige Schrift subsistiert gleichzeitig in mehreren kanonischen Formen," in *Studien zu Propheten und Religionsgeschichte,* ed. A. Schenker (Stuttgart: Katholisches Bibelwerk, 2003), pp. 192-200; Gilbert, "Textes exclus, textes inclus: Les enjeux," in *L'autorité de l'Écriture,* ed. Jean-Michel Poffet (Paris: Cerf, 2002), pp. 51-70; and Raedy, "What Happened to the Vulgate?"

8. We can posit that God used and continues to use the various authentic forms of Scripture, the unique wordings and particular features of the Hebrew, Greek, and Latin texts, to reveal aspects of the richness of the deposit of faith in ways that speak to diverse cultures in their own linguistic idioms.[68] This can be seen as part of the divine accommodation or syncatabasis.

9. Knowledge of the Septuagint and the Vulgate is often essential for understanding the liturgical use of a biblical text or for understanding the use of a text in patristic preaching. Study of the works of the Church Fathers is both essential to coming to a complete understanding of Scripture in both its literal and spiritual senses and helpful in learning how to communicate that understanding in preaching and teaching. The writings of Pope Benedict XVI, his academic and pastoral writings and his homilies, make frequent reference to readings peculiar to the Septuagint and the Vulgate. Attention to his underlying assumptions and explicit conclusions about these versions can be helpful in learning to think with the Church about the Word of God and the textual pluriformity of the Old Testament.[69]

---

68. Farkasfalvy, commenting on approaches to Scripture in the Middle Ages, writes: "Students of the biblical texts remained interested in textual variants but not necessarily with the intention of eliminating them for an amended text. Rather, the variants were regarded as parallel paths offering access to the deeper riches of the biblical text and were handled not as competitors from among which one had to choose, but as complements entitled as such to 'equal opportunity' in representing the original text." Farkasfalvy, *Inspiration & Interpretation*, p. 144. His remark holds true in general for the patristic era as well.

69. An example of this is found in *Verbum Domini* 12. The Pope refers to Isaiah 10:23 in its Greek form, a text cited by St. Paul in Romans 9:28. He shows concisely how the Septuagint of Isaiah known to the Fathers (Origen) and cited by the Apostle was understood in a spiritual sense, calling attention as he does so to the unity of the Old and New Testaments. It is worth noting that the Pope is quoting in this section not from an academic lecture but from a homily he gave at Christmas in 2006. He has a great gift of explaining in simple terms the sometimes complex biblical roots of Christian thought.

CHAPTER 10

How the Liturgy of the Hours Provides an Effective Means for Teaching the Book of Psalms

Kelly Anderson

Teaching the Book of Psalms presents unique and distinctive difficulties. Since the Psalter is composed of one hundred fifty prayers, each deeply beautiful in its own right, a sweeping overview fails to convey the richness and splendor of each. But even a sweeping overview is nearly impossible. There is no narrative structure, storyline, or characters, nor are there agreed-upon overarching themes and ideas. Further complicating the matter is that the Psalter is used more than any other biblical book in the liturgy. Only the Book of Psalms is read at every Mass, and the Liturgy of the Hours is largely composed of psalms. Coupled with these inherent difficulties, an instructor usually has only a limited amount of time to present this diverse, complex book. For example, at St. Charles Borromeo Seminary, the psalms are part of the course on Wisdom Literature. So, besides plowing through Proverbs, Job, Ecclesiastes, Sirach, the Song of Songs, and Wisdom, the professor also has the happy task of covering all of the psalms. A friend of mine, a theology professor at Villanova, recently groused that every time she has attempted to teach the psalms she has "blown it." She had discovered the same thing I had: it is simply impossible within the confines of a classroom to convey the depth, beauty, and richness of these prayers.

This essay suggests that the best way to resolve these difficulties rests in a both/and approach — to use both modern research and the Liturgy of the Hours (LOH). I would not advocate teaching any other biblical book in light of its liturgical use, nor would I maintain that such a practice has a place in a college or university. However, the psalms have a particular place in the Liturgy, and the *telos* of seminarian study is different than that of a college student. For a seminarian who will be in a parish for most of his priestly life, learning the psalms in the context of the LOH may be the most fruitful and sensible of all possibilities. For, "a privileged place is naturally taken by the Liturgy of the Hours, the prayer of the Church par excellence, destined to give rhythm to the days and times of the Christian year, offering, above all with the Psalmody, the daily spiritual food of the faithful."[1] This essay will first examine why teaching the psalms via the LOH is the most felicitous method and then offer some practical considerations for such an endeavor.

Presenting the Psalms in the Liturgy of the Hours

The psalms should be presented in light of the LOH for two basic reasons. First, presenting seminarians with only the "latest" in biblical research ill-equips them for their mission. During the past fifty years of scholarship on the psalms many new trajectories and developments have come forth, which, while fascinating and exciting, may prove to be irrelevant in a very short time. They lack the credibility that only further research and time can bring. Since priests have few opportunities to keep abreast of modern research, teaching them what is current may prove futile in the end. This would be especially true if such research falls flat or changes dramatically. Further, the Church has always read the psalms in the light of Jesus Christ, which is what the liturgy invites us to do. Such a reading began in the New Testament itself, and the LOH continues this long tradition.

A Brief Overview of Modern Research

Let us examine the movement and fluidity of modern research. Modern scholars on the psalms have moved away from two older trajectories, that of form and rhetorical criticism. The towering influence of Hermann Gunkel's form criticism has waned. Gunkel classified the psalms according to types and genres and then determined where each type would have fit into the worship of Israel (i.e., its "setting in life" or *Sitz im Leben*). His types included laments (individual and communal), thanksgiving, praise, royal psalms, prophetic exhortations, etc. Sigmund Mowinkel, who expanded and

---

1. *Message to the People of God of the XII Ordinary General Assembly of the Synod of Bishops*, no. 9.

revised Gunkel's research, proposed a cult-functional method, concluding that the New Year Festival was the setting for many of the psalms. However, due to a lack of concrete evidence and its largely inductive character, this latter proposal has largely been abandoned.

In 1968 James Muilenburg advocated that form criticism be supplemented with rhetorical criticism.[2] This type of study seeks to identify and categorize various literary features of each individual psalm. The most prominent are parallelism, repetition, chiasms, and structures of the psalm itself.

Currently, there is growing interest among scholars to understand the Book of Psalms as a coherent theological work that moves toward a final goal. The watershed moment was Gerald H. Wilson's 1985 thesis *The Editing of the Hebrew Psalter.*[3] According to Wilson, there are two major and distinct segments to the Psalter: 2–89 (the first three books of psalms: 1–41; 42–72; 73–89) and 90–145 (the last two: 90–106; 107–150). The first segment contains three strategically placed royal psalms (2, 72, and 89), which are the first psalm of Book I and the last psalms of Books II and III respectively. These psalms focus on the kingship of David and the eventual demise of his kingdom. The last segment, 90–145, answers the lament of the first by focusing on Moses (seven of the eight references to Moses occur in Book IV), the Torah of God, and the universal kingship of *Yhwh*, who is the true king of Israel, not David. Thus, Books I-III celebrate the reigns of David and Solomon and lament the dark days of oppression during the divided kingdoms and Babylonian exile. They also address the apparent failure of the Davidic/Zion covenant theology. Books IV-V anticipate and rejoice in Israel's restoration to the land and the reign of *Yhwh* as king.

Wilson also maintained that Psalm 1 and the final five psalms (146–150) function as an introduction and conclusion. Psalm 1 seems to be intentionally positioned as an introduction to the whole Psalter. Beginning with "Happy are those . . . who delight in the Law of the Lord," the psalm introduces the benefits of one who reads and follows the message of the Psalter. Thus, Psalm 2 could have been the beginning of the initial first collection (2–89) with Psalm 1 added on later.[4] Further, the last five psalms are a con-

---

2. Cf. J. Clinton McCann Jr., "Psalms-Introduction," in *New Interpreter's Bible,* vol. 4 (Nashville: Abingdon, 1996), pp. 641-77, here 652.

3. Gerald H. Wilson, *The Editing of the Hebrew Psalter,* Society of Biblical Literature Dissertation Series 76 (Chico, CA: Scholars Press, 1985).

4. Patrick D. Miller ("The Beginning of the Psalter," in *The Shape and Shaping of the Psalter,* Journal for the Study of the Old Testament: Supplement 159 [Sheffield: Sheffield Academic, 1993], pp. 83-92, here 84-85, and *Interpreting the Psalms* [Philadelphia: Fortress

clusion of praise that was also added at the final stages of the editing of the Psalter.

Wilson argued that the editorial work produced a holistic book that seeks to move beyond the exilic experience of Israel and to provide a future grounding for faith in *Yhwh*. Wilson also maintained that "the shape of the canonical Psalter preserves a tense dialogue (or a dialogue in tension) between the royal covenantal hopes associated with the first two-thirds of the Psalter (1–89) and the wisdom counsel to trust *Yhwh* alone associated with the final third (Psalms 90–150)."[5] Wilson continued to write and refine his theory in several articles until his untimely death in 2005.

However, not all scholars are convinced of the validity of a holistic reading of the psalms, nor of its importance. R. Norman Whybray remained unconvinced that the psalms were meant to be read as a holistic, pious work or that there was any systematic redaction of either the royal or wisdom psalms.[6] Erhard S. Gerstenberger stated, "In short, the Psalter does not contain a summa of theological thought or any kind of theological system but a treasury of experiences accumulated by generations of people who lived in the region where the cradle of our own civilization stood."[7] John Day maintains that

> [i]t is apparent that any attempt to find one grandiose scheme to account for the ordering of the psalms is bound to end in failure. On the other hand, careful study of the Psalter reveals that its criteria are not completely haphazard and that a whole series of criteria have been operative. Sometimes the editors have put together psalms with the same superscriptions. On other occasions, it is possible to discern thematic reasons, common catchwords or genres which have led to particular psalms being placed next to each other.[8]

Roland Murphy even questioned how pertinent a holistic reading of the Psalter would be: "I would agree with [James L.] Mays that it is 'possible

---

Press, 1986], pp. 81-93) has argued that Psalms 1 and 2 are linguistically and thematically bound and should be read together.

5. Gerald H. Wilson, "Shaping the Psalter: A Consideration of Editorial Linkage in the Book of Psalms," in *The Shape and Shaping of the Psalter,* pp. 72-82, here 81.

6. S. Jonathan Murphy, "Is the Psalter a Book with a Single Message?" *Bibliotheca Sacra* 165 (2008): 283-93, here 290-91.

7. Erhard S. Gerstenberger, *Psalms: Part I: With an Introduction to Cultic Poetry* (Grand Rapids: Eerdmans, 1988), p. 36.

8. John Day, *Psalms,* Old Testament Guides (Sheffield: Sheffield Academic, 1990), p. 111.

and useful to read a psalm as part of the book of Psalms,' in other words, to give to a specific psalm the context of a book to which it belongs, but I think that its usefulness would be relatively limited."[9]

Other scholars have accepted the idea that the Psalter was redacted in order to form a holistic book with a coherent message. However, what exactly that message is continues to be debated. Two scholars who disagree with the overriding themes presented by Wilson are J. Clinton McCann Jr. and David C. Mitchell.

McCann argues that the emphasis of the book is on instruction, saying the Psalter is "to be read and heard as God's instruction to the faithful."[10] This is indicated by Psalm 1, which functions as the introductory invitation to receive God's instruction, as well as Psalm 2, which contains the central theological message that the Lord reigns.

Mitchell contends that the Psalter does not look back to the experience of the exile, but forward.[11] Using the eschatological program of Zechariah 9–14 as a blueprint, he argues that a similar theology exists in the Psalter. He maintains that the Psalter is essentially prophetic with an eschatological and messianic agenda. The Davidic kingship forms the basis for the eschatological hope of a messianic figure. He identifies the movement as an eschatological gathering of Israel to the homeland, followed by the judgment of the nations and the worship of God by all the nations on Mount Zion.

One could cite more examples.[12] However, I think it is clear that modern scholarship is involved in a rather vigorous debate concerning the editing

9. Roland E. Murphy, "Reflections on Contextual Interpretation of the Psalms," in *The Shape and Shaping of the Psalter*, p. 23.

10. J. Clinton McCann Jr., *A Theological Introduction to the Book of Psalms: The Psalms as Torah* (Nashville: Abingdon, 1993), pp. 9-10.

11. David C. Mitchell, "Lord Remember David: G. H. Wilson and the Message of the Psalter," *Vetus Testamentum* 56, no. 4 (2006): 526-48, and *The Message of the Psalter: An Eschatological Programme in the Books of the Psalms,* Journal for the Study of the Old Testament: Supplement 252 (Sheffield: Sheffield Academic, 1997). Mitchell's assessment agrees with that made by Brevard S. Childs, *Introduction to the Old Testament as Scripture* (Philadelphia: Fortress Press, 1979), pp. 508-25, especially 517-18.

12. For a recent overview, see Murphy, "Single Message?" pp. 283-93; D. M. Howard, "The Psalms in Current Study," in *Interpreting the Psalms*, ed. David Firth and Philip S. Johnston (Downers Grove, IL: InterVarsity, 2005), pp. 23-40. Also well done is his earlier article "Editorial Activity in the Psalter: A State of the Field Survey," in *The Shape and Shaping of the Psalter,* Journal for the Study of the Old Testament: Supplement 159 (Sheffield: Sheffield Academic, 1993), pp. 52-70, although now somewhat dated. Also excellent is Mitchell's overview in *Message of the Psalter,* pp. 15-65.

of the Psalter and its consequences.[13] It remains to be seen where this re-search will lead and what developments or consequences of these studies are forthcoming.

We all would agree that priests are quite busy. Furthermore, we have probably all experienced that what they learn in the seminary about certain topics sticks with them. At times when I listen to a homily from a priest who graduated from the seminary some thirty years ago (or even ten years ago!), he uses references and research from that time. Priests do not have time to update themselves on the latest scholarship, research, and developments once they enter parish life. What a priest learns in the seminary remains his foundation. It would then be shortsighted to teach our seminarians only these approaches that remain debated or are in continual development.

The Church's Tradition

The Church has read the psalms christologically all her life. To read the psalms in light of our tradition inserts the priest in a long line of spiritual richness that began in the New Testament and continued nearly two millennia. Research tendencies come and go, but this aspect of the psalms has remained stable and is an integral part of the life of the Church and her liturgy.

From the patristic era until the Age of Enlightenment the psalms were

---

13. Presented here is the briefest of overviews. Also debated is the possibility of more than one canon for the Book of Psalms. The discovery of the Psalm manuscripts at Qumran has raised questions concerning the text and canon of the psalms. The most important of these discoveries is the Psalms Scroll (11QPsᵃ), which contains portions of thirty-nine psalms from the Psalter as well as some others. Due to the different order of psalms and the presence of extrabiblical psalms, including four previously unknown, some scholars have postulated that this scroll represents a variant tradition or another authoritative canon. Holding this view are Gerald H. Wilson, "The Qumran Psalms Manuscripts and the Consecutive Arrangement of Psalms in the Masoretic Psalter," *Catholic Biblical Quarterly* 45 (1983): 377-88; "The Qumran Psalms Scroll Reconsidered: Analysis of the Debate," *Catholic Biblical Quarterly* 47 (1985): 624-42; and Peter W. Flint, *The Dead Sea Psalms & the Book of Psalms,* Studies on the Texts of the Desert of Judah, vol. 17, ed. F. García Martínez and A. S. van der Woude (Leiden: Brill, 1997). Others have argued that the scroll was not an alternative canon, but rather a liturgical book or a collection of lyrics. Cf. P. W. Skehan, "A Liturgical Complex in 11QPsᵃ," *Catholic Biblical Quarterly* 34 (1973): 195-205; Mitchell, *Message of the Psalter,* pp. 22-23. Finally, a renewed interest in Hebrew poetry with regard to the Psalter ought to be mentioned as well.

largely read with the understanding that they point to the future and that their completion is found in the person of Jesus Christ and his kingdom. The psalms were seen as prophetic in nature, and their messianic content discerned through a typological reading. Mitchell summarized his view, saying:

> Among sixteenth-century Christians, the general hermeneutic of Psalms interpretation differed little from that of the previous two millennia, in the essentials of recognizing the Psalter's literary integrity and future-predictive purpose, although in specifics, such as Luther's "destructione synagoge," it varies from rabbinic literature. Similar views prevailed until the early nineteenth century.[14]

A typological reading of the psalms remains absolutely valid as *Dei verbum* teaches us: The principal purpose to which the plan of the old covenant was directed was to prepare for the coming of Christ, the redeemer of all and of the messianic kingdom, to announce this coming by prophecy (see Luke 24:44; John 5:39; 1 Pet. 1:10), and to indicate its meaning through various types (see 1 Cor. 10:12) (*Dei verbum* 15).

To read the psalms as a means of knowing Jesus Christ offers the seminarian a sound way of praying the LOH that will nourish him all his life. Amidst the tidal wave of theories, research, and movements, the seminarian, if schooled in the LOH and the Church's tradition, need not get lost in rapid scholarly developments, some of which may fizzle out. The seminarian, and later the priest, has the assurance that he prays in the tradition of the Church, and that his prayer is both the prayer of Christ to the Father, and the prayer of the bride to the bridegroom.[15] The seminarian can, and should, explore many forms of criticism or hermeneutics, but an integral reading of Sacred Scripture should always be his foundation and bedrock.[16]

The psalms could be presented around the basic framework of the LOH, which is constructed around two frames, light and symbolic days. The fundamental symbol for the primary hours is light, a theme that can be traced back to the Old Testament (Pss. 18:29; 27:1; 36:10; 44:4; Isa. 9:1; 60:19-20; Mic.

---

14. Mitchell, *Message of the Psalter*, p. 40.

15. *Sancrosanctum concilium* 83-85.

16. *Dei verbum* 12 explains the proper exegesis of Sacred Scripture: "But, since Holy Scripture must be read and interpreted in the sacred Spirit in which it was written, no less serious attention must be given to the content and unity of the whole of Scripture if the meaning of the sacred texts is to be correctly worked out. The living tradition of the whole Church must be taken into account along with the harmony which exists between elements of the faith."

7:8; Hab. 3:4) as well as to the paganism of the Mediterranean world through the prominent use of sun imagery.[17] Christians applied this image to Christ, and it is a pervasive theme in the New Testament, especially the Johannine literature (Luke 2:32; John 1:4-9; 3:19-21; 8:12; 9:5; 12:35-36; 12:45-46; Acts 9:3; 1 Tim. 6:16; 1 John 1:5-7; 2:8; Rev. 21:23; 2:5).[18] The whole of the LOH revolves around the theme of light.

In Lauds, the rising sun indicates that the darkness of the night is overcome, and the pray-er thanks and praises God for another day. As much as possible, the choice of the first psalm makes some allusion to the morning and praise.[19] The second, a psalm chosen from a different part of the Bible, is also a hymn of praise, while the last psalm has the strongest character of praise. Note how the reference to light finds its way in the climactic moment of Lauds: *In the tender compassion of our God the dawn from on high shall break upon us, to shine on those who dwell in darkness and the shadow of death, and to guide our feet into the way of peace* (Luke 1:78-79).

In Vespers, which may have originated from the rite of *Lucernarium*, the passing of day reminds those praying of the darkness of Christ's passion and death, and of the passing nature of all creation.[20] The pray-er asks pardon for the sins of the day and prays for protection for the coming night.[21] Vespers is also a prayer of thanksgiving, being prayed at the hour of the Last Supper. God is thanked for the graces of the day, especially for the grace of the risen Christ.

The first psalm is a prayer of the evening, mentioning either the evening or prayer at evening, and the lighting of the lamp (although this is not always accomplished). The other psalms are chosen either for their christological character or their paranetic and moral character, or because they appeal for conversion.[22] A hymn from the New Testament follows, inviting the pray-er to read the psalms in the light of Christ. This is accentuated by a short reading from the New Testament, which has a moral exhortation. The climax is the *Magnificat,* the great thanksgiving and praise of the Church.

17. Robert Taft, *The Liturgy of the Hours in the East and West: The Origins of the Divine Office and Its Meaning for Today* (Collegeville, MN: Liturgical Press, 1986), p. 348; see also pp. 348-52.

18. Taft, *Liturgy of the Hours,* p. 489.

19. Jordi Gibert Tarruel, "La Nouvelle Distribution du Psautier dans la Liturgia Horarum," *Ephemerides Liturgicae* 87 (1973): 325-82, especially 349, 356-60.

20. Taft, *Liturgy of the Hours,* p. 355.

21. Taft, *Liturgy of the Hours,* p. 355.

22. Tarruel, "Nouvelle Distribution," p. 349.

The Office of Readings, which used to be called Matins, was the prayer of the night. The Fathers and other spiritual writers exhorted Christians, especially those in contemplative life, to engage in consistent nocturnal prayer. The night is a time of heightened intimacy, a time of love, but it is also a time of severe temptation and sin. The character of this prayer encompasses both of these dimensions. The psalms and readings are meant to be a special moment of intimacy savored with the Lord, while also being a plea for strength against encroaching temptations and sinful desires.

In Night Prayer, or Compline, the psalm invites the pray-er to abandon himself confidently in the repose of the night, which prefigures the repose that comes to us all.[23] Note that the climactic moment of the prayer, the *Nunc Dimittis,* has a reference to light: *a light for revelation to the Gentiles and for glory to your people Israel* (Luke 2:32).

The LOH is also crafted around Friday and Sunday, the two most symbolic days.[24] Friday is the day when the death of the Lord is commemorated. As such, it is a day of penance and the psalms address that. As the week moves closer to Friday, the first psalm in Lauds lessens in its praise and turns to a plea of one in danger. The culminating moment is Friday, where the pray-er makes a powerful plea for forgiveness. Sunday, of course, is the celebration of Easter; thus, the psalms are those of great praise. This spirit of praise continues on Monday and the subsequent days until the tone gradually changes to one of sorrow and penitence once again.

The New Testament additions in the LOH also invite the pray-er to read the psalms christologically. The third prayer hymn of Vespers is taken from the New Testament. Additionally, the three hymns at the end of the primary hours (the *Benedictus, Magnificat,* and *Nunc Dimittis* — all culminating moments) invite the pray-er to read the psalms and prayers of the Old Testament as fulfilled in Jesus Christ.

To conclude, the LOH is meant to be an actualization of the Paschal Mystery with the pray-er intimately entering into the Passion of Christ, living his experiences and, via the psalms, discovering his life, inner emotions, and thoughts. It is the voice of Christ that resonates within the psalms.[25] This daily, profound contact with the word of God is meant to enable the person to make decisions to live as Christ, treading the path of daily conversions, or to refuse him. *Indeed, the word of God is living and active, sharper than any*

---

23. Tarruel, "Nouvelle Distribution," p. 349.
24. Tarruel, "Nouvelle Distribution," p. 349.
25. Cf. *Sacrosanctum concilium* 83-85.

two-edged sword, piercing until it divides soul from spirit, joints from marrow; it is able to judge the thoughts and intentions of the heart (Heb. 4:12). Thus, the continual praying of the LOH calls a person to greater intimacy, obedience, and love of Jesus Christ.

Furthermore, the LOH constitutes the prayer life of the Church, the prayer that priests and religious are required to pray and laypeople are encouraged to pray. Introducing the psalms within the framework of the LOH would be a great benefit to our seminarians, who need to make this prayer one of the foundations of their priestly life. By noting the revolving themes of light, the days of the week, and the hour where the psalm is prayed, the priest has at his disposal an excellent means for categorizing and contextualizing the psalms. While scholars continue to debate if the movement of the Psalter is didactic, sapiential, or eschatological, the priest may be better served reading the psalms within the movement of the LOH.

The LOH is modern in form but ancient in scope. Therefore, reading the psalms in light of our long tradition will help the priest and seminarian encounter Jesus Christ.

Practical Considerations

Any modern scholarship on the psalms that needs to be presented can be done within the framework of the LOH. In other words, modern research does not have to be set aside (nor ought it be!) but can be subsumed into the reading of the LOH, which the Synod of Bishops in 2008 exhorted the faithful to do.

> Exegetical knowledge must, therefore, weave itself indissolubly with spiritual and theological tradition so that the divine and human unity of Jesus Christ and Scripture is not broken. In this rediscovered harmony, the face of Christ will shine in its fullness and help us to discover another unity, that profound and intimate unity of Sacred Scriptures.[26]

Since the students are earning graduate degrees from our institutions, it is necessary that they have a grasp of recent research and scholarship. We would ill-equip them for service if they cannot talk broadly on current

---

26. *Message to the People of God of the XII Ordinary General Assembly of the Synod of Bishops,* no. 6.

developments or read a recent article on the subject of the psalms. At the same time, the final scope needs to be that of encountering Jesus Christ.

In my opinion there appear to be four sections that need to be presented as an introduction to the psalms. First, there should be an overview of the Psalter, which should include the division of the Psalter into five books, noting the various collections within them. The student ought to be aware of the titles of the psalms and how these contribute to forming the various categories. The instructor could also discuss various canonical issues, especially in light of the Dead Sea Scrolls. A second trajectory should be an overview of Hebrew poetry, as well as a presentation of literary and rhetorical devices within the psalms themselves. Third, instructors ought to give a presentation of form criticism and genres. Gunkel's ideas still affect nearly all other branches of work, and these provide a useful means for discussing psalms. Most commentaries assume a rudimentary knowledge. Finally, a brief overview of the research that deals with the editing of the Psalter ought to be presented. Since this research is still in flux, however, it might not be beneficial to spend a lengthy amount of time on it. I would offer that these four tools should be sufficient for a more in-depth look at the psalms. A few articles could also be assigned to fill out the student's knowledge on these topics.

Once an introduction has been made, an overview of the LOH could be presented, complete with the overall theological thrust of the prayers, looking at the basic ideas and symbols of the LOH.

The instructor could choose one day, either a Friday or Sunday, and lead the students through each of the hours. Beginning with the psalms of Lauds, the instructor could trace the development of the day through Compline.

Each psalm could be first looked at as a microcosm, using such techniques as literary or rhetorical criticism. The particular structure, language, genre, etc., could be identified along with its supposed *Sitz im Leben.* At that point, the field of interest should widen and the psalm could be examined in light of its context, first in that hour (for example, Lauds) and then the day in general. The seminarian could learn how to *read* the psalms by employing modern methods, but *pray* the psalms to encounter Jesus Christ.[27] Thus, the seminarian would learn modern methods in an ancient context. The seminarian could then, eventually, take one of the hours, or even a day, from the LOH and demonstrate that he has learned to do this type of exegesis himself.

---

27. An example of this can be found in John Paul II, *Psalms and Canticles: Meditations and Catechesis on the Psalms and Canticles of Morning Prayer* (London: Catholic Truth Society, 2004).

Conclusion

The Book of Psalms is a difficult book to teach within the confines of a class-room. Teaching the psalms within the LOH seems to be the most beneficial to the seminarian in light of the inherent difficulties the book presents, cou-pled with the lack of concrete instructional time. Such a method accentuates the role of the psalms in the liturgy and provides the seminarian a means of cultivating his spiritual life. Modern methods of exegesis need not be ig-nored, but rather used to develop an understanding of Jesus Christ via the psalms.

I am not unaware of the pitfalls such a methodology carries with it. It would be easy to "over-spiritualize" the psalms or see types of Jesus Christ to the point of being ridiculous. Also risky is neglecting the excellent strides modern research has made on the psalms, thus reducing them to a subjective reading. There is also, admittedly, a disadvantage in not studying the Psalter as it stands. However real these difficulties may be, they weigh against the importance of presenting the seminarians a concrete, longstanding meth-odology for reading the psalms.

As an academic, I love to explore new trends and tendencies with my students. This has its place and is laudable. However, as a servant of the Church and my students, it is necessary to put their needs first. And the first task of a seminarian, as well as that of his professor, is to encounter the person of Jesus Christ. Perhaps in teaching the psalms, this is best done via the LOH.

CHAPTER 11

Combining Synchronic and Diachronic Methodology in Teaching the Pentateuch

Michael Magee

Some years ago, a lay professor of the Old Testament recounted to me her early days in the study of scientific biblical exegesis and teaching. She remembered her enthusiasm upon being given the opportunity to gain knowledge of the methodologies of scientific biblical exegesis, but also her anxiety regarding whether Catholics could be expected to be receptive to reading the Bible with the help of such historical-critical methodologies. She stated that the lay students whom she had taught, to her pleasant surprise, had received her instruction with the same enthusiasm that she herself had experienced. Even so, she had been dismayed to find that many seminarians balked at historical-critical methodologies. On these seminarians she disappointedly pinned the label of "fundamentalist."

On the basis of my own experience of seminary instruction in biblical studies in the late 1980s, which had also relied heavily on methodologies such as source criticism, form criticism, redaction criticism, and tradition history, I must admit that I felt a certain sympathy for the students the professor was describing, even if I also felt a high regard not only for her own competence but also for her delight in the insights yielded by these methodologies. I wondered whether the discontentment that she had encountered had indeed been motivated by a minimalization of the human history of the divinely inspired biblical text that could justifiably be termed "fundamentalist," as her words seemed to suggest. In my own case, as I believe to be the case also in regard to the students that I now see in class, discomfort with diachronic methodology may indeed appear at the outset to be motivated by a misguided protectiveness of the divine role in the history of the sacred texts, as if one's focus on the human aspect of the texts would endanger this. However, this particular type of anxiety is usually not difficult for the professor to help the student to overcome. More persistent is the fear that too lopsided a tendency toward the dissection of the biblical text and the choice of a hidden world behind the text — rather than the text itself — as the primary object of study, leaves the student ill-equipped to approach the text either as nourishment for personal prayer, as an adventure to be lived, or as an engaging message to be preached. Such concerns on the part of seminarians should not be dismissed too quickly. While the account that I give here is somewhat autobiographical, it is intended to illustrate what I have found so far to be the most effective manner of combining synchronic and diachronic methodologies in the teaching of the Pentateuch in a seminary curriculum.

During the course of my own higher studies of Sacred Scripture in preparation for teaching, maintaining a high degree of attention to the Pentateuch, I focused as much as I could on approaches to the text that would be helpful in supplementing the findings of diachronic methods that I was sure would always be necessary in biblical instruction, at least as an effective key to the history of modern exegesis of the Pentateuch.

There were many possible synchronic approaches that were available for such consideration. Careful attention to the original-language texts, including word studies and alternative ways of translating key passages, provided one avenue. Rabbinic studies provided a fresh alternative that often yielded insights surprisingly amenable to a Christian reading of key passages. The reading of the Pentateuch within the context of the entire canon of both Testaments, and an underscoring of elements found to be foundational for New Testament or later dogmatic theology, would certainly be warranted in a seminary curriculum. The terminology and insights provided by narratology in particular seemed to provide an excellent guide for the consideration of the Pentateuch in its global integrity, however justified might be the ascertainment of additional layers of meaning inherent in smaller units as studied by various diachronic methods. While diachronic methods would certainly be destined to retain their rightful place in biblical study, it seemed to me in the mid-1990s that a renewed emphasis on synchronic methods constituted the wave of the near future.

Planning the Course

Having completed the Licentiate in Sacred Scripture in 1997 and spending a decade in other assignments before finally preparing to teach the Pentateuch in a seminary curriculum in 2007, I was eager to supplement my reading of Pentateuchal criticism by means of the most recent studies that I could find. To my great surprise, diachronic studies were still very much in evidence. Furthermore, some of the findings of diachronic Pentateuchal study that had always seemed at least mildly upsetting to unsuspecting seminarians or other students being introduced for the first time to scientific biblical study, such as the presence of multiple sources, the ascertainment of the influence of extrabiblical currents of thought, and of a later dating of composition than previously believed, had only become far more radical in the past twenty years.

It was amusing to see that some seminarians were delighted when they happened to notice the title of one book that I was reading, *A Farewell to the Yahwist?*,[1] but their delight was dampened by the realization that in this recent study, von Rad's version of the Yahwist was being supplanted certainly not by a renewed Moses setting out to regain his lost turf, but rather by a bewildering array of much later hypothetical sources lumped together only as "non-Priestly." Another recent work, Thomas Römer's important study of *The So-Called Deuteronomistic History,* seemed to yield a fascinating picture of the coming together of that part of the Bible, but in using anything in it I shuddered to think of the reaction if I should ever dare to let seminarians know of some of its more provocative assertions, such as the affirmation that the Davidic United Kingdom "may well be a Deuteronomistic invention."[2] The speculation that divine providence might have employed Persian imperial authorization in the process by which the Pentateuch became widely diffused and revered as Israel's Torah seemed consonant at least in some way with the biblical text itself, as for example in Ezra 7; even so, the further speculation that such factors — and perhaps even still later developments extending into the Hellenistic and Hasmonean periods — might have influenced even the very composition of the Pentateuch seemed even a far more radical revision of the likely dating of that composition than John Van Seters's earlier hypotheses of a quarter century ago, which had already seemed so radical when they were first encountered.[3]

1. Thomas B. Dozeman and Konrad Schmid, eds., *A Farewell to the Yahwist? The Composition of the Pentateuch in Recent European Interpretation,* Symposium Series 34 (Atlanta: Society of Biblical Literature, 2006).

2. Thomas Römer, *The So-Called Deuteronomistic History: A Sociological, Historical, and Literary Introduction* (New York and London: T. & T. Clark, 2007).

3. On the developments seen to have likely taken place in the Persian period, cf. the diverse contributions in Gary N. Koppers and Bernard M. Levinson, eds., *The Pentateuch as*

In the preparation of a syllabus for the study of the Pentateuch for the seminarians in 1st Theology during the first year that I taught it, one initial attempt consisted of a division of the semester more or less evenly between diachronic and synchronic methodologies. The texts chosen for the two respective parts of the semester were the *Introduction to Reading the Pentateuch,* by Jean-Louis Ska of the Pontifical Biblical Institute,[4] to be used as a guide to the diachronic methodologies, and an older work, *The Book of the Torah: The Narrative Integrity of the Pentateuch,* by Thomas W. Mann, to be used for the synchronic reading, principally from the standpoint of narrative criticism.[5] Thus dividing the semester, the principal remaining question was which of the two approaches should be covered first.

Beginning with the diachronic methodologies seemed to offer the advantage of proceeding in the manner of a history of modern Pentateuchal criticism beginning with Baruch Spinoza, Richard Simon, and Jean Astruc and up to the present day, then ending the semester with a synchronic approach that the seminarians would perhaps enjoy more, so that the semester would end with their positive assessment of the course and, hopefully, of the Pentateuch itself. On the other hand, the opposite sequence seemed convincingly to be argued by Ska himself, in the Preface of his *Introduction,* as he explains why he begins his study with an overview of the Pentateuch in its final, canonical form, "because diachronic, analytical readings always follow synchronic readings and synthesis of the data. If the whole is greater than the sum of its parts, it is important to consider the whole before looking at the 'sum.'"[6] The final draft of the syllabus therefore projected that the class would begin with the synchronic reading, and only subsequently focus on diachronic methodologies.

The result of that plan over the first semester of teaching the Pentateuch was precisely what I had expected, and it was not very satisfactory. After several sessions presenting introductory material such as the historical back-

---

Torah: New Models for Understanding Its Promulgation and Acceptance (Winona Lake, IN: Eisenbrauns, 2007). As an example of a study placing the solidification of the Pentateuch's status as late as the Hellenistic and Hasmonean periods, cf. Reinhard G. Kratz, "The Legal Status of the Pentateuch between Elephantine and Qumran," in *The Pentateuch as Torah,* pp. 77-103.

4. Jean-Louis Ska, *Introduction to Reading the Pentateuch* (Winona Lake, IN: Eisenbrauns, 2006).

5. Thomas W. Mann, *The Book of the Torah: The Narrative Integrity of the Pentateuch* (Louisville and London: Westminster John Knox Press, 1988).

6. Ska, *Introduction to Reading the Pentateuch,* p. x.

ground of the kingdoms and empires of the Ancient Near East, the original languages of the text, and an initial survey of the raising of various questions concerning authorship, and the overall structure of the Pentateuch, the first half of the semester followed Mann's essentially narratological presentation of the contents of the Pentateuch in its present form. The students enthusiastically attuned themselves to the focus on such dimensions of the text as narrative tension (for example, in the question of who would carry on Abraham's legacy), the implications of a dramatic slowing of narrative time (for example, with the beginning of the Abraham cycle or the sojourn at Sinai), and dramatic reversal (as in the masterpiece of the Joseph cycle's surprise ending, at least from the perspective of the characters). Such tools provided them with guidelines for presenting the essential message of the story to others, as they could see themselves doing either in preaching or in teaching. Of course, this survey also provided an occasion to point out certain characteristics in the text, such as the presence of doublets, which would be picked up again in the context of a presentation of diachronic methods of exegesis.

When the focus shifted more heavily onto the more analytical and diachronic, analytical methods, however, the tone of the class became less enthusiastic as gauged by the students' responses to the lectures, and some of the students clearly struggled to give the same attention as they had before. They struggled also with questions such as why a single author would not necessarily have employed different titles for the deity, and thus why such a phenomenon must necessarily be seen to indicate the presence of multiple sources. They questioned whether conclusions drawn from the hints noted by modern critics of a redactor's hand — such as apparent insertions, resumptive repetitions, explanatory glosses, and such linguistic markers as "again" or "that is" — might amount to an anachronistic superimposition of modern expectations on an ancient text. They observed the rise and fall of such hypotheses as the supposed role of G. von Rad's "small historical creed" or M. Noth's tribal "amphictyony" and wondered aloud how profitable it could possibly be simply to jump aboard the latest theories only to see them suffer the fall into the same foreseeable obsolescence as their predecessors.

By the end of the semester, most of the seminarians were convinced that the findings of modern historical-critical scholarship did not necessarily contradict a belief in the divine inspiration of the biblical text. They were able to see that any denial of the same would constitute a neglect of the human role in the composition of Sacred Scripture, and thus a fall into an error in its regard that would be analogous to Monophysitism in Christology. They were not all as thoroughly convinced, however, of the real utility of such scholarship for pastoral ministry, except perhaps as a body of knowledge necessarily pertaining to the academic competence of the Priest, which could shield him from a charge of ignorance and allow him to meet modern scholarship on its own terms. Few seemed to believe that diachronic studies of the Pentateuch would provide them with much assistance for preaching. Even if such study sought to do justice to the human role in the composition of the text, it seemed to provide little practical assistance, doing little or nothing to help the student grasp the sense of the whole. Such an appraisal seemed to be solidified by the students' written assignments: on the one hand, the preparation of a homily based on a passage from the Pentateuch found in the weekday Lectionary for Mass, and on the other, a comparison of the exegesis of a single text found in a modern commentary and that found in a rabbinic or patristic work. One student summed up the prevailing reaction of the class when he stated in his evaluation at the end of the 2008 Spring Semester that "[t]he first half of the course was very interesting and engaging. The second half was much less so, even though it was necessary."

Reevaluating and Restructuring the Course

Upon my beginning to teach the Pentateuch to seminarians for the second time in the spring of 2009, time constraints prevented the execution of a previously desired project of redesigning the course in a way that would prove more satisfying. Accordingly, the syllabus distributed at the beginning of that semester was changed little from the previous year. The flow of the course, however, seemed to provide an invitation to make significant changes as the course unfolded, especially since this year's class was even more interactive than their predecessors had been for this course.

Some of this year's more inquisitive students confided that upon entering into the semester, they had really been interested almost exclusively in the Book of Genesis. That accounted for their wealth of questions, which proved insightful enough to suggest an early abandonment of the planned timetable for the rest of the semester and a reduction of the amount of time that would be allocated to the diachronic methods at the end. As the semester proceeded, however, the narrative reading of the Pentateuchal narrative piqued the students' interest in the later books no less than in Genesis, and the enriching class discussions continued. The result was that by the midterm exam, scheduled a week past the midpoint of the semester, the class had not advanced beyond the Book of the Covenant following immediately upon the Decalogue in the Book of Exodus. At this pace, it seemed clear that by the time the semester ended, there would be no time at all left for a focus on diachronic methods in their application to the Pentateuch.

Since their total omission seemed unacceptable, I settled, almost accidentally, upon the solution that I now think to be the optimal one for combining synchronic and diachronic methodologies in the teaching of the Pentateuch: that is, to present the contents of the Pentateuch in the form of a synchronic reading spanning the entire semester, but to insert into the overall plan diachronic readings of specific texts chosen carefully so as to show that this kind of analysis of the text could be useful without detriment to the overall integrity of the text, and might even enhance one's understanding of the passage while facilitating its integration into a broader theological context.

Some attention to doublets and other indications of multiple sources had already been occasioned by the initial reading of Genesis in its final canonical form. The consideration of the law codes provided a further opportunity for showing the reworking of the same or similar material by different human authors. Since the planned section of the course that would have focused more intensely on literary problems in the narrative texts of the Pentateuch did not materialize in the end because of time constraints in the Spring 2009 Semester, it will probably be necessary in a future reworking of the course to give more attention to this aspect in the context of the initial synchronic reading of Genesis in future years. Thus implemented as a momentary intensification of focus on specific texts within the context of a synchronic reading of the whole, the attention given to the more analytical approaches to individual texts did not arouse the same discomfort in seminarians as had their allocation to an entire separate section of the course in the previous year.

Modern critiques of historicity in the Pentateuchal texts had also occasioned some volatile reactions on the part of students in the previous year, but during the second year, the insertion of the presentation of such critiques within an overall reading of the Pentateuch in its canonical integrity provided a chance to choose moments when the critiques would not emerge as a potential attack on the Faith itself, even if they might have seemed so if treated in isolation, and even if some such theories might be open to question on other grounds.

A good example would be such a critique regarding the actual historical existence of precisely the twelve eponymous ancestors of the tribes of Israel as sons of that Patriarch. When such critiques of historicity were presented as a theme in their own right, as part of a presentation of diachronic methodology, the student might recoil at the mere question of such a doubt being cast, and wonder how much of the story would be left in the end if so basic an element could be called into question. However, when the Patriarchal narratives were presented within the context of an overriding synchronic reading, also within the context of the whole biblical canon, it more readily could be seen, for example, that the significance of an aspect of the narrative such as the twelve-tribe federation is not threatened with nullity by questions of actual historicity. Admittedly, there are some such historical critiques that continue to seem somewhat more threatening to the very essence of the Faith: for example, the calling into question of the very existence of Abraham. His importance as the ancestor of Christ arguably seems to render his historical existence a necessary component of biblical faith. Nevertheless, the use of a prior overarching method that enables one to ascertain first and foremost the message of the integral Pentateuch on the basis of a synchronic reading prevents many disturbances to the Faith that might accrue on the basis of isolated critiques of individual elements of historicity.

When the parallel contents of the law codes of the Pentateuch were encountered for the second or third time in the reading of the books of Moses in their canonical form, this recurrence, as noted before, provided an obvious occasion for showing students the manner in which the same material had apparently been reworked by various human authors at different times in Israel's history. It also provided the opportunity to show how changing circumstances in the life of the people led to specific alterations in the presentation of the material, such as the emphasis on a central shrine and on a king in the Deuteronomic Code with its likely ties to the reform of Josiah, or the absence of any reference to the Land in the Holiness Code of Leviticus with its likely exilic provenance. Even so, when these were encountered successively over the course of a survey of the canonical form of the Pentateuch rather than as a project of comparison abstracted from the whole, what emerged more readily and more clearly was the insight that the reworking of the material could be regarded as somewhat akin to the evolution of dogma in the Church, with the parallel processes in the Bible and in the Church seen as mutually validating. This was so even if the order in which the law codes are encountered in the Pentateuch should likely be regarded as somewhat different from the order in which they developed chronologically: i.e., with the Covenant Code of Exodus remaining first, but with Leviticus's Holiness Code probably developing later than the Deuteronomic Code.

As already mentioned, the critique of a naïve notion of Mosaic authorship has become so basic to Pentateuchal study that it pertains to the initial introduction of such a course, so that a brief history of this critique had been mentioned even before beginning the synchronic reading of the canonical form of the text. Nevertheless, it seemed also that the seminarians would be shortchanged if there were no mention at some point of the latest serious conjectures regarding the dating of the composition of the Pentateuch. Even so, if treated in isolation as a theme in its own right, it might be upsetting to students that the last century's distancing of the time of composition from the narrated events has only widened further in more recent scholarship. When the overall presentation followed a synchronic reading, however, it proved possible to introduce the question of dating and also of the conjecture of chronologically successive strata of the text in a manner that — far from proving to be an obstacle to a coherent synchronic reading — in some cases actually proved helpful in resolving problems, theological as well as literary, that had been encountered in such a synchronic reading.

A relatively complex instance of such a diachronic analysis of the text, for example, occurs in Römer's *So-Called Deuteronomistic History*, where this author sees three successive strands of material dated to the Assyrian period, the neo-Babylonian period, and the Persian periods, respectively. Deuteronomy 7:1-5 is ascribed by Römer to the latest stratum, namely the Persian period, and Römer notes the "ideological, non-realistic character of these verses" as evidenced by the fact that one part of the passage forbids intermarriage with peoples whose very continued existence already seems to be negated by the command to exterminate them in verses 1-2.

Interestingly, such an ascription of this text to a later stratum actually helps to resolve a troubling theological question that naturally arises in the synchronic reading prior to such analysis: namely the question of how and why God could have ordered the extermination of innocent peoples. On the basis of an uncritical synchronic reading alone, that would necessarily be the apparent sense of the text. However, when this part of the text is seen as a product of the Persian period, then it can be read not as an actual command given by God, prior to the conquest, that the peoples must be exterminated, but as an encapsulation within the narrative of an imperative residing on a different plane and actually belonging to a much later date, the Persian period, decrying the same intermarriage and the consequent threat of religious syncretism just as is found in a close parallel — likely contemporaneous according to Römer — namely Ezra 9.[7] In this perspective, the interpretation of violent invectives in spiritual rather than physical terms, such as might typically be seen in patristic readings of such texts, actually does not seem far from the mark after all.

Conclusion

In employing a synchronic reading of the Pentateuch for the basic structure of the entire course, it seems advisable to do so on the basis of one principal methodology, and Thomas Mann's principally narrative reading seemed to function admirably for this purpose. Besides interposing diachronic readings of particular passages at carefully selected points, it proved helpful also to choose appropriate points to introduce readings to texts based on other synchronic methods, such as rabbinic readings of the Decalogue and the story of the Burning Bush,[8] or St. Ambrose's commentary on the Joseph cycle, or Roland Barthes's structuralist reading of the story of Jacob and the Angel in Genesis 32:22-32.[9] What proved most effective in any event was the use of one consistent synchronic reading as the backbone of the Pentateuch course, with the use of other methodologies exemplified by their application to individual passages carefully selected along the way to capitalize on the specific strengths of each. Such a division of the syllabus proved more effective than either structuring the course primarily on the basis of diachronic methodologies, on the one hand, or dividing the course equally between synchronic and diachronic methods, on the other. The utility of such a choice, furthermore, is due not to any lack of openness that today's seminarians have toward scholarly exegetical methodology, whether synchronic or diachronic. Instead, such a choice in teaching the Pentateuch is called for by the seminarians' openness to their own future ministry, in which they know they will be called upon to unfold for God's people, not the prehistory of the biblical text, but rather its divine unity and its everlasting message.

---

7. Römer, *The So-Called Deuteronomistic History,* p. 170.

8. For this, useful examples were drawn from Menahem Kasher's *Encyclopedia of Biblical Interpretation* (New York: American Biblical Encyclopedia Society, 1967).

9. Barthes's structuralist interpretation of this passage is described by John Barton in *Reading the Old Testament: Method in Biblical Study* (London: Dartman, Longman & Todd, 1984), pp. 116-19.

Contributors

KELLY ANDERSON, SSL, St. Charles Borromeo Seminary, Philadelphia, PA

SCOTT CARL, SSL, Director of the Monsignor Jerome D. Quinn Institute of Biblical Studies, The St. Paul Seminary School of Divinity of the University of St. Thomas, Saint Paul, MN

DENIS FARKASFALVY, O.CIST., STD, University of Dallas, Dallas, TX

PABLO GADENZ, STD, Immaculate Conception Seminary, Seton Hall University, South Orange, NJ

MARY HEALY, STD, Sacred Heart Major Seminary, Detroit, MI

MICHAEL MAGEE, STD, St. Charles Borromeo Seminary, Philadelphia, PA

FRANCIS MARTIN, SSD, Dominican House of Studies, Washington, DC

BRANT PITRE, PhD, Notre Dame Seminary, New Orleans, LA

STEPHEN RYAN, O.P., PhD, Dominican House of Studies, Washington, DC

JAMES SWETNAM, S.J., D.PHIL, Professor Emeritus, Pontifical Biblical Institute, Rome

CHRISTIAN D. WASHBURN, PhD, The St. Paul Seminary School of Divinity of the University of St. Thomas, Saint Paul, MN

PETER S. WILLIAMSON, STD, Sacred Heart Major Seminary, Detroit, MI

Index